**DATE DUE**

# Professionals Versus the Public

# Professionals Versus the Public:

## Attitudes, Communication, and Response in School Districts

### Harvey J. Tucker
### L. Harmon Zeigler

New York and London

**PROFESSIONALS VERSUS THE PUBLIC**
**Attitudes, Communication, and Response in School Districts**

Longman Inc., New York
Associated companies, branches, and representatives
throughout the world.

Developmental Editor: Nicole Benevento
Editorial and Design Supervisor: Judith Hirsch
Cover Design: Dan Serrano
Manufacturing and Production Supervisor: Kris Becker
Composition: Book Composition Services
Printing and Binding: LithoCrafters Inc.

This work was developed under a grant from the U.S. Office of Education,
Department of Health, Education, and Welfare. However, the content does
not necessarily reflect the position or policy of that Agency, and no
official endorsement of these materials should be inferred.

**Library of Congress Cataloging in Publication Data**

Tucker, Harvey J., 1948-
    Professionals versus the public.

    (Professional book series)
    "Written under the auspices of the Center for Educational
Policy and Management, University of Oregon."
    Bibliography: p.
    1.  Communication in education—United States.
2.  Education—United States—Public opinion.  3.  Public
opinion—United States.  I.  Zeigler, L. Harmon, 1936-, joint
author.  II.  Oregon. University. Center for Educational
Policy and Management.  III.  Title.
LB2847.Z44      379'.153'0973      79-16483
ISBN 0-582-28141-5

# Contents

List of Figures and Tables                                    ix
Acknowledgments                                               xiv

**1. School Governance in Theory and Practice** .................  1
   Experts and Laymen in School Governance .............  1
   Responsiveness and School Governance ................  4
   School Governance Research .........................  8
      The Hierarchical Style of School Governance ........  8
      The Bargaining Style of School Governance .........  13
      Polyarchy and School Governance .................  17
      Governance Styles in Perspective ..................  18
   Behavior and Responsiveness .........................  19
   Notes .............................................  21

**2. Methodology** ...............................................  23
   Subjective and Objective Data .......................  24
   The Demand-Response Log ...........................  24
   Identifying a Sample ................................  25
      Choosing Twelve School Districts ..................  26
   Recruitment of Field Observers .......................  30
      Training of Field Observers ......................  30
      Quality Control ..............................  31
   Survey Research ....................................  31
   The Demand-Response Log in Detail ..................  32
   Summary ..........................................  41
   Notes .............................................  42

**3. Unarticulated Preferences of Experts and Laymen** ............  43
   Agenda Attitudes and Preferences ....................  43
   Preference Aggregation ..............................  45
   Congruence .......................................  46
   Program Expenditure ...............................  46
   Program Approval ..................................  52
   Performance Satisfaction ............................  56
   Controversial Issues ................................  61
   Efficacy ..........................................  65
   Representation in Perspective ........................  68
   Notes .............................................  72
   Appendix: Survey Questionnaire .....................  72

**4. School Board Meetings: A Selective View** ...................  77
   **Key Events and Meetings** .............................  78
      COLDREN CORNERS ...........................  78

MEETING WITH MOST TOTAL DEMANDS .............. 79
MEETING WITH MOST PUBLIC DEMANDS ............ 80
BARWIG PARK ................................. 80
MEETING WITH MOST TOTAL DEMANDS .............. 81
MEETING WITH MOST PUBLIC DEMANDS ............ 81
NELSONVILLE ................................. 82
MEETING WITH MOST TOTAL DEMANDS .............. 83
MEETING WITH MOST PUBLIC DEMANDS ............ 83
LEEVILLE .................................... 83
MEETING WITH MOST TOTAL DEMANDS .............. 85
MEETING WITH MOST PUBLIC DEMANDS ............ 86
KENTINGTON .................................. 86
MEETING WITH MOST TOTAL DEMANDS .............. 88
MEETING WITH MOST PUBLIC DEMANDS ............ 89
MACKTOWN .................................... 89
MEETING WITH MOST TOTAL DEMANDS .............. 90
MEETING WITH MOST PUBLIC DEMANDS ............ 90
BALLARD CITY ................................ 91
MEETING WITH MOST TOTAL DEMANDS .............. 93
MEETING WITH MOST PUBLIC DEMANDS ............ 93
DRUMMOND FALLS ............................. 94
MEETING WITH MOST TOTAL DEMANDS .............. 95
MEETING WITH MOST PUBLIC DEMANDS ............ 96
HARTSHORNE HTS. ............................. 97
MEETING WITH MOST TOTAL AND MOST PUBLIC
DEMANDS .................................... 98
GRAHAMDALE ................................. 99
MEETING WITH MOST TOTAL DEMANDS ............. 100
MEETING WITH MOST PUBLIC DEMANDS ........... 100
STUMONT .................................... 101
MEETING WITH MOST TOTAL DEMANDS ............. 102
MEETING WITH MOST PUBLIC DEMANDS ........... 102
Conclusions ......................................... 103
The Public: An Arroyo .............................. 104

5. School Board Meetings: A Comprehensive View ............... 108
Actors and Attendance ............................... 108
Actors at School Board Meetings .................. 108
Attendance ....................................... 110
The Agenda of School Board Meetings ................. 111
How Similar Are the Agendas of the
Eleven School Districts? ........................ 121
Agenda-Setting ...................................... 123
Participation in School Board Meetings ................. 126

Nature of Communication ............................. 129
   Demands: A Further Analysis ..................... 136
   Demands and Most Important Issues ............... 139
Policy Proposal ...................................... 140
Voting .............................................. 141
Superintendent Defeats .............................. 144
   Stumont: ........................................ 145
      CONTRACT WITH LOCAL TELEVISION STATION ... 145
      AIR-CONDITIONING FEASIBILITY STUDIES
         AUTHORIZATION .......................... 147
      PURCHASE ORDER FOR BAND UNIFORMS ........ 147
      RECLASSIFICATION OF ADMINISTRATIVE POSITION 147
      CONTRACT WITH CHAMBER OF COMMERCE ...... 148
   Leeville: ........................................ 148
      BUSING EXTENSION ......................... 148
      NEW TEACHER HIRING PROCEDURES ........... 149
      REDUCTION IN FUTURE BUDGET .............. 149
   Coldren Corners: ................................ 149
      TUITION WAIVER .......................... 149
      MILITARY EDUCATION PROGRAM .............. 150
      SMOKING AT SCHOOL BOARD MEETINGS ........ 150
      CENTRAL MENU PLANNING .................. 150
      TUITION WAIVER .......................... 150
      BUSING ELIGIBILITY ........................ 151
   Kentington: ..................................... 151
      REPORT ON GROUP USING SCHOOL FACILITIES ... 151
   Summary of Superintendent Defeats ............... 151
Nonunanimous Votes ................................ 152
Conclusion ......................................... 153
Notes .............................................. 155
Appendix .......................................... 156

6. Administrative Cabinet Meetings ......................... 157
   The Agenda of Cabinet Meetings ..................... 157
   Agenda-Setting ..................................... 168
   Participation in Cabinet Meetings ..................... 170
   The Nature of Communication at Cabinet Meetings ....... 172
   The Demand Cycle .................................. 174
   Substance of Demands .............................. 177
   Conclusion ........................................ 178
   Notes ............................................. 178

7. Private Communications ................................ 179
   Sources of Private Contacts ......................... 180

Purpose of Private Contacts ........................... 183
Agreement and Disagreement in Private Communications .. 185
Scope of Request ..................................... 189
Subject of Private Contacts .......................... 196
Public Preferences and Three Modes of Communication ... 199
Conclusion ........................................... 200
Notes ................................................ 201

**8. Responsiveness** ........................................ 202
Agenda Responsiveness ................................ 203
Symbolic Responsiveness .............................. 208
Service Responsiveness ............................... 211
Policy Responsiveness ................................ 214
    Policy Responsiveness at Public Meetings .......... 214
    Policy Responsiveness in Private Contacts ......... 217
Influence Responsiveness ............................. 219
Differential Responsiveness in Private Communication .... 223
Responsiveness in Perspective ........................ 224
Notes ................................................ 228

**9. Preference, Communication, and Response** ................. 229
Preference ........................................... 230
Communication ........................................ 231
Response ............................................. 232
A Broader Perspective ................................ 233

Bibliography ............................................. 243
Index .................................................... 247

# List of Figures and Tables

Figure 1.1. Responsiveness Linkages .......................... 21


Table 2.1. Demographic Characteristics of School Districts ....... 29
  Form #1 Main Meeting Form .................... 34
  Form #2 Motion and Action Summary for Meetings . 35
  Form #3 Superintendent-Board Member Follow-Up . 36
  Form #6 Constituent Interview .................... 38
  Form #4 Screening Questionnaire for Superintendent
    or Board Members .................... 39
  Form #5 Conversation Report: Interview Guide for
    Superintendent or Board Members ...... 40


Table 3. 1. Most Important Issues from General Public Survey ... 44
Table 3. 2. Most Important Issues from School Official Surveys .. 44
Table 3. 3. Program Expenditure Preferences: Public ............ 47
Table 3. 4. Program Expenditure Preferences: Elite ............. 49
Table 3. 5. Program Expenditure Preferences: Officials .......... 50
Table 3. 6. Program Expenditure Attitude Congruence .......... 52
Table 3. 7. Program Approval: Public ......................... 53
Table 3. 8. Program Approval: Elite .......................... 54
Table 3. 9. Program Approval: Officials ....................... 55
Table 3.10. Program Approval Attitude Congruence ............. 57
Table 3.11. Performance Satisfaction: Public ................... 58
Table 3.12. Performance Satisfaction: Elite ................... 59
Table 3.13. Performance Satisfaction: Officials ................. 60
Table 3.14. Program Satisfaction Attitude Congruence .......... 60
Table 3.15. Issues: Public ..................................... 61
Table 3.16. Issues: Elite ...................................... 62
Table 3.17. Issues: Officials .................................. 63
Table 3.18. Issue Attitude Congruence ......................... 64
Table 3.19. Efficacy: Public ................................... 65
Table 3.20. Efficacy: Elite .................................... 66
Table 3.21. Efficacy: School Officials ......................... 67
Table 3.22. Efficacy Attitude Congruence ...................... 68
Table 3.23. Whose Attitudes Do School Officials Best Represent? . 69
Table 3.24. Modal Orderings .................................. 70
Table 3.25. Average Orderings ................................. 71

Table 4. 1. Most Important Issues in District Narratives ......... 103
Table 4. 2. Distribution of Demands: Overall and Public ......... 105
Table 4. 3. Days of Greatest Public Demands ................. 106


Table 5. 1. Attendance at School Board Meetings .............. 111
Table 5. 2. Purpose and Resolution of Discussions at School Board
Meetings ....................................... 112
Table 5. 3. Distribution of Topics at School Board Meetings ..... 113
Table 5. 4. Proportion of School Board Discussions Concerned with
Important Issues ............................... 115
Table 5. 5. Distribution of Statements at School Board Meetings,
by Topic ....................................... 116
Table 5. 6. Proportion of School Board Statements Concerned with
Important Issues ............................... 117
Table 5. 7. Regression of Statements and Discussions at School
Board Meetings ............................... 118
Table 5. 8. Disproportionate Intensity of Discussions at School
Board Meetings ............................... 119
Table 5. 9. Disproportionality of School Board Discussions Con-
cerned with Important Issues .................... 120
Table 5.10. Difference Scores for Discussions—School Board Meet-
ings ......................................... 121
Table 5.11. Difference Scores for Statements—School Board Meet-
ings ......................................... 122
Table 5.12. Agenda-Setting at School Board Meetings ........... 124
Table 5.13. Participation in School Board Discussions .......... 127
Table 5.14. Statements at School Board Meetings .............. 128
Table 5.15. Distribution of Statements by Public .............. 129
Table 5.16. Percent of Various Types of Statements at School
Board Meetings ............................... 130
Table 5.17. Superintendent Statements ........................ 131
Table 5.18. School Board Statements ......................... 132
Table 5.19. Public Statements ................................ 134
Table 5.20. Public Statements by Group Spokesmen ............. 135
Table 5.21. Public Statements by Unaffiliated Individuals ........ 135
Table 5.22. Demand Articulation ............................ 136
Table 5.23. Negative Demand Articulation .................... 137
Table 5.24. Negative Demands as a Proportion of all Demands ... 138
Table 5.25. Conflict at School Board Meetings ................. 139
Table 5.26. Correspondence Between Issues of Greatest and Least
Conflict and Issues from Public Surveys, School
Official Surveys, and Narratives ................. 140
Table 5.27. Policy Proposals ................................. 141
Table 5.28. Voting Decisions ................................ 144

Table 5.29. Cases of Board-Superintendent Opposition .......... 146
Table 5.30. Schubert Index of Cohesion in Dissent in Three Districts 154
Table 5.31. Lone Dissent in Three Districts ................... 154


Table 6. 1. Purpose and Resolution of Discussions at Cabinet Meetings
............................................. 158
Table 6. 2. Distribution of Topics Discussed at Cabinet Meetings . 159
Table 6. 3. Proportion of Cabinet Discussions Concerned with
Important Issues ............................. 160
Table 6. 4. Distribution of Statements at Cabinet Meetings, by
Topic ........................................ 162
Table 6. 5. Proportion of Cabinet Meeting Statements Concerned
with Important Issues ......................... 163
Table 6. 6. Regression of Statements and Discussions at Cabinet
Meetings ...................................... 163
Table 6. 7. Disproportionate Intensity of Discussions at Cabinet
Meetings ...................................... 164
Table 6. 8. Difference for Discussions—Cabinet Meetings ........ 165
Table 6. 9. Difference Scores for Statements—Cabinet Meetings .. 166
Table 6.10. Correlation Between Cabinet and Other Meeting Dis-
cussions ...................................... 167
Table 6.11. Correlation Between Cabinet and Other Meeting State-
ments ........................................ 167
Table 6.12. Agenda-Setting at Cabinet Meetings ................ 168
Table 6.13. Participation in Cabinet Discussions ............... 170
Table 6.14. Statements at Cabinet Meetings ................... 171
Table 6.15. Percent of Various Types of Statements at Cabinet
Meetings ...................................... 172
Table 6.16. Request and Supply of Information as a Proportion
of all Statements ............................. 173
Table 6.17. Demands as a Proportion of all Statements ......... 174
Table 6.18. Timing of Demands at Cabinet Meetings ............ 175
Table 6.19. School Board and Administrative Cabinet Demand
Articulation Overtime ......................... 175
Table 6.20. Conflict at Cabinet Meetings ..................... 176
Table 6.21. Correspondence Between Issues of Greatest and Least
Conflict of Issues from Public Surveys, School
Official Surveys, and Narratives ................ 177


Table 7. 1. Recipients of Private Communications ............. 180
Table 7. 2. Source of Private Communications with School Board 181
Table 7. 3. Source of Private Communications with Superintendent 182
Table 7. 4. Purpose of Private Communications with School Board 184

Table 7. 5. Purpose of Private Communications with Superintendent .......................................... 184
Table 7. 6. School Board Agreement with Constituent ........... 186
Table 7. 7. Superintendent Agreement with Constituent ......... 186
Table 7. 8. Modal Purpose of Most Frequent Source of Private Communications with School Board ................. 187
Table 7. 9. Modal Purpose of Most Frequent Source of Private Communications with Superintendent ............... 188
Table 7.10. Modal Purpose of Private Communications by Source 189
Table 7.11. Distribution of Private Communications by Scope of Requests: All School District Officials ............... 191
Table 7.12. Distribution of Public Demands at School Board Meetings by Scope of Request ..................... 191
Table 7.13. Distribution of Private Communications with School Board by Scope of Request ...................... 192
Table 7.14. Distribution of Private Communications with Superintendent by Scope of Request ................ 192
Table 7.15. Modal Action Requested of School Board by Scope of Request ......................................... 193
Table 7.16. Modal Action Requested of Superintendent by Scope of Request ...................................... 194
Table 7.17. Topic of Private Communications with School Board . 195
Table 7.18. Correlations Between School Board Private Communications Topics and School Board Meeting Discussion Topics ............................... 196
Table 7.19. Proportion of Private Communications with School Board concerned with Important Issues ........... 197
Table 7.20. Topics of Private Communications with Superintendent ......................................... 198
Table 7.21. Correlations Between Superintendent Private Communications Topics and Cabinet Discussion Topics . 199
Table 7.22 Proportion of Private Communications with Superintendent concerned with Important Issues .......... 200

Table 8. 1. Agenda Responsiveness—Public Preferences ......... 204
Table 8. 2. Agenda Responsiveness—Elite Preferences .......... 206
Table 8. 3. Agenda Responsiveness—School Officials' Preferences 206
Table 8. 4. Symbolic Responsiveness—Opportunity for Public Participation ..................................... 209
Table 8. 5. Symbolic Responsiveness—Constituent Perception of School Officials ............................... 210
Table 8. 6. Service Responsiveness: Action .................... 212
Table 8. 7. Service Responsiveness: Satisfaction ............... 214
Table 8. 8. Opportunity for School Board Policy Responsiveness . 215

Table 8. 9. School Board Policy Responsiveness ............... 215
Table 8.10. Public Satisfaction with Response at School Board
           Meetings ...................................... 217
Table 8.11. Policy Responsiveness for Private Contacts: Action .. 218
Table 8.12. Policy Responsiveness for Private Contacts:
           Satisfaction ................................... 219
Table 8.13. Public Influence at School Board Meetings ......... 221
Table 8.14. Public Influence in Private Contacts ............... 221
Table 8.15. Rankings of Districts on Responsiveness Indices ..... 225
Table 8.16. Intercorrelations of Responsiveness Indices ......... 227


Table 9. 1. Significant Correlates of Responsiveness ........... 234

# Acknowledgments

This book is a product of a long-term research effort conducted through the Center for Educational Policy and Management of the University of Oregon and funded by the National Institute of Education. The book, however, does not necessarily represent the views of this agency. Important contributions were made by a number of people. We gratefully acknowledge the help of Martin Burlingame and Jon Schaffarzick of the National Institute of Education. Larry Pierce, Anne Schneider, and L. A. Wilson II were colleagues at various stages of the project. Jane Feldman, L. Dallas Hardison, Henry Steveson, and Harold Wingfield were research assistants. Helpful manuscript reviews were provided by William Boyd, Judith Gruber, Robert Lineberry, Arnold Meltsner, and Paul Peterson. Dale Mann, Sam Kirkpatrick, Bruce Robeck and Roby Robertson gave us encouragement and ideas. Nicole Benevento and Linda Salmonson of Longman lent editorial expertise.

We also acknowledge the cooperation of superintendents, administrators, and school board members in the 11 school districts of our study. They must remain anonymous as must the field researchers who recorded observational data. Finally, we would like to recognize the important role of Robert Graden, business manager of the Center for Educational Policy and Management. Our research project enjoyed the support of university, state, and federal organizations. Bob's assistance in coordinating these disparate entities was invaluable. We found refreshing his belief that the goals of our research and the goals of our supporting institutions were frequently compatible.

# 1

# School Governance in Theory and Practice

Public school districts in America are units of local government. As is the case with other governments, school districts were created to provide goods and services. The direct beneficiaries of public schools are, of course, students and parents. However, all members of society gain by the production and dissemination of knowledge. Thus, in America, education is a public good: everyone benefits and everyone pays. As a result, educational governance is of potential concern to all. Educational professionals and the lay public agree that some degree of school district responsiveness to constituents is essential.

## Experts and Laymen in School Governance

The ideal of responsiveness in school governance is reflected in the American tradition of local control of public schools at the primary and secondary levels. Local governments—including school districts—because of their unique position in the American federal system, their size and proximity, both physical and psychological, to constituents, are expected to be the most responsive. Thus, when the central queries of political science are asked of school governance: who gets what, when and how? one might expect that the distribution of influence will favor the laymen.

Traditional democratic theory holds that political influence ought to follow lines of legal authority. Administrators in school districts (superintendents, central office staff and principals) should follow the instructions of their constituents (the public). The board appoints the superintendent and may remove him at any time. The superintendent is an administrative officer similar to a city manager. The school board is the elected representative speaking for the public. Even when the board is appointed by an elected official, as is the case in Chicago and New Haven (Peterson, 1976; Dahl, 1961), its function is still presumed to be a representative one. Hence, the major source of political influence is popular support, and the norm of policy decision-making is responsiveness to public desires and preferences.

The increasing complexity of 20th-century political, social, and economic life presents a major challenge to the notion of democratic control of government. The political influence of technological elites has captured the imagination of social scientists, and for good reason. In a technological age, especially one in which the conservation of scarce resources replaces the distribution of abundant resources as a focus of policy, elected officials are frequently required to deal with issues containing components too sophisticated for them to comprehend. Thus, they turn to experts for information, and expert knowledge is easily transformed into a political resource for the acquisition of influence.

Recognition of the growing importance of experts has caused social scientists to reevaluate their empirical and normative models of policy formation. A newer model of governance, which might be called a technological model, sees the implementation of information systems and management science techniques causing a fundamental change in the governing process. Problems and policy alternatives are now seen as too complex for the public and its representatives to evaluate. Legislators solicit and follow the recommendations of professional administrators. The major source of power is information, and the new norm of policy decision-making is deference to expertise.

Proponents of the technological models stress the importance of experts as "new political actors." However, in that portion of the political process concerned with educational policy-making, experts are certainly not new. Although historical interpretations may vary, there is consensus that educational experts, the superintendent and his professional staff, had become influential, if not dominant actors by the 1920's.[1] The increase in political influence of experts in education predated similar developments in other arenas of decision-making. Thus, the major tenet of the technological model, deference to expertise, is a well-established norm in modern educational governance. Problems and policy alternatives in educational governance are seen as essentially technical in nature, and too complex for the public and its lay representatives to understand and evaluate.

Thus, there is considerable ambivalence concerning the applicability of the democratic and technological approaches to school governance. On the one hand, the formal status of school districts as local units of government and the tradition of local control of education indicate that the democratic approach is appropriate as a normative and empirical model of school governance. On the other hand, the growth of educational expertise, the reform movement of the early 20th century (which attempted to remove educational governance from the political arena), and the modern requirement, now universal, that school administrators be professionals with degrees from recognized colleges of education, suggest that the technological approach is more appropriate.

The democratic approach is most clearly approximated by descriptive models such as bargaining and polyarchy, especially the latter (Dahl and Lindblom, 1953; Dahl, 1971). The technological approach is closely matched by the hierarchical model of decision-making (Dahl and Lindblom, 1953). Past research suggests that the technological model is the most appropriate description of educational governance.[2] However, the contention that hierarchical models and technological approaches are no longer empirically correct has appeared recently in both popular and academic literature. The argument is that an increasing politicization of education has changed the climate in which school officials work, to the extent that deference to experts can no longer be regarded as the preponderant form of policy-making.[3]

On the surface, the turbulence of the 1960's certainly seemed to have contributed to a politicization of education. Popular accounts of highly publicized conflicts portrayed professionals as struggling vainly against a variety of powerful interest groups. Professionals, themselves, were active in promoting the view of the "beleaguered superintendent." One observer quotes from the ranks of the beleaguered superintendents to support his contention that the world of the superintendent, as seen from the inside, is far more conflictual than the world as described by students of educational policy-making:

> The American school superintendent, long the benevolent ruler whose word was law, has become a harried and embattled figure of waning authority . . . brow-beaten by once subservient boards of education, teachers' associations, and parents, the superintendent can hardly be blamed if he feels he has lost control of his destiny. . . . Administrative powerlessness is becoming one of the most pervasive realities of organizational life [Maeroff, 1974, pp. 1, 29].

While some might be inclined to dismiss such testimony as self-serving, the view has to some extent been echoed by scholars such as Boyd (1976), who argues that the model of professional dominance is no longer correct. Similarly, McCarty and Ramsey (1971) conclude that

> One can hardly avoid the view that today's educational administrator is engulfed in a pressure-packed set of constraints. . . . individuals previously without power are becoming aware of the strength that can be marshalled if they work together. . . . the tension so apparent throughout American society has galvanized school boards into the political arena with a vengeance [McCarty and Ramsey, 1971, pp. 163, 211, 213].

The upshot of this controversy has been a renewed interest in the question, "Who governs schools?" This new interest is shared by practitioners and scholars in educational administration, political science, sociology, and other social sciences. Social scientists who see a technological revolution as changing the basis of governmental decision-making are interested in exploring the technological decision-making approach so well supported in educational administration literature. Simultaneously, students and practitioners of educational administration who see increasing politicization of educational governance are interested in exploring topics such as lay participation and conflict resolution.

It's important to note that those who see the demise of technological and hierarchical decision-making assert that the change has been quite recent. They would argue that the change from hierarchical to more conflictual decision-making has been within the past five to ten years. As a result, the research finding that hierarchy is the most frequent mode of school district governance is now presumably outdated.

Thus, we come full circle. The reform movement of the early 20th century was implemented because school governance was seen as *too* responsive to individual and organized interests, and *too* democratic. A shift to technological decision-making was seen as appropriate and desirable. Thus, the normative and empirical view of school governance changed from one supporting a traditional norm of democracy to one supporting a technological approach. But recently, students and practitioners of educational administration have argued that the technological approach and hierarchy no longer accurately describe school governance. The shift is due, not to a change in the desires of school administrators and school board members, but rather to a change in the political and socioeconomic environment in which schools must operate. The 1960's and early 1970's have been characterized by increasing politicization, expecially in terms of increasing demands from ethnic, racial, and other minority groups. School districts have not been immune to the changing political environment which has affected other governmental units. Consequently, there are theoretical and empirical reasons to expect that both educational experts and the lay public are important, active participants in policy-making at the local school district level.

## Responsiveness and School Governance

Since schools are public governments, most laymen would assume that they "should do what the people want," that is, they should be responsive. No matter how decisions are made, Americans believe that the content of government decisions should not be at variance with public sentiment, however one chooses to measure this sentiment. In other words, responsiveness should exist independently of the quantity and quality of lay participation.

As we shall discuss later, responsiveness itself is a multidimensional concept capable of several definitions, each of which is capable of multiple operational definitions. However one chooses to define and operationalize responsiveness, it is a key notion in the tradition of American democracy. As the authors of a recent study of city councils put it, "in a democracy the degree to which the governors are responsive to the preferences of the governed is the *sine qua non* of whether democracy, in fact, exists" (Eulau and Prewitt, 1973, p. 24). Similarly, Sidney Verba and Norman Nie argue that "responsiveness is what democracy is supposed to be about" (1972, p. 300). Beyond agreement upon responsiveness as the key to democracy, however, there is no clear agreement about how one decides whether or not a government is, in fact, responsive.

We suggest that the process by which a decision is made may be independent of the extent to which its content is responsive. It is possible to identify two distinct schools of thought on the matter of defining responsiveness. One school we will designate as representational, the other as congruence. The representational school argues that responsiveness is a relationship between the leaders and the led. In this relationship the "people" make demands. They actively communicate their expectations to decision-makers, who, in turn make responses which attempt to satisfy the demands. The decision-makers, if they are responsive, hear what is being said, develop a series of alternative means of satisfying demands, mediate conflicting demands, and ultimately reach a decision which is formulated in response to the most dominant or the most persuasive set of demands. The key concept here is one of activity, both in the making of demands and in the response to demands. Thus, according to the representational school, decision-makers are unresponsive if they do not comply with, or at least consider, preferences expressed to them directly by their constituents.

In their description of city councils, Eulau and Prewitt make explicit use of the representational model.

These councils appear to be altogether immune to pressures emanating from the public; no identifiable public voices, whether sporadically or permanently organized, intrude into their deliberations. These councils may or may not be acting in the interests of the represented, but they are clearly not acting in response to the represented [1973, pp. 426–427].

Eulau and Prewitt deem these city councils unresponsive, because they ignore constituent demands. It is important to note that the presentation of such demands is necessary in order for responsiveness to exist. Without demands there can be no response. According to the representational school, decision-makers, irrespective of their desire to be responsive, cannot be so until they are presented with constituent demands.

The representational school assumes the existence of demands which are communicated from constituents to governments. This is a rather strict requirement, which is frequently not met in the real political world, especially in the world of educational governance. Accordingly, we identify a second school of thought, which is the congruence school. The requirements here are less severe. The congruence model of responsiveness assumes merely that constituents hold general attitudes and expectations. They need not communicate such expectations to the decision-makers. Responsiveness exists when the policy actions of the government reflect the attitudes and expectations of its constituents. Hence, responsiveness under the congruence model may be the result of shared attitudes between rulers and ruled. As one proponent of this model suggests, "We judge a legislature to be more representative of its citizens if the opinions of the representatives on a broad spectrum of relevant issues closely parallel those of citizens on the same issues" (Luttbeg, 1974, p. 440).

Of course, it is also possible that representatives will, on occasion, act according to what they perceive to be the wishes of citizens, even though they do not personally agree. Such actions would have the same effect as actually sharing values. In either case, however, leaders must accurately perceive citizens' expectations, must either agree or suspend personal judgment, and, by implication, must become active in implementing citizen preferences.

All these acts might be undertaken without any of the various forms of political communication so vital to the representational model. A decision-making body might be quite free of demands from interest groups, informal organizations, or interested and active individuals. Unresponsive in the first sense (that is, not responding to communication), it could be quite responsive in the second sense (that is, the actions they undertake are compatible with the expectations of constituents). Indeed, one could argue that precisely because a decision-making unit is so responsive in the sense of accurately perceiving the priorities of citizens there is no need for the communication so crucial to the representational model.

There is a third notion of responsiveness which we will not consider in this book. A government is responsive to the extent that it detects and responds to problems and needs, whether or not those problems and needs are perceived by citizens. The representational and congruence models both posit responsiveness as a relationship between citizens and government. This third school posits responsiveness as a relationship between government perceptions and government response to these perceptions. There is no necessary relationship between rulers and ruled in this third model.

Whatever the merits of this model of responsiveness, it is clearly irrelevant to a discussion of democratic governance. On the other hand, this model of responsiveness is one frequently favored by professional educational administrators who argue that because of their expertise, they alone are able to perceive the educational needs of the community. Some go so far as to reject lay claims when they do appear. We choose not to pursue a needs model of responsiveness, not only because it is so alien to American democracy, but, more importantly, because it is incapable of empirical verification. As it applies to an individual school official, the model is circular. Both perception of and reaction to needs originate with the individual. Thus, whenever an action occurs it is by definition because of a perceived need. Unfortunately, only behavior can be observed. Insofar as individuals are concerned, discrepancies between need perceptions and reaction are theoretically impossible and empirically unobservable.

It is possible, of course, to apply the needs model of responsiveness to a group of government officials. If officials are unanimous in their perceptions and actions, the model is again circular. If officials disagree in their perceptions of need, the tautological linkage between perception and reaction no longer exists. The behavior of officials as they compare needs assessments and alternative policies is observable.

The primary goal of this study is to explore the extent to which school district officials are responsive to the preferences of their lay publics. Given our interest in both representational and congruence responsiveness, we shall be concerned with lay preferences, the process of communication and decision-making in school districts, and the content of decisions. These three elements have been employed by Dahl and Lindblom (1953) to designate four ideal styles of governmental decision-making: hierarchical, bargaining, polyarchal, and market.

In hierarchical decision-making processes, most decisions are made by the leaders of the organization. They decide when, under what conditions, and with whom to consult, if outside advice is desired. There are typically infrequent opportunities for nonleaders to displace leaders. As these processes are applied to school districts, the superintendent is the key decision-maker. School boards act less as decision-making bodies and more as communication links between the superintendent and the public. The major norms for decision-making are the professional values and expertise of the administrative staff. Ideas for change, innovation, and alternative decision-making modes come through professional communication channels. Thus, frequent direct communications between school district officials—that is, superintendents, central administrators, school board members—and members of the lay public are seen as unnecessary under the hierarchical style of decision-making.

In organizations which rely on bargaining, decisions are negotiated by various leaders representing groups with competing goals. Each leader or group has enough power to block the attainment of goals of the other leaders. Bargaining, therefore, refers to methods for resolving differences among leaders by making mutually beneficial exchanges and compromises. In public school systems this suggests that superintendents, school boards, and interest group leaders have goals which may vary from issue to issue, and from participant to participant. More importantly, these actors each control important and varied resources. The interdependencies thus created set up situations in which bargaining can take place. School officials bargain with community leaders, who command resources needed by the schools. As a result, opportunities for nonprofessional values to be represented in the decision-making process exist whenever people holding these values control some resource needed by school officials. The extent to which school officials will be responsive to outside values is dependent upon the distribution of resources among community leaders and the intensity of preferences among these leaders.

Bargaining is a familiar decision-making process in American politics. Bargaining, for example, between executives and legislators, is the norm in American national politics. Bargaining between school boards and superintendents is not the norm preferred by school board members or school administrators.[4] Therefore, this style may be of limited applicability in studying school politics.

It is important to note that bargaining can take two separate forms.[5] The first form, which might be called "bargaining among school officials," holds that the superintendent, the school board, and other school-based interests (teachers' union, employee organizations, principals, etc.) engage in both cooperative and conflictual behavior in the day-to-day resolution of school problems. The second form of bargaining holds that bargaining occurs between school officials and outside interest groups. The school board, superintendent, and other school officials are seen to form a unitary group, which must bargain with non-school groups, such as municipal, county and state governments, the federal government, taxpayers' organizations, civil rights groups, and racial groups. These two types of bargaining are not mutually exclusive. It is possible for an interest group to align itself with some school officials in opposition to others. For example, a group might create opposition between the board and superintendent and side with one of these two major contestants. Additionally, bargaining can assume either a pluralistic or ideological nature.[6] Pluralistic bargaining is characterized by short-term conflict on varying issues and changing coalitions. In short, the situation is fluid. Ideological bargaining is more stable and the factions are more durable in their composition. Participants are organized according to long-term ideological beliefs and preferences. Thus, the coalitions are likely to be involved in major and long-term decisions. Ideological bargaining focuses on bargaining between school officials as a unit, and external actors. Pluralistic bargaining focuses on bargaining among school officials who may be aligned with interest groups outside the school district organization. Since school officials hold a common set of ideological predispositions, we would not expect ideological bargaining to occur among school officials.[7]

The third style, polyarchy, assumes that laymen control adequate resources to dominate most decision-making situations. Leaders compete for the support of nonleaders, both to gain office and to achieve support for programs that are being considered by the organization. In school systems, polyarchal decision-making would be characterized by widespread citizen participation in school decisions. Superintendents and school boards would openly solicit the opinions of various publics on most issues. Within the district, most decisions would be made by committees comprised, in part, of public members. Thus, a key distinction between bargaining and polyarchy is that under the former, participation is limited to interest groups while under the latter, participation by both groups and unaffiliated individuals is possible. Polyarchal decision-making also assumes that implementation of school programs would involve maximum community participation.

Many public organizations have attempted to create polyarchal processes by bringing outside individuals and groups into their decision-making processes. Sometimes this has been required by law. For example, the community control movement has attempted to give parents more decision-making authority in school governance.[8]

The norm of polyarchy is widely shared among theorists of American democracy.[9] But the norm of polyarchy is *not* favored by school administrators, school board members, or teachers' groups. Although polyarchy is regarded as ideal by democratic theorists, it is not regarded as ideal by administrative theorists concerned with educational problems.

The final decision-making style that Dahl and Lindblom discuss is the price or market system in which consumers control decisions by purchasing desired services. This model is inapplicable to most aggregate government organizations. There have been some few attempts to implement a market system of education but these experiments have been short-lived.[10] Thus, while the market system (sometimes called the voucher system) is a well-developed theoretical notion, discussed by such scholars as Christopher Jencks (1972) and Milton Friedman (1962), at present it lacks an empirical counterpart.

Thus, the three styles of governance applicable to school districts range from maximum individual participation in decision-making, to formal decision-making based on individual and group participation and support, to decision-making based on competing interest groups, to decision-making by professional experts restricted, not by explicit communications from constituents, but by professional goals and expectations. These ideal types can be ordered in terms of the relative participation and influence of government officials—experts—and the public—laymen. The major theme of this inquiry will be the relative roles experts and laymen play in school governance. For hierarchy to be the most appropriate description, experts should predominate in most decisions. For bargaining to be most appropriate, there should be a balance between experts and groups of laymen, or between groups of experts. For polyarchy to be most appropriate, the preferences of laymen should predominate in most cases.

## School Governance Research

Dahl and Lindblom's four styles of governance provide convenient categories for summarizing past research on school governance which focus directly on relations between government officials and their constituents.

## THE HIERARCHICAL STYLE OF SCHOOL GOVERNANCE

No school system is explicitly designed to concentrate authority hierarchically. Legal authority is divided between a lay school board and its administrative designees. Hierarchical administrative decision-making systems occur when the representative function of the lay board is eroded. How this comes about can be seen best by analyzing the decision resources available to school boards and superintendents. From the normative view of society in which symbols associated with popular sovereignty have such high salience, the mere act of representation is a potential resource. If the school board is perceived—at least by the superintendent—as being a potential mobilizer of various publics, its power is enhanced.

Although legal authority and representative function are the most universal of the potential resources available to school boards, others may exist in specific districts. In their study of a rural community in upstate New York, for instance,

Vidich and Bensman (1960) discovered that the school board was closely allied with prevailing community elites. Others have found this to be the case in communities characterized by an allegedly monolithic elite structure (Kimbrough, 1964). However, Gittell and Hollander's comparative analysis of six urban districts (1968) finds little evidence of interaction, much less alliance between school boards and community elites. Hence, the participation of key members of the community power system is a potential resource available to some, but not all, school boards. The political elite(s) of a community may—depending upon the issue, the community, the style of the board—be available as a board resource.

The superintendent's resources are more limited in scope but potentially more effective than the board's. His fundamental resource is his professional expertise in matters pertaining to education. The relationship between administrative experts and elected laymen is hardly unique to school districts. Other examples which come most readily to mind are city council and city manager, and legislative committee and executive department in both state and federal governments. Shared authority is common in all these situations, yet there is something special about the expertise of the superintendent of schools. In the rest of the world educational governance is the responsibility of professionals who are not expected to be directly accountable to laymen. The tradition of lay participation in educational governance is almost uniquely American. However, "Americans accord greater deference to superintendents than they do to most other public professionals" (Martin, 1962, p. 50). This deference allows the school superintendent to assume more authority than his administrative counterparts in other governments.

The claim for expert status by the superintendent is buttressed by another tenet of educational governance in America: the separation of education and politics. As a consequence, educational decision-making has been insulated from broader based political conflict. The "reforms" of 1890–1910—initiated in response to the growing influence of urban political machines—produced two principles which are still followed by school officials: (1) the separation of policy-making from administration, and (2) the concentration of authority in the office of the superintendent. Keeping politics out of the schools also meant minimizing the legitimacy of conflict, and hence the legitimacy of "outside" participation as represented by pressure groups (Salisbury, 1967). In contrast to overtly political bodies, such as state legislatures or city councils, school boards and administrators define pressure groups as outside the proper influence system (Hess and Kirst, 1971). The "normal" resource of an interest group is the perception by a decision-maker of its legitimacy (Zeigler and Baer, 1969). Admittedly, perceptions of legitimacy vary from group to group, issue to issue, and so on, but there is a general assumption on the part of most public officials that groups have a right to be heard. Superintendents do not share in this assumption (Crain, 1968, pp. 115–128). Further, only about half the school board members accept the legitimacy of group originated demands (Jennings and Zeigler, 1971). When traditional political action is seen as illegitimate, interest group influence will be minimal, as in New York:

> In the last two decades, education in New York City has become amazingly insulated from political and public controls. One could accurately describe the situation as an abandonment of public education by key forces of political

power within the City. . . . Weber's theory of the emergence of a specialized bureaucracy monopolizing power through its control of expertise characterizes the role of the education bureaucracy in New York City. The claim that only professionals can make competent judgments has been accepted. Civic and interest groups have responded ambivalently. On the one hand they accept the notion of the professional competence of the bureaucracy, but at the same time express a hopelessness regarding their ability to change the system [Gittell, 1967, p. 209].

To a lesser degree, teachers suffer from a comparable denial of legitimacy. They are nonmanagerial employees of the school district. Their role in setting school district policy is analogous to that of line employees in other large public or private organizations. Similarly, students and parents are not granted any special legitimacy because they are the primary clients of public education. In short, neither lay interest groups external to the school district, nonmanagerial employees, nor clients of the school district are seen as legitimate challengers to the authority of professional educational administrators.

The relative insulation of boards and superintendents from the constraints of political conflict, leaves us with the task of understanding how boards and superintendents share their power. Superintendents, like city managers, are products of the increasing complexity of educational policy and the demand for efficiency. In the early years of the public school system, the authority to manage schools was in the hands of school boards. Boards had leaders, raised money, selected texts, and even interviewed prospective students (Callahan, 1966). However, in the middle of the 19th century, schooling rapidly became compulsory and free. Simultaneously, America was experiencing the Industrial Revolution, with its accompanying population explosion and urbanization. As schools grew in size and complexity lay boards no longer had time or skills to continue management. Various schemes (including the currently popular "community school," or the division of large cities into small districts, each with its own board) were tried; but finally the boards gave up. In the latter half of the 19th century, boards began to hire professional administrators who slowly and inexorably began to assume not only administrative but also policy-making authority (James, 1967).

Around 1895 school boards were threatened with the loss of virtually all authority. Superintendents proposed the responsibility for instructional policy be turned over to them exclusively. Once appointed, superintendents were to be independent of boards and not subject to dismissal until the expiration of long-term contracts. Boards—still able to tap partisan political resources—managed to win this fight, retaining their authority to hire and fire superintendents. Thus, the shape of educational policy-making was set: each contestant retained some resources (Callahan, 1966). Indeed, noting the erosion of school board powers, Carlson (1972) maintains that the board's most important contemporary function is selecting a superintendent. Winning the fight to retain authority over the hiring and firing of superintendents did not, of course, do much more than keep retreat from turning into rout.

Consolidation of school districts to achieve managerial economies became a major component of the ideology of "scientific management." Since 1932, $4/5$ of the school districts in the United States have disappeared, while pupil populations have increased by 15 million. This consolidation has further increased the size of school districts. The ratio of board members to student population has increased from 1 to 46 in 1932 to 1 board member to 300 pupils in 1967 (James, 1967). Further, superintendents predict—and approve—even more centralization in the future (Andes, *et al.,* 1971). Clearly, the complexity which limits the viability of lay control of educational governance is increasing.

Hines's (1951) 50-year history of the Eugene, Oregon, school board illustrates the trends which James and Callahan outlined. Hines's study shows the gradual assumption by superintendents of the responsiblity, first for the instructional program, then for the selection and supervision of the professional staff. From these beachheads the superintendents expanded their domain to budget preparation and fiscal control, purchasing, school site selection, plant management, and public relations. The assumption of board powers was gradual and not invariably uncontested. Conflict erupted at each new expansion of superintendent authority and was not necessarily resolved during the incumbency of the superintendent that initiated the change. But the general thrust of the transfer of power is unmistakable when viewed over the long sweep of time.

According to Hines, the first erosion of board power occurs when the superintendent (and central office staff) assumes control over the instructional or educational program. The educational program is the core of educational policy—it is the most significant output of the school district. Yet, it is the first area to be delegated by the board to the superintendent. Virtually all studies which classify issues coming to the attention of the board find that the educational program receives scant school board attention.

> It is common knowledge that boards of education devote little time and thought to the problems of the educational program *per se* [Greider, *et al.,* 1961].

A systematic study of a national sample of school districts by Zeigler and Jennings, with Peak (1974) provides additional support for the earlier generalizations. In this study, it was posited that the superintendent would have a well-developed idea of an appropriate educational program for his district, and that the board's function would be to react (much in the manner of Congress reacting to the initiative of the "chief legislator," the President). The examination of the interplay between boards and superintendents confirmed that the former respond to the initiatives of the latter. Superintendents either directly or indirectly control their school boards' agendas: only 4 percent of the boards surveyed exercised independent agenda-setting authority. Superintendents also advance policy proposals which are nearly always enacted by boards. In only ¼ of the school districts did a majority of board members report that they would *ever* oppose a recommendation concerning educational programs made by their superintendent.

As one superintendent in an earlier study, referring to the board members and the educational program, candidly observed,

> They don't know anything about it; but the things they *know* they talk about, like sidewalks, sites, and so forth. I let them go on sometimes because I don't want them to talk about curriculum [Kerr, 1964, p. 51].

The basic resource of the board is its representative capacity. However, Zeigler, *et al.* (1974), found that relatively few boards have been able to escape superintendent domination and assert their representative resources. How does it come about that the representative resource is under-utilized? A fundamental contributing factor is the board's image of its opportunities. Dykes states that "what the school board does depends in large measure on the board's view of itself in relation to its responsibilities" (Dykes, 1965, p. 11).

Dykes's assertion allows one to classify boards along a continuum according to the degree to which they accept either a representative or "professional" role. A board that sees itself principally as a mechanism through which various segments of the community can participate in the formation of educational policy will behave much differently than one that views its role as being a protective buffer between the experts who run the schools and the public. In the former instance, public support or opposition will be a salient input for the board. In the latter case, the *professionally* oriented board is less inclined to perceive and act upon expressions of popular values. Such boards will place greater reliance on technical expertise. The board which subordinates its representative responsibilities to what it perceives to be its responsibilities to professional educators is likely to accept an administrative definition of its job and hierarchical governance.

Gross, Mason, and McEachern's seminal study of school boards and superintendents in Massachusetts makes it clear that, from the point of view of the superintendent, the two roles are incompatible and the professional role is preferred. Degree of professionalism was measured by reaction to the following statement: "In deciding issues the board members should vote as representatives of important blocs or segments." The modal superintendent response was "absolutely must not"; and 58 percent of the board members agreed with this reply (Gross, *et al.*, 1958, p. 225).

A majority of American school boards tend to perceive their roles as being consistent with the values of professional educators. In other words, the majority of boards define educational governance in such a way as to give superintendents hierarchical authority. Rather than serving as a conduit to channel popular views to administrators as per the bargaining or polyarchy models, boards define their job as "selling" the administration's program to segments of the community.

Not surprisingly, there is a significant positive relationship between board professionalism and superintendent dominance: superintendents dominate because boards want them to (Peak, 1971). As Lipham, Gregg, and Rossmiller put it: "board members [tend] to engage in role avoidance—delegating the decision-making power to the superintendent of schools." Lipham and his colleagues found, for instance, that 90 percent of school board members thought that they should not serve as spokesmen for segments of the community; yet slightly over ¼ of the citizens thought this was a good idea (Lipham, Gregg, and Rossmiller, 1969).

The McCarty and Ramsey (1971) report does contain a graphic description of a typical professional board:

> The superintendent of schools made certain that no issue came up that would raise the ire of any board member. . . . Therefore, there was very little in the way of controversy, argument, debate, or the like. . . . School board meetings were very short since they were confined to approving the recommendations of the superintendent. . . . Much of [the superintendent's] work was done behind the scenes. He frequently contacted board members . . .

and probably knew exactly how every vote would be beforehand. This allowed him the option of failing to bring up issues that might lead to a confrontation or raise some question regarding his authority.

Perhaps the key issue in the decision-maker role is that of selecting board members. . . . The school board itself urged people to run . . . and they usually did so unopposed. . . . Candidates were always suggested by the superintendent . . . in terms of their name, the person's prestige in the community, his talent for being down to earth on the crucial issues, and his compatibility with the other board members [McCarty and Ramsey, 1971, pp. 173–174].

Those who hold that hierarchy best describes board-superintendent relations acknowledge there are variations in this pattern. Board members, occasionally, become articulate and superintendents occasionally lose. The insulation of the schools from laymen cannot be guaranteed. This lay participation is a prerequisite for both the bargaining and polyarchy styles of school governance.

## THE BARGAINING STYLE OF SCHOOL GOVERNANCE

The relatively closed educational system in America is one which the various articulate publics have found remarkably impermeable. At the risk of redundancy, it is worth repeating that school governance in America is symbolically democratic. As we have seen, however, lay control is not a principle which guides most interactions between educational professionals and the lay board and public. Martin, perhaps most severe among those who expose this conflict between symbols and reality, laments:

Thus is the circle closed and the paradox completed. Thus does the public school, heralded by its champions as the cornerstone of democracy, reject the political world in which democratic institutions operate [Martin, 1962, p. 89; see also Salisbury, 1967, pp. 408–420].

Legitimacy—the key to successful negotiation between government officials and various publics—is difficult to establish. Information—a basic resource in the arsenal of the lobbyist—is hard to pry loose from the iron grip of the superintendent.[11] Clearly, the opening of school districts to constituent demands hinges upon the extent to which educational decision-makers conceive their role as legitimately entailing acknowledgment of and response to such demands. On this score, we find that the mass public, in keeping with its attachment to the symbols of democracy, is least inclined to accept the notion that school board members should follow their own judgment. While not denying the fact that in most cases the public does not know what it wants, board members typically do *not* view their role as representing the public; ⅔ of them believe they should follow their own judgment. Even more adamant are superintendents. Three-fourths of them believe board members should be "delegates" rather than "representatives" (Zeigler, *et al.*, 1974, p. 121).

The bargaining style holds that school administrators, board members, and lay interest group leaders all participate in school governance because all hold important resources. We have seen, however, that the normal political resources available to laymen in other governmental arenas are severely constrained by the mores of school district governance. Nevertheless, school boards and superintendents have some interaction with the lay public. To get more precisely at the nature of this interaction, Zeigler, et al. (1974), categorized school boards according to the legitimacy and responsiveness each accorded to group demands as per the bargaining mode.

It is only when one moves into the complexities of urban life that there is any appreciable communication between formal organizations and elected and appointed school officials. Not only do such officials have a positive effect toward groups (i.e., accord them legitimacy), but they see more of them. However, even in those urban, group-oriented districts, interest group activity is sporadic at best. Indeed, urban districts are group oriented only in comparison to small-town and rural ones. Thus, group activity posited by the bargaining model occurs only part of the time in a minority of school districts.

Whereas the Zeigler, et al. conclusions about the paucity of group life are based upon comparative surveys, Smoley's (1965) study of pressures on the board of school commissioners in Baltimore provides corroboration by an exhaustive case study. Using minutes of the board and some additional published sources, he considered over 2,300 issues during a seven-year period. Smoley revealed that even in a large city interest groups are largely uninvolved.

Of the 2,389 issues considered by the Board of School Commissioners, only 207 included participation by outside groups—less than ten percent! Furthermore, much of the participation which did take place contained no hint of attempted influence, but was action in the performance of official functions to provide service to the Baltimore school system [Smoley, 1965, p. 180].

Smoley's analysis also provides insight into how superintendents can use their resources to minimize external demands. Superintendents usually set agendas for board meetings and load them with trivia—nuts and bolts problems of administration which neither boards nor interest groups can understand. At first glance, the inclusion of administrative tasks in the agenda may seem risky, but the strategy is successful. Immersed in trivial administrative matters rather than major issues of educational policy, boards do not provide a forum for interest arbitration. Over 2,000 of the 2,389 decisions concerned staff personnel and the school building program. Only a handful related to instructional affairs. Most issues were routine and quickly resolved. The skillful use of trivia is a powerful weapon which can diminish the opportunity for bargaining while it enhances the conditions of hierarchy.

Further problems for bargaining appear when one probes into the distribution of activity among types of groups. The results are unequivocal: the most active voice is that of the PTA, followed (distantly) by teachers (Smoley, 1965; Gross, 1958; Zeigler et al., 1974). Almost ⅔ of the board members in the Zeigler et al. study cited the PTA; about ⅓ recalled demands by teacher groups. After these two, the list declines through civil rights groups (29%); various business, professional and service clubs, down through the much feared but relatively quiescent right-wing groups (13%) to the rarely active labor organizations (3%). At this point, let us note that most interest group action is undertaken by members of the school district "family." There is an "establishment" tinge to the group spectrum.

If the usual decisional climate is ideologically cool, there is no gainsaying the fact that it does, on occasion, become quite heated. When issues lose their routine, technical flavor and strike deep at emotions, then school officials may find themselves in the midst of group-dominated conflict which can be resolved only by bargaining and compromise. Such conflicts surrounding the resolution of episodic issues are rare but usually spectacular.

Granted that schools are now commonly described as the center of turmoil (teacher strikes, student revolts, taxpayer revolts, busing, community control, and the like), even in the 1960's relatively placid districts probably outnumbered the tempestuous ones. Some districts cope with their problems over a long period of time with a minimum of strife. Others—those which capture the imagination of the mass media—seem to be caught up in perpetual conflict. What may best characterize school district phenomena of this type is a model of episodic crisis (Iannaccone, 1967; Campbell, 1968, pp. 50–52).

What happens when episodic crises erupt? When the district population becomes antagonized, support for school policy dwindles, group demands increase, and the interaction between educational decision-makers and unattached individuals decreases (Jennings and Zeigler, 1971; Jennings and Zeigler, 1972a). The prerequisite conditions for bargaining come into existence. Imagine, for example, a school district beset by scandal or fiscal chaos. As popular support dwindles, an increase in group demands outside the district "family" occurs. As public confidence in the district continues its descent, the loss of confidence is articulated and given explicit focus by interest group leaders. They pinpoint, according to their own objectives and interests, the specific aspects of discontent to which they will address their efforts. The decline in popular support becomes less generalized as group activity increases. Groups clearly thrive in an atmosphere of conflict between the governed and the governors. Such a condition of stress is a precipitant condition for group activity, irrespective of the social complexity of the community. The board and superintendent are in a stage of siege. The threatening environment of hostile group activity surely sets educational governance apart from other public decision-making processes. Where group conflict is normal, bargaining is an accepted mode of resolution.

School boards, unlike most governmental bodies, are accustomed to communications from unaffiliated individuals which consist of cues rather than demands (Summerfield, 1971). Such cues may have affective content, but quite often simply consist of feedback to the board concerning their actions. When individual communication does consist of preferences on pending policies, such preferences are not seen by school officials as vigorously made demands.

Group communications, more often reflecting the *ressentiment* of the masses, are addressed toward serious ideological conflict except when coming from supportive organizations such as PTA's (Peterson, 1976). Can organizations translate their anger into observable phenomena? If not, their activity would make little difference, since school boards and superintendents would have little evidence of the state of public opinion. The evidence is that group activity is strongly associated with financial defeats, teacher firings, and superintendent turnovers (Zeigler *et al.*, 1974). Small wonder that groups are feared! Of particular interest is a strong association between the activities of political organizations and superintendent turnovers. When superintendents insist that education and politics do not mix, they are not just mouthing platitudes. Again, there is strong incentive for superintendents to use their resources to buffer themselves against "outside" groups.

Linkage opportunities are reduced appreciably by the self-perpetuating recruitment pattern characteristic of school boards. When, as is frequently the case, incumbent board members are able to perpetuate their influence by bringing like-minded colleagues to the board, interest group activity (and individual communications as well) tapers off considerably. Boards in these circumstances appear almost akin to closed corporations, insulating themselves from the hue and cry of interest group politics. Boards and superintendents value a public display of unity, and generally eschew identification with group originated values and public conflicts.

The only groups welcomed into such dynasties are PTA's and, less often, teachers. Their comparative acceptance stems from their semiofficial status. Furthermore, their typical participation does not reflect the conflict specified by the bargaining model.

The PTA—with its membership strongly biased with respect to social characteristics in a manner comparable to school boards—functions not as a demand generating group, but rather as a buffer or defense mechanism. It does not translate mass hostility into specific demands, but rather communicates the policy of the board and superintendent to its clientele. It coopts potentially disruptive parents, defusing conflicts before they begin (Dahl, 1961, p. 155; Koerner, 1968, p. 26).

Teachers' organizations (the local affiliates of the National Education Association and of the American Federation of Teachers) occupy a curious place in the array of group activity. Of all the groups engaging (however sporadically) in efforts to influence the content of educational policy, teachers should have the highest legitimacy. They are not outsiders. Yet teachers' organizations are a distinct second in group activity to the PTA. In spite of some very visible collective bargaining activities, teachers' organizations are relatively unconcerned with most school district policy issues. They generally confine their activity to narrowly defined issues, such as teacher hirings, firings, conditions of work, and salaries (Pierce, 1975).

Bargaining, then, appears to be a rather pale alternative to hierarchy. The groups which bargain successfully are generally "establishment," and the range of alternatives is generally modest. Bargaining in school politics does not generally appear the bargaining of the normal political process. Peterson's (1976) study of Chicago school politics is the most recent confirmation of the difficulty of bargaining in school governance. Peterson documented the existence of intense ideological bargaining among Chicago school board members. Nevertheless, he concluded that

> information necessary to hold subordinates accountable for their most important activities was virtually impossible to obtain, and for this reason alone the board of education necessarily had limited impact on the educational processes in the city of Chicago. . . . Chicago's school system was thus in many ways isolated from external political forces and highly dependent on its educational staff for information, recommendations, and policy executions [Peterson, 1976, pp. 126–127].

Thus, even though bargaining is extremely well-developed in Chicago's municipal governance, it is not the predominant style of school district governance.

## POLYARCHY AND SCHOOL GOVERNANCE

Unfortunately, the empirical literature on polyarchal school governance is extremely limited. This reflects both school administrators' rejection of lay participation as a legitimate normative model of policy-making and the inapplicability of polyarchy as a description of school policy-making.

More so than other units of local government, school districts are insulated from the erratic winds of community conflict by political institutions. Such devices as at-large, nonpartisan elections minimize the link between public preferences, group demands, and elected and appointed officials. Although it may make intuitive sense to speculate that the larger school districts which resulted from consolidation would encompass greater social heterogeneity and hence greater group conflict, this has not occurred. The reforms which increased the size of school districts also changed the structure of elections. Partisan, ward-based elections were replaced by nonpartisan, at-large elections. Today, about 75 percent of school board members are elected on a nonpartisan basis; about 73 percent are elected at-large. Ward elections increase the likelihood that grievances, which are likely to be neighborhood based, will be articulated in political campaigns. Similarly, partisan elections place the educational decision-making process within the mainstream of electoral politics. The primary function of political parties in elections is the mobilization of constituent participation. Political parties are also important institutions which educate, aggregate, and focus public opinion. Thus, the isolation of school governance from partisan politics serves to insulate schools from public opinion.

This insulation can be documented in both the quantity and quality of competition for elected school board positions. More than 34 percent of school board members initially gain their seats by appointment or through uncontested elections. Of those school board members who do face electoral competition, 44 percent report no important substantive differences from their opponents (Zeigler, *et al.*, 1974, pp. 25–73).

As a result, school board elections attract the participation of few constituents:

Voting in school board elections has been historically lighter than in general elections. It is hard to be certain why this is true, but a number of contributing factors are easily identified. First, in most school districts elections are deliberately scheduled to be held in the off year and in the off season so as to remove them as completely as possible from any association with regular political elections. Second, the very low level of competition among candidates leads to less excitement and controversy. Third, the nonpartisan nature of school elections makes it difficult for the voter to differentiate among the candiates; he is not able to rely on any perceptions he might have about what sort of policies a Democrat or a Republican might pursue. Fourth, school board members typically do not establish a stable, identifiable constituency; instead, as the hearings confirmed, they tend to insist that they represent equally all segments of the school district. If all the candidates at least profess to represent all the people equally there is little reason to get too excited about which one wins. Furthermore, the absence of a clearly identified constituency undoubtedly reduces the general level of active involvement in campaigning with a consequent reduction in the enthusiasm of voters. Fifth, the mass media devote little attention to these elections. Finally, it is not at all uncommon for school board candidates to run unopposed. When this occurs low voter turnout is perfectly understandable [Reed and Mitchell, 1975, pp. 194-195].

In his landmark study of decision-making in New Haven, Robert Dahl found in public education "reciprocal relationships between leaders and constituents through which constituents exert a good deal of *indirect* influence on the decisions of leaders" (Dahl, 1961, p. 159, emphasis in original). He concluded that direct influence over decisions in public education seems to be exerted almost entirely by public officials and that the number of citizens who participate directly in important decisions bearing on the public schools is small. Thus the leading proponent of polyarchy failed to find the widespread citizen participation, constituent control of important resources, and competition by leaders for constituent support specified by that model in his examination of the politics of educational governance.

Since Dahl's study, a number of innovations have been employed to stimulate constituent participation and influence in school governance. The cluster of phenomena loosely referred to as "decentralization," "neighborhood government," the "community revolution," "participation," "citizen involvement," etc., have been studied by LaNoue and Smith (1973). The dominant purpose of the decentralization movement was to increase constituent participation in the making of school policy, especially by the poor and those not previously involved. In certain respects that goal was achieved: new activists have emerged as participants in school politics. However, the new elite that has emerged to represent ghetto residents functions much like traditional elites. There has been no massive grass-roots citizen involvement in poor neighborhoods. LaNoue and Smith conclude that "decentralized school structures have not yet overcome the traditional barriers to political participation," and go on to observe that "on the basis of available evidence, it does not appear likely that mass citizen involvement could be induced under any imaginable system of local control of schools" (LaNoue and Smith, 1973, p. 229).

Thus, while polyarchy may be a useful concept to describe decision-making on some issues in some school distrcts, it has never been advanced as an empirical model which applies to the preponderant style of decision-making in any school district.

## GOVERNANCE STYLES IN PERSPECTIVE

The hierarchy, bargaining, and polyarchy concepts describe decision-making processes which occur in school districts. Examples of each mode exist simultaneously in virtually all school districts. Thus, in a given school district, a hierarchical relationship may exist between superintendent and school board, school board members may bargain with each other on a limited number of issues, and episodic crises may stimulate polyarchal participation. Furthermore, demand for some academic student classes may be met by quasi-market mechanisms.[12] However, when attention is turned to the predominant mode of decision-making at the district level, all styles are not equally prevalent.

Our survey of the empirical literature on educational governance indicates the relative frequency with which the hierarchy, bargaining, and polyarchy models apparently reflect the predominant styles of governance extant in American school districts today. It is the consensus of educational administrators, political scientists, and students of public administration that the greatest number of school districts are characterized by hierarchy; the next greatest number are characterized by bargaining; and few, if any, are characterized by polyarchy.

### Behavior and Responsiveness

While the hierarchical, bargaining, and polyarchy styles are useful heuristic concepts for organizing basic notions of governance and past research in educational governance, they are unsatisfactory models to guide empirical research. The styles were originally developed to characterize large societies. The fact that examples of decisions reflecting each style exist simultaneously within a single governing unit creates considerable difficulty in identifying a single appropriate style of decision-making. For example, in a given school district, in a given year, there may be thousands of students making "market" decisions concerning classes. Dozens of decisions concerning PTA activities may be polyarchal. Bargaining may characterize a single textbook adoption question. Finally, all school district expenditure decisions may be proposed by the superintendent and unanimously affirmed by the school board, as specified by hierarchy.

The dilemma is clear. How is one to aggregate numerous decisions made by different actors at different levels of government? Decisions are perceived as varying in importance by the most directly involved individuals and hence have varying scopes of impact. Furthermore, in a larger perspective, the market alternatives presented to a student may have been developed in a hierarchical system.

Another reason why these models are inadequate is that they are concerned only with process or, in our terms, representational responsiveness. Hierarchy, bargaining, and polyarchy focus mainly upon communication processes involving governmental officials and their constituents. Such communications are a prerequisite for representational responsiveness but may be irrelevant to congruence responsiveness. Congruence responsiveness exists to the extent that governmental policy is connected with constituent preference. The process whereby such congruence is achieved is of little moment.

Our notions of responsiveness can be summarized by reference to four key concepts (see figure 1.1):

1) unarticulated constituent preferences,
2) articulated constituent preferences,
3) preferences of governmental officials,
4) behavior of government officials.

Our concern is with preferences and behavior of the lay public and the preferences and behavior of school district officials. Our concept of responsiveness focuses explicitly upon the policy behavior of government officials. Thus, in figure 1.1 congruence responsiveness is represented by the linkage of unarticulated constituent preferences and behavior of government officials, and representational responsiveness is the linkage between articulated constituent preferences and the behavior of government officials.

The needs model of responsiveness discussed earlier is the linkage between preferences of governmental officials and their behavior. Such linkage between preferences of constituents and those of governmental officials does not fit our model of responsiveness. Although attitude matching and, in some cases, attribute matching is sometimes offered as a measure of responsiveness, in our terms, attitude congruence does not measure responsiveness. Attitudes of government officials may, in some sense, *represent* attitudes of constituents, but officials do not *respond* to constituents by their attitudes. Only by their actions can government officials be responsive.

Our concept of responsiveness is a subset of the broader idea of representation. Although we will investigate all elements and all linkages in figure 1.1, our primary concern will be with the two responsiveness linkages.

To measure congruence and representational responsiveness, information on three of the four variables in figure 1.1 is necessary. First, it is necessary to collect information on unarticulated constituent preferences. Second, it is necessary to collect information on communications (articulated preferences), between members of the public—laymen—and members of the school decision-making establishment—the experts. Finally, it is necessary to collect information on the decision-making behavior of school officials. The congruence model of responsiveness holds that there will be correspondence between community preferences and the content of decisions. The representational school of responsiveness holds that there will be correspondence of communications between experts and laymen and the decision-making process. The congruence model does not make any assumptions about process. It limits concern to the content of decisions. The representational model is concerned both with process and with content. The paradoxical situation exists in which a decision can be responsive according to the congruence model, but unresponsive according to the representational model. The key is the linkage between unarticulated lay preferences and articulated lay preferences. It may well be the case that the articulate minority of citizens do not express the desires and preferences of the inarticulate majority.

It should be made clear that our concept of school district policy is broadly defined. Thus, when we explore school district decision-making process, we will be concerned, not only with decisions made by school board members, but also with discussions at school board meetings, and with the agenda of school policy-making in its largest sense. Additionally, we will be concerned with interactions and decisions made in private. These points will be discussed in the following chapter, which describes the methodology of our inquiry.

This book will attempt to describe the communications network of school governance. We are concerned with who says what, to whom, and with what effect. Our primary interest is in the relationship between experts and laymen and the responsiveness of the former to the latter. Chapter 2 describes the methodol-

FIGURE 1.1

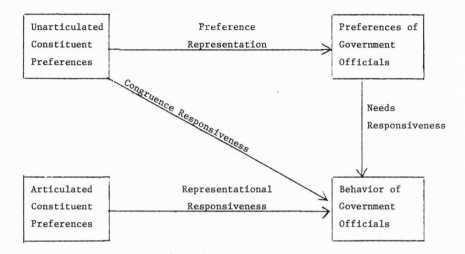

ogy of the study. Chapter 3 presents data on attitudes and preferences of school district officials and their constituents and explores how representative the former are of the latter. Chapters 4, 5, 6, and 7 consider communications and decision-making at school board meetings, administrative cabinet meetings, and private contacts between school experts and the lay public. Chapter 8 addresses the problem of responsiveness. Chapter 9 highlights major findings and suggests directions for further research.

## Notes

1. See, for example, Tyack (1974) and Guthrie (1975).
2. See, for example, Martin (1962), Gittell (1967), James (1963), Carlson (1972), and Zeigler and Jennings (1974).
3. Boyd (1976) is a leading proponent of this view.
4. See, for example, Zeigler and Jennings with Peak (1974), and texts on educational administration such as Greider, Pierce and Rosenstengel (1961), Campbell, Bridges and Nystrand (1977), and Knezevich (1969).
5. See Peterson (1976).
6. *Ibid.*
7. See Gross (1958).
8. See, for example, Aleshire (1972), Gittell, *et al.* (1972), Fantini (1971a, b), Hallman (1972), Jenkins (1972), LaNoue and Smith (1971), Levin (1972), Marcson (1971), Sussmann and Speck (1973), and Usdan (1969).
9. For example, Dahl (1971).
10. Areen and Jencks (1971), Arons (1971), Binderman (1972), Bureau of School Service

and Research (1972), Center for the Study of Public Policy (1970 and 1971), Coons, Sugarman and Clune (1970), Coons and Sugarman (1971), Friedman (1962), Ginsberg (1971), LaNoue (1972), Lyon (1971), and Mecklenberger (1972).
11. On the resources of lobbyists, see Zeigler and Baer (1969).
12. Peterson (1976), for example, argues that a variety of decision-making styles existed simultaneously in Chicago.

# 2
# Methodology

The theoretical interests outlined in the previous chapter make it imperative to collect systematic information on three classes of variables. First, it is necessary to collect information on community opinion, that is, the unarticulated attitudes and preferences of constituents (most broadly defined) of school districts. Second, information on explicit communication between laymen in the school districts and expert school officials is required. Finally, the third class of variable is information on the decision-making process conducted by elites once demands have been articulated by either experts or laymen. Additionally, information on school officials' unarticulated preferences is desirable. In short, it is essential to collect both attitudinal and perceptual information as well as objective data concerning communications and decision-making in public school districts.

This is by no means an original quest. Harold Lasswell (1948) once urged political scientists to study "who says what, in what channels, to whom, with what effect." As simple as this paradigm is, it directs one toward a host of complex problems. The most enduring of all concerns in political science—power or influence—is inexplicably linked to communication. A cannot exercise power over B without some form of communication from A to B. The communication may be direct, even brutal. Or, it may be indirect and difficult to identify. Thus, when we are dealing with such large units as school districts and trying to understand their internal processes, relationships with other institutions, and relationships with constituents, we focus naturally on communications.

The congruence model of responsiveness posits a direct relationship between community preferences—even though they may be unarticulated—and decisions made by school district elites. The methodology for determining community preferences is relatively straight-forward and well-developed in social science research. Community preferences may be ascertained by use of survey research techniques. However, analysis of decisions and decision-making processes is much more problematic. In order to establish relationships between preferences and decisions, a complicated analysis of communications in the manner of Lasswell is necessary.

An analysis of communications is also necessary to evaluate the representational model of responsiveness. This model defines responsiveness as a direct function of explicit communications between laymen and experts. Thus, it is necessary to undertake a complex analysis of communications processes, both between laymen and experts and among experts, in order to assess congruence and representational responsiveness. Therefore, we will attempt as complete a description as possible of the pattern of communications in public school districts.[1] We define communications as a set of premises transmitted from one unit to another. Our foci are (a) the source of communication, (b) the content of communication, (c) the source of response, and (d) the content of response.

## Subjective and Objective Data

It would be ideal to collect both objective and subjective data concerning communications. Communications research has emphasized that how one views the content of communication is related to how one views the source of communication. One's frame of reference significantly affects how one interprets the communication. Burns (1954), for example, often found that when a superior claimed to give a subordinate instruction the subordinate would note that he had been given advice. Similarly, a school board member's request for information from the superintendent may be variously interpreted as an incident of support, neutrality, or opposition by different observers. These subjective distortions are particularly troublesome if one's intent is to describe patterns of communications and influence.

Unfortunately, subjective data alone will not provide a sufficient data base for this study. Two problems arise in the use of perceptual data. The first problem is familiar to all social scientists who employ the observations of participants: quite often their reports do not agree. Given a conflict in perception, the researcher is at a loss to assess reality. A second, and more basic problem, is that individuals often do not accurately recall and report their own behavior and perceptions. Burns (1954) asked executives in a business organization to keep records of people with whom they talked, and what they said. He then asked them what they *thought* they did. Comparing observation with interview, Burns found sharp discrepancy between administrators' perceptions of what they were doing and the actual record. The probability of such discrepancy is, of course, increased as the period of recall is lengthened. For example, school officials asked to recall the incidence of conflict over an entire school year may base their reports, not on the hundreds of decisions made, but on a smaller number of "important" issues. Clearly, individual recall provides an imperfect record of events, regardless of whether one's interest is in reconstructing objective or subjective data sets.

## The Demand-Response Log

Our attempt to resolve these problems was to conduct longitudinal comparative research that incorporated both systematic observation of events and periodic recording of participants' perceptions. During the nine-month 1974–75 academic year, we collected data on the flow of communications and decisions in 11 public school districts in the United States and Canada, utilizing an interrelated set of data collection techniques which we call "The Demand-Response Log." The Demand-Response Log consists of objective and perceptual data concerning both public and private communications. Objective records of all statements and decisions made at central school board meetings, meetings of the superintendent and his administrative cabinet, and other formal meetings (for example, regional board meetings, public hearings, etc.) were recorded by two trained observers in each school district. School board members and superintendents and other senior school district administrators were interviewed regularly to record their perceptions of presentations made by members of the public—laymen—at meetings. Those who made presentations at public meetings were interviewed concerning their perceptions of how they had been received by school district officials at the meetings and of any other communications. Thus, the Demand-Response Log records both objective and perceptual data concerning communications between experts and laymen in public forums.

The Demand-Response Log also records information concerning private contacts between experts and laymen collected in regularly scheduled interviews with school board members, superintendents, and other senior school district administrators who were specifically designated by the superintendent to receive communications from members of the lay public. Since these communications occurred in private it was not possible to obtain objective data concerning the interaction. Our data concerning private communications between experts and laymen is limited to the perceptions of the experts. Because of the confidential nature of the private communication, it was not possible for us to collect perceptual data from the laymen's point of view.

Data on community preferences were collected by use of an opinion survey on school policy. The survey was conducted among samples of the mass public, leaders of interest groups, and other active individuals in the school district, and school board members and senior administrators in each school district. Thus, we have attitudinal and perceptual data concerning the preferences of both experts and laymen. We also have objective and subjective data on the communications process between experts and laymen. Finally, we have both objective and subjective data about the decision-making process in public school districts. To recapitulate, information on unarticulated preferences of the mass public, private and public communications between school district officials and their constituents, and policy decisions made at school board and administrative cabinet meetings were collected. Hence, the empirical bases of this book are both objective and perceptual data relevant to the query: who says what, to whom, with what effect?

## Identifying a Sample

Given the decision to attempt a comprehensive description of communications, only a limited number of school districts could be studied. Furthermore, since the analysis required a sustained commitment on the part of a school district, we were constrained by access problems. Nevertheless, we attempted to select a sample of districts that would reflect, albeit incompletely, the variety of school districts in America. We attempted to include school districts that fell across the range of size, location, demographic attributes, formal decision rules, and informal decision processes.

Choosing an appropriate number of research sites was made somewhat difficult by various constraints imposed upon the researchers. First, we were proposing a longitudinal study which would take nine months. The vast amount of data we intended to collect would be relatively expensive. Thus, the cost of research limited the sample size. Second, because the Demand-Response Log instruments were so intensive and the quantity of data to be collected so great, the problem of data management also contributed to limit the number of school districts involved in the project. The chief data management problem was quality control. Field personnel had to be trained to observe and record behavior. After training, continuous monitoring of incoming data would be necessary to produce Demand-Response Logs which would be accurate and comprehensive. If, for example, the data coming in from a district were incomplete, we would have to identify and collect missing data promptly. The problem of coordinating a network of field observers also limited the sample size.

On the one hand, to increase the generalizability of findings, we wanted to have as many school districts involved in the project as possible. On the other hand, the constraints of access, time, money, and quality control limited the number of districts which could be included in our study. We sought a compromise between the desire to include a sizable number of districts and the realities of the limitations imposed upon data collection by the research design. The final decision made in connection with the funding agency was to conduct a nine-month longitudinal study in 12 school districts.

## CHOOSING TWELVE SCHOOL DISTRICTS

In the summer of 1974 we faced the task of selecting 12 school districts to participate in the Responsiveness Project. Given our theoretical interests, we attempted to select school districts which would represent a range of environmental and structural characteristics including different types of interactions between school experts and laymen characterized by the hierarchical, bargaining, and polyarchal styles of decision-making. We recognized from our previous work and the works of others that the probability of identifying hierarchical districts was substantially higher than that of bargaining districts, which was higher than that of polyarchal districts. Selecting districts which would represent varying size, location, wealth, etc., was relatively easy. Selecting districts with varying decision-making styles was problematic. Rather than select districts at random, we decided to gather information, albeit subjective information, concerning the preponderant style of decision-making in candidate school districts.

We turned, first, to data reported in Zeigler, *et al.* (1974). Variables from that study, which had theoretical relevance to styles of governance, were isolated. The districts in that study were then classified according to the hierarchical, bargaining, and polyarchal modes of decision-making. Unfortunately, those data were not sufficient to lead us to 12 school districts which might participate in the Responsiveness Study. There were two interrelated problems. First, the number of school districts which could be classified according to each model with confidence was extremely small, approximately twenty. Second, we could not be confident that the classification of those twenty districts was still accurate. The data for the Zeigler, *et al.* (1974) study were collected in 1968. There was a high probability that some updating of data would be necessary.

In order to update the 1968 data on the twenty districts, we developed questionnaires. The questionnaires were administered to persons within each candidate school district who were quite familiar with the schools. In some instances this was a school administrator. In other instances faculty members in nearby universities were contacted. We also solicited newspaper reporters who regularly covered the schools and other community influentials to respond to our questionnaire concerning the candidate school districts. Additional candidate districts were nominated by our colleagues at the Center for Educational Policy and Management and by questionnaire respondents. Questionnaires were then administered to persons in these additional districts. Through this procedure, we developed a ranking of about one hundred candidate districts from those likely to employ hierarchical through those likely to employ the bargaining mode, to those likely to employ the polyarchal mode of decision-making.

Attention was then turned to enlisting 12 school districts to participate in the Responsiveness Project. This was no mean task. For one matter, school officials, especially superintendents and school board members, were being asked to give up quite a bit of time to the Responsiveness Project. We were requesting a minimum of one 30-minute interview every two weeks with these school officials. Additionally, the data we desired were likely to be, in many cases, quite sensitive. Not all school officials were willing to divulge information concerning the contacts they had with constituents in private. Third, some school officials were concerned about the impact our data might have on their districts. Although we did not intend our data collection activities to be an experimental intervention, the presence of project personnel and the release of preliminary data could result in unpredictable publicity and public reaction.

Complicating the risks to districts was the fact that we were proposing an unprecedented and comprehensive study of all communications and decision-making in school districts. Evaluative statements were perceived by many to be unavoidable. Given our desire and stated purpose to describe processes of communication and to develop indicators of responsiveness, statements comparing school districts' performances would be forthcoming. Thus, in addition to risks concerning divulging what might be private and sensitive information, participating school districts would be placing themselves in jeopardy of being described as either unresponsive or less responsive than other school districts in our study.

These risks were only partially obviated by our guarantee to school districts and participants within school districts of anonymity. Anonymity could be guaranteed with regard to material prepared for scholarly audiences. But total anonymity locally during the conduct of the study was impossible. Since our study was federally funded, the material we forwarded to the National Institute of Education could be obtained under the Freedom of Information Act. The known and potential costs of participating in our study were substantial.

Our procedure for recruiting school districts to participate in the Responsiveness Study was as follows. First, candidate school districts were provided with a prospectus concerning the project. Interested districts were then visited by a representative of the project, who spoke with both school administrators and school board members. In some instances, a return visit was made to give further information and to request participation. It is interesting to note that, in about half of the districts which decided to participate, the superintendent was able to decide in favor of participation without formal approval from the school board. In the others, participation was decided by a formal vote of the school board in a public meeting. Through this process, by September 1974, 12 school districts had agreed to participate in the study.

Although each of the districts which we selected had been thoroughly informed of our intentions, we soon encountered some access problems as the data collection began. Each district was provided with a contract which specified that in exchange for the provision of data to the district it would remain in the study for nine months. Unfortunately, in two school districts it became apparent within a few weeks that the data required for our study would not be forthcoming. In one of these school districts the superintendent had been informed that he would be dismissed at the end of the academic year. As a result, he was no longer willing to participate or intercede on our behalf with the school board members who became hesitant to participate. In a second location, litigation was initiated against the school district by the federal government shortly after the initiation of data collection. Given this crisis, the superintendent and school board members were no longer willing for the comprehensive and potentially sensitive data required for the Responsiveness Project to be collected. Thus, within a month and a half of initiation, it was necessary to discontinue data collection in two of our 12 school districts.

Given the unexpected expense of (1) losing two school districts, (2) recruiting school districts from our reserve lists, and (3) identifying and training project representatives for the reserve districts, it was possible to replace only one school district. Thus, the final number of school districts in the Responsiveness Project was 11. We started with 12 in September of 1974, lost two in the first few weeks of data collection, and substituted one in early November of 1974.

The major demographic characteristics of the 11 school districts are portrayed in table 2.1. The Census Bureau geographical designations for each are as follows: Stumont [2] and Hartshorne Heights—South Atlantic; Leeville—New England; Barwig Park and Macktown—East North Central; Ballard City—West North Central; Nelsonville and Grahamdale—Mountain; Coldren Corners and Drummond Falls—Pacific. Kentington is located in Western Canada.

Size of district is measured in terms of the size of the standard metropolitan statistical area (SMSA) and city in which it is located, and school district enrollment. On the first measure our districts range from a low SMSA population of 62,000 in Kentington to a high of 1.4 million in Drummond Falls. City size ranges from 29,000 in Hartshorne Hts. to 530,000 in Drummond Falls. Student enrollments range from 21,000 in Coldren Corners to 112,000 in Stumont. Thus, our sample includes examples of relatively low enrollment districts in low population areas (Coldren Corners, Barwig Park, Kentington), high enrollment districts in low population areas (Grahamdale, Hartshorne Hts.), low enrollment districts in high population areas (Macktown, Leeville, Nelsonville), and high enrollment districts in high population areas (Stumont, Ballard City, Drummond Falls).

The districts also vary widely with regard to racial composition and wealth. With respect to race, the range is from one percent minority enrollment in Coldren Corners to approximately forty-four percent in Grahamdale. Wealth, measured by annual per pupil expenditure, ranges from a low of approximately one thousand dollars in Grahamdale to a high of about one thousand eight hundred dollars in Drummond Falls.

Table 2.1 also presents the tentative designations of preponderant decision-making style in each district based on subjective and objective information gathered prior to the initiation of data collection. Four districts were designated as hierarchical, four as bargaining, and two as polyarchal. Kentington, a Canadian district, represented a market style in the extreme range of choices available to parents with respect to educational philosophies which guided individual schools.[3]

To summarize, our sample of 11 districts was selected to be broadly representative of a range of characteristics of school districts extant in America. However, examples of districts located in the largest metropolitan areas and extremely small school districts are absent.

TABLE 2.1

DEMOGRAPHIC CHARACTERISTICS OF SCHOOL DISTRICTS

| District | Approx. Population SMSA 1972 | Approx. Population Major City | School District Enrollment 1974-75 | % Negro and Spanish Heritage Pupils, in Central Cities, 1970 | | Approx. Per Pupil Expenditures 1974 | Tentative Style Classification |
|---|---|---|---|---|---|---|---|
| | | | | Below High School | High School | | |
| Coldren Corners | 225,000 | 76,000 | 21,151 | 1.4 | 1.1 | 1580 | H |
| Barwig Park | 353,000 | 126,000 | 23,915 | 17.4 | 14.4 | 1329 | B |
| Nelsonville | 744,000 | 175,000 | 27,325 | 12.8 | 10.0 | 1352 | H |
| Leeville | 645,000 | 176,000 | 29,000 | 4.3 | 2.0 | 1320 | B |
| Kentington | 61,761 | 61,000 | 29,561 | n.a. | n.a. | 1172 | M |
| Macktown | 549,000 | 197,000 | 34,804 | 19.1 | 14.2 | 1265 | H |
| Ballard City | 1,304,000 | 507,000 | 56,700 | 28.7 | 26.7 | 1523 | B |
| Drummond Falls | 1,400,000 | 530,000 | 70,000 | 13.1 | 10.4 | 1796 | B |
| Hartshorne Hts.* | 297,539 | 29,000 | 77,332 | 14.2 | 13.9 | 1233 | H |
| Grahamdale | 357,000 | 243,000 | 83,386 | 43.5 | 39.1 | 1037 | P |
| Stumont | 636,000 | 528,000 | 111,957 | 28.0 | 27.1 | 1152 | P |

* School District includes several cities

H = Hierarchy
P = Polyarchy
B = Bargaining
M = Marketing

## Recruitment of Field Observers

The Demand-Response Log instruments were developed prior to the selection of school districts for the study. Once the participating districts were identified, it was necessary to recruit two field observers in each district and to train them in the use of the Demand-Response Log instruments. Needless to say, a great deal of the ultimate success or failure of the project would rest upon the ability of the observers to carry out their data collection tasks. It was essential to hire the highest quality individuals and to train them to collect reliable data. Not only were they required to use the Demand-Response Log correctly and thoroughly, they were also required to interview school officials and to establish a satisfactory working relationship with them.

The process of hiring field observers began in each school district with the superintendent and personnel department. All school districts were given the option of participating in the selection of observers. About half of the districts participated in the selection process to the extent of suggesting candidates. In most cases, our districts were located near a university or junior college. The social science and education departments at such schools were alternate sources of nominations. Finally, we ran advertisements in local newspapers to enlarge the applicant pool. The candidates were then interviewed by a representative of the project.

Field observers were selected with care. Nevertheless, some had to be replaced during the data collection period. Unfortunately, we can offer few generalizations concerning an optimum procedure for selecting data collection personnel. We found excellent personnel from a variety of backgrounds and experiences. Some of our best field observers were college students. Some of our worst field observers were college students. In some school districts we were fortunate enough to recruit highly trained professionals. Our team of field observers included university professors and former school administrators. However, some were poor data collectors and had to be replaced. In retrospect, we see that the requirements for the data collection tasks of our project were not limited to ability to follow instructions so that information collected would be both accurate and reliable. It was also necessary for the field observer to employ a personal style that would put both highly educated school administrators and a range of school patrons at ease during personal interviews. Unhappily, it is easier to identify individuals who are likely to be conscientious and capable in an objective sense than it is to identify individuals who possess the requisite charm.

## TRAINING OF FIELD OBSERVERS

Once our field observers were selected it was necessary to train them in the use of Demand-Response Log instruments. The object of training was to teach skills to give us assurance that all data would be collected in a consistent manner. Observer training was divided into three basic parts. The first was study of an extensive written description of the project, its objectives, instruments involved, and their use. The second was seminar discussion of the purpose and use of data collection instruments. Finally, simulation exercises employing specially developed video tapes were used to reinforce the previous two approaches and to prepare the observers for actual meetings and interviews.

Only the third element of our observer training, simulation exercises, is somewhat unique. The goal of field observation of meetings was to obtain a comprehensive record of all communications and decisions made at those meetings. Unlike most research projects we did not have a narrow focus which identified "relevant" data. Our training sought to teach, not what interactions to observe and record, but how to observe and record all interactions. We gave field observers no discretion.

Video tapes of simulated meetings were used extensively in the training. The tapes were reconstructions of actual meetings which had been attended and recorded by project staff as the data collection instruments were developed. The training progressed from simple to complex interactions so that later portions of the tapes included ambiguous situations, complicated events, and rapid interchanges. The speed and complexity of later taped interaction was actually greater than that which would likely occur at any meeting our observers would attend. Interview training was conducted according to the program developed by the Survey Research Center at the University of Michigan.

## QUALITY CONTROL

The division of responsibilities, therefore, was between 22 field observers in 11 districts and a staff at the University of Oregon. Observers were to send information to us weekly. Staff members examined this information to insure completeness. To sensitize the observers to the milieu of the district and to familiarize us with the ongoing flow of events, we asked each observer to read and clip the local newspapers, in addition to their other activities. We also subscribed to these newspapers. Close communication was maintained with each observer so that errors could be corrected and missing information supplied.

### Survey Research

Another major set of data collected was information about the preferences of citizens living within each school district. A community survey instrument was developed in the spring prior to the data collection and was pretested in the summer. The sampling technique was a stratified random sample that gave all residents an equal opportunity of being selected. The primary source of potential respondents was the city directory.

A general questionnaire was augmented by an addendum of approximately 10 questions concerning issues of major concern in each district. These latter questions were undertaken in consultation with each school district, primarily as a service to them. At the beginning of the academic year, the questionnaires were administered by mail and were returned over a period of three months.

Although survey pretest yielded a response rate of 63 percent, the actual survey produced a response of 20 percent. An examination of the socioeconomic characteristics of survey respondents and those of the community at large indicated that respondents were over-representative of upper socioeconomic status and educational levels, and were most active in educational policy. Thus, our community sample is biased heavily in favor of the public attentive to school matters.

It is interesting to note that in one school district several of the questions from our community survey were administered in a questionnaire distributed to people who attended public hearings. A comparison of the questions common to our survey and their survey was made, which indicated that the distribution of the responses was virtually identical. Although this independent confirmation exists for only one district, it is so strong that it strengthens our belief that the responses to our community survey are representative of those laymen attentive to school governance issues.

Our survey instrument was also administered to school officials and to samples of community elites. The procedure for surveying the former group was straightforward: during the data collection period, our field observers distributed the survey instrument to school board members, superintendents, and senior school district administrative staff designated by superintendents. The procedure for surveying the community elites was a bit more complicated. Toward the end of the data collection period the Demand-Response Logs were reviewed to identify individuals in each school district who were frequent participants. This list of active laymen was augmented by soliciting the names of active and influential constituents from superintendents and school board members. The latter list was quite uneven from district to district. In most of the districts, school officials attempted to give us a list of active laymen who represented the entire range of opinions and preferences extant in their community. A few school districts, however, limited their nominations to such individuals as officers of parent-teacher organizations, and members of school board advisory committees. We recognized that these latter nominees were quite likely to express opinions favorable to the school district. We did not use these biased lists. As a result, the number of questionnaires sent to community elites in each school district varied from approximately twenty-five to eighty. The response rates from community elites were approximately eighty percent. However, given the small sampling universe we obtained a rather restricted data base for assessing the preferences of community elites.[4]

## The Demand-Response Log in Detail

We now turn to a detailed description of the elements of the Demand-Response Log. It will be recalled that the purpose of the Demand-Response Log was to capture as completely as possible the universe of communications between expert school officials and lay constituents in each school district. We were interested in studying public communications from both an objective and a subjective point of view. We were interested in capturing information on private communications from the point of view of the school official who was contacted. Such systematic observation of behavior is relatively rare in social science research. Therefore, it was necessary to try a variety of instruments, modifying them as we went along. The Demand-Response Log instruments were developed in the nine months prior to the initiation of data collection in our sites.

Pretesting and refinement of the Demand-Response Log instruments were undertaken by using the instruments to record communications processes in city council meetings, faculty meetings, and a variety of public meetings—including school board meetings—in the greater Eugene area. We initially believed that a limited amount of information could be selectively recorded. We quickly discovered, however, that a more reliable procedure was to have the field observer record as much as possible a universe of communication. We therefore moved from a procedure of selective recording to universal recording.

To explicate the use of the Demand-Response Log instruments, we present an excerpt of information as it was received from the field prior to coding. The excerpt begins a sample of the Main Meeting forms, form #1. The information on the extreme left column of the form reveals that the events took place at a school board meeting in district aa (items 8–9), on the bb day of September, 1974 (items 10–15). The meeting had an audience of 30 people (items 46–48), and was recorded by observer number 0 (item 69, bottom, middle of form). The sequence number of the first form (of a series) is 0072 (upper left corner), and the matter before the board is a discussion of whether the district should lend books to private school students. This is agenda item number six, lower left center. Mr. X, the father of a student, is making a "demand" of the school board. Mr. X is a white male who does not purport to be respresenting anyone other than himself. Mr. X's remarks concern district policy on lending books to private school students. He says that the law requires that books be lent, yet the distirct is not lending books. Mr. X reads a letter he wrote to the commissioner of education. There is no obvious audience reaction.

Board member E, a white male, asks Mr. X when his letter was sent. Mr. X, as coded on form sequence number 0073, answers E's question. Board member A, a white female, then asks Mr. L, the board's legal counsel, if the Law Department is aware of the information required by the board on the book lending issue. L, a white male, answers yes (sequence number 0074). There has not yet been any obvious audience reaction to any of the speakers.

Mr. X then remarks that other districts are lending books and asks why the law isn't being followed in this district (sequence number 0075–0076, not shown here). Board member D, a white male, tells Mr. X that he is wrong; Mr. X replies that other districts in other towns in the area are lending books to private school students. In a previous discussion it was brought out that the board is waiting for a legal opinion on the constitutionality of the law requiring book lending. Board member C assures Mr. X that the issue is under consideration and will be settled. Mr. X agrees and his appearance before the board is ended.

Since this is also the end of discussion on the topic of book lending, a form #2 follows to summarize the action taken. Again, the date of the meeting, the district code (items 8–9), and the agenda item appear. (The sequence number of the last speaker is coded as 00762—corresponding to Mr. X's final statement as the *second speaker* on form 0076.) The substance of discussion is summarized on the form, and the action taken is coded according to three dimensions: type of decision is "no decision," outcome is "tabled," type of action is "other"—refer to legal counsel. It is recorded that all parties present showed a medium degree of interest in the topic, and that there were no discernible emotional reactions. Finally, item 67 indicates that follow-up interviews will be attempted with Mr. X, the superintendent, and board members.

The follow-up interview with the superintendent of district aa on the topic of lending books is recorded on a form #3, "Superintendent-Board Member Follow-Up." The district identifier and interview data are recorded in the upper left corner, as is the sequence number of the Main Meeting form where the topic

FORM #1 -- MAIN MEETING FORM

<u>1</u> : <u>0</u> : <u>1</u> : <u>a</u> : <u>a</u>
5  6  7  8  9

SOURCE __MR. X__     REPRESENTING __FATHER OF STUDENT__ RECIPIENT __BOARD__

DATE OF MEETING
<u>0</u> : <u>9</u> : <u>b</u> : <u>b</u> : <u>7</u> : <u>4</u>
10 11  12 13  14 15

TOPIC __LENDING OF PUBLIC BOOKS TO PRIVATE SCHOOL STUDENTS.__

__LAW IS MANDATORY!__

__READS LETTER HE WROTE TO COMMISSIONER OF EDUCATION__

**LAW REQUIRES LENDING OF BOOKS — DISTRICT IS NOT LENDING BOOKS**

TO BE CODED BY CASEA
SOURCE ONE

<u></u> : <u></u> : <u></u> : <u></u> : <u></u> : <u></u>
16 17  18  19  20  21

RECIPIENT ONE

<u></u> : <u></u> : <u></u> : <u></u> : <u></u> : <u></u>
22 23  24  25  26  27

TOPIC

<u></u> : <u></u> : <u></u> : <u></u> : <u></u> : <u></u>
28 29  30  31  32  33

| STATEMENT (01.) (51-52) | Demand, Recommendation in Favor<br>02. Demand, Recommendation Opposed<br>03. Request Info.<br>04. Supply Info.<br>99. Don't Know | CHARACTERISTICS OF SPEAKER (01) (53-54) | 01. White Male<br>02. White Female<br>03. Black Male<br>04. Black Female<br>05. Spanish Male<br>06. Sp. Female<br>07. Other Male<br>08. Other Female | REACTION TO SPEAKER (code only when <u>obvious</u>) (55-58) |
|---|---|---|---|---|

                    Ap. Opp. Mixed Ignore
Supt. 1  2  3  4
Aud. 1  2  3  4
B/Pres.1  2  3  4
Board 1  2  3  4

SOURCE TWO

<u></u> : <u></u> : <u></u> : <u></u> : <u></u> : <u></u>
34 35  36  37  38  39

SOURCE __BOARD MEMBER E__ REPRESENTING __BOARD__ RECIPIENT_____

TOPIC __LENDING BOOKS__

__DATE OF LETTER?__

RECIPIENT TWO

<u></u> : <u></u> : <u></u> : <u></u> : <u></u> : <u></u>
40 41 42  43  44  45

| STATEMENT 01. (59-60) | Demand, Recommendation in Favor<br>02. Demand, Recommendation Opposed<br>(03) Request Info.<br>04. Supply Info.<br>99. Don't Know | CHARACTERISTICS OF SPEAKER (01) (61-62) | 01. White Male<br>02. White Female<br>03. Black Male<br>04. Black Female<br>05. Spanish Male<br>06. Sp. Female<br>07. Other Male<br>08. Other Female | REACTION TO SPEAKER (code only when <u>obvious</u>) (63-66) |
|---|---|---|---|---|

                    Ap. Opp. Mixed Ignore
Supt. 1  2  3  4
Aud. 1  2  3  4
B/Pres.1  2  3  4
Board 1  2  3  4

NUMBER OF PEOPLE IN AUDIENCE
<u>0</u> : <u>3</u> : <u>0</u>
46 47 48

TYPE OF MEETING (49-50)

(01.) School Board
02. Executive Board
03. Administrative Cabinet
04. Public Meeting
05. Other (specify)

AGENDA ITEM (67-68)

01  02  03  04  05  (06)  07  08  09  10

11  12  13  14  15  16  17  18  19  20

21  22  23  24  25  26  27  28  29  30

31  98 (not an agenda item)

<u>0</u> : <u>2</u>
69 70

DO YOU PLAN A FOLLOW-UP INTERVIEW FOR:

SOURCE ONE ___
       71

SOURCE TWO ___
       72

02-08-28-74
FORM #2--MOTION AND ACTION SUMMARY FOR MEETINGS

FOR OFFICE USE ONLY

INSTRUCTIONS: FILL OUT ONE OF THESE FORMS WHENEVER AN ACTION IS TAKEN, SUCH AS A MOTION, A VOTE, A DECISION WITHOUT A VOTE, AND SO ON. YOU SHOULD HAVE ONE OF THESE FORMS, AT LEAST, FOR EACH ITEM ON THE AGENDA.

Sequence # of Last Speaker          Date of Meeting  _09-bb-74_

_0  0  7  6  2_
 1  2  3  4  5                       Motion by _____

_____ _a_ _a_
 6   7   8   9          Agenda Item # _6_                34-35    DESCRIPTION OF MOTION OR TOPIC: (DESCRIBE BELOW
                                                                  AND CODE CATEGORIES ON THE LEFT)
                       Main Motion = 1               36
__ __ __ __ __ __      Amendment   = 2                        _LENDING OF PUBLIC SCHOOL_
10 11 12 13 14 15
                       TYPE OF DECISION (Circle One)            _BOOKS TO PRIVATE SCHOOL_

__ __ __ __ __ __      01. Roll call vote                      _STUDENTS — DECISION WILL_
16 17 18 19 20 21      02. Hand vote                 37-38
                       03. Voice vote                          _COME AFTER LEGAL OPINION_
                       04. No vote
__ (LEAVE BLANK) __    (05.) No decision                       _ON CONSTITUTIONALITY_
22 23 24 25 26 27      06. Agenda item omitted
                                                               _OF LAW REQUIRING_
                       OUTCOME
__ __ __ __ __ __                                              _LENDING IS OBTAINED._
28 29 30 31 32 33      1. Vote, passed
                       2. Vote, failed
                       3. No second                  39
                       (4.) Tabled
                       5. Other (specify)

                       TYPE OF ACTION

                       01. Direct decision by group
                       02. Refer to Committee        40-41
                       03. Refer to Superintendent
                       04. Refer to Board
                       05. Refer to Administrator
                       (06.) Other Action (specify)
                       _REFER TO COUNSEL_

VOTING RESULTS

INSTRUCTIONS: MEMBER OF THE BOARD OR OTHER GROUP SHOULD BE LISTED ALPHABETICALLY BY YOU SO THAT "A" ALWAYS STANDS FOR THE FIRST MEMBER, "B" FOR THE SECOND, "C" FOR THE THIRD, AND SO ON. BE SURE TO SUPPLY US WITH A LIST OF THE MEMBERS' NAMES AND THEIR CODES. IF THE VOTE IS BY VOICE OR HAND, ESTIMATE THE TOTAL VOTE AND RECORD THOSE YOU COULD OBSERVE.

| | (42) A | (43) B | (44) C | (45) D | (46) E | (47) F | (48) G | (49) H | (50) I | (51) J | (52) K | (53) L | (54) M | (55) N | (56) O | (57) P | (58-59) TOTALS | (60) SUPT. POSITION |
|---|---|---|---|---|---|---|---|---|---|---|---|---|---|---|---|---|---|---|
| Yes | 1 | 1 | 1 | 1 | 1 | 1 | 1 | 1 | 1 | 1 | 1 | 1 | 1 | 1 | 1 | 1 | ____ | 1 |
| No | 1 | 2 | 2 | 2 | 2 | 2 | 2 | 2 | 2 | 2 | 2 | 2 | 2 | 2 | 2 | 2 | ____ | 2 |
| Abstain | 3 | 3 | 3 | 3 | 3 | 3 | 3 | 3 | 3 | 3 | 3 | 3 | 3 | 3 | 3 | 3 | ____ | 3 |
| Absent | 4 | 4 | 4 | 4 | 4 | 4 | 4 | 4 | 4 | 4 | 4 | 4 | 4 | 4 | 4 | 4 | ____ | 4 |

|  | | DEGREE OF INTEREST | | | EMOTIONAL REACTION (if any) | | |
|---|---|---|---|---|---|---|---|
| | | High | Medium | Low | Delighted | Angry | Mixed |
| 61-62 | Board | 1 | (2) | 3 | 1 | 2 | 3 |
| 63-64 | Audience | 1 | (2) | 3 | 1 | 2 | 3 |
| 65-66 | Supt. | 1 | (2) | 3 | 1 | 2 | 3 |

Do you intend follow-up interviews?
67          (1. Yes)
            2. No

FORM #3--SUPERINTENDENT-BOARD MEMBER FOLLOW-UP                                03-08-28-74

PERSON INTERVIEWED  Supt. of GG

TOPIC  LENDING OF SCHOOL BOOKS TO
       PRIVATE SCHOOL CHILDREN

FIRST SCHOOL BOARD MEETING
CODING FORM CODE

0 : 0 : 5 : 4   1
1   2   3   4    5

0 : 3 : a : a
6   7   8   9

DATE OF INTERVIEW

0 : 9 : b : b : 7 : 4
10  11  12  13  14  15

TO BE CODED BY CASEA

16  17  18  19  20  21

RECIPIENT

22  23  24  25  26  27

TOPIC

28  29  30  31  32  33

POSITION
1. In favor
2. Oppose
3. Neutral
4. Other
9. Don't Know
34

FINAL SCHOOL BOARD
MEETING
CODING FORM CODE

35  36  37  38  39

DATE OF MEETING

40  41  42  43  44  45

---

|  | NAME  Students | NAME  Mr. X | NAME |
|---|---|---|---|
| Do you recall (name)'s presentation before the school board about (topic)? | RECALL  1. (Yes)  2. No  (45) | RECALL  1. (Yes)  2. Yes  (54) | RECALL  1. Yes  2. No  (62) |
|  | SOURCE ONE  0 : 0 : 6 : 8  47  48  49  50 | SOURCE TWO  0 : 0 : 7 : 2  55  56  57  58 | SOURCE THREE  63  64  65  66 |
| Did you agree or disagree with what (name) said about (topic)? | AGREEMENT (51) 1. (Agree)  2. Neutral  3. Disagree  9. No Opinion | AGREEMENT (59) 1. (Agree)  2. Neutral  3. Disagree  9. No Opinion | AGREEMENT (67) 1. Agree  2. Agree  3. Agree  9. No Opinion |
| Did (name's) presentation effect your position on (topic)? | EFFECT (52) 1. Effect  2. (No Effect)  3. Negative Effect  9. No Opinion | EFFECT (60) 1. Effect  2. (No Effect)  3. Negative Effect  9. No Opinion | EFFECT (68) 1. Effect  2. No Effect  3. Negative Effect  9. No Opinion |
| Do you feel that (name) is satisfied with the action that was taken? | SATISFACTION (53) 1. Satisfied  2. Neutral  3. (Dissatis-fied)  9. No Opinion | SATISFACTION (61) 1. Satisfied  2. Neutral  3. (Dissatis-fied)  9. No Opinion | SATISFACTION (69) 1. Satisfied  2. Neutral  3. Dissatisfied  9. No Opinion |

DOES RESPONDENT INTEND TO DO ANYTHING FURTHER ABOUT THIS MATTER?   1. (Yes) (70)
                                                                   2. No

(If yes, describe)  Asking City Solicitor's opinion on
Constitutionality of Issue

REMARKS

CONTINUED TO
ANOTHER FORM?
1. Yes   (71)
2. (No)

36

addressed by constituents first appears. In this case, the topic was introduced at the school board meeting before Mr. X spoke. Form #3 is topic specific, and is designed to record a superintendent's or board member's reaction to as many as three constituents who spoke on the topic. Mr. X was the second constituent to speak at the board meeting about the lending of school books to private school children. The superintendent of district aa remembers Mr. X's presentation before the board and agrees with his point of view; the presentation had no effect on the superintendent's position, however. The superintendent perceived that Mr. X was dissatisfied with the action taken at the board meeting. The superintendent does intend further action on the matter once he has obtained advice from legal counsel.

The perceptions of Mr. X are obtained by interviewing him, using form #6. The topic is entered by the logger as a part of the first question. Mr. X says he favors loaning school books to private school students. Mr. X mentions two prior contacts that he has made: with the superintendent at the meeting and with the Commissioner of Education. No action has been taken by either one. Mr. X believes he had an effect on the superintendent, although on form #3 the superintendent says that Mr. X did not have an effect. The citizen believes that board members A, B, and C agree with him but that board member D does not. He thinks the superintendent has not taken a position even though the superintendent indicated on form #3 that he is in agreement with Mr. X.

As this excerpt from our Demand-Response Log file for the aa district demonstrates, our instruments record demand events which take place at school board meetings from three different perspectives. First, forms #1 and #2 record incidents from an objective perspective. Second, form #6 records incidents from the perspective of constituents making demands. And the third, form #3 records demand events from the perspective of decision-makers—the superintendent and the school board members. These forms record both substance and procedure. Moreover, they record the reactions of all parties to both the substance of topics and the procedure of decisions or nondecisions.

The Demand-Response Log also contains instruments to record information on private communications. The next excerpt describes a private contact between a constituent and the superintendent in school district xx. Form #4 is a summary of Superintendent X's nonpublic constituent contacts for the week ending September 24. In this particular week, the superintendent had approximately fifteen contacts from constituents over a wide range of topics.

Form #5 records Superintendent X's recollection of one of the contacts summarized on form #4. A Mrs. Articulate, representing a local PTA, requested that lunch periods be lengthened to 55 minutes, and that Superintendent X take action to effect the change. Superintendent X didn't have a firm position on this request at the time of the interview. He reported that the request did have some effect on his position, but the contact had only a small effect on Mrs. Articulate's position. The request is currently pending, and Superintendent X estimates that Mrs. Articulate is neither satisfied nor dissatisfied with the action taken so far. It should be noted that Superintendent X classified Mrs. Articulate's request as a school finance matter, and that similar reports are recorded for the other nonpublic contacts Superintendent X had that week.

The typical division of labor between the two field observers in each district was as follows: one attended and reported school board and school board commit-

FORM #6--CONSTITUENT INTERVIEW     06-08-28-74

TO BE CODED BY CASEA

Date of Interview _____    Your Name **A . LOGGER** _____

$\overline{1}$ $\overline{2}$ $\overline{3}$ $\overline{4}$ $\overline{5}$  Person Interviewed **MR X**   Phone # _____

$\overline{6}^{0}$ $\overline{7}^{6}$ $\overline{8}^{a}$ $\overline{9}^{a}$  Group Affiliation, if any, of person interviewed **NONE** _____

1. Hello, my name is (your name). I'm working on a nation-wide research project which includes a study of the (name of district/city) public school system. I understand that you have expressed an interest in

$\overline{10}$ $\overline{11}$ $\overline{12}$ $\overline{13}$ $\overline{14}$ $\overline{15}$

(STATE THE TOPIC OF INTEREST AND WRITE IT HERE) **LOANING PUBLIC Sch. Books to Priv. Sch.**

$\overline{16}$ $\overline{17}$ $\overline{18}$ $\overline{19}$ $\overline{20}$ $\overline{21}$  It would be very helpful for our study if you could tell me what your position **Students**
is on (topic). (IF NEEDED) Do you favor or oppose (topic)? (RECORD COMMENT BELOW)

$\overline{22}$ $\overline{23}$ $\overline{24}$ $\overline{25}$ $\overline{26}$ $\overline{27}$  Position

$\overline{28}$ $\overline{29}$ $\overline{30}$ $\overline{31}$ $\overline{32}$ $\overline{33}$  (01. Favor)    **IT'S A LAW**
02. Oppose

2. Since the beginning of the school year, have you contacted any of the school
$\overline{34}$ $\overline{35}$  officials, the school board, superintendent, or other public officials about this matter? (IF YES, ASK):

$\overline{36}$ $\overline{37}$ $\overline{38}$ $\overline{39}$ $\overline{40}$ $\overline{41}$  Who did you talk to? (RECORD EACH CONTACT THE PERSON HAS MADE)

$\overline{42}$ $\overline{43}$ $\overline{44}$ $\overline{45}$ $\overline{46}$ $\overline{47}$  1. **SUPERINTENDENT** _____   3._____

2. **LETTER TO COMMISSIONER** _____   4._____
**OF ED.**
$\overline{48}$ $\overline{49}$ $\overline{50}$ $\overline{51}$ $\overline{52}$ $\overline{53}$  (FOR EACH CONTACT RESPONDENT HAS HAD, ASK THE FOLLOWING QUESTION)

3. Did you ask (official) to take some specific action, or were you mainly interested
$\overline{54}$ $\overline{55}$ $\overline{56}$ $\overline{57}$  in expressing your viewpoint to them, or what? (RECORD ANSWER BELOW AND THEN ASK): What did (official) do about the matter? (RECORD ANSWER BELOW AND THEN REPEAT THE
$\overline{58}$ $\overline{59}$ $\overline{60}$ $\overline{61}$  QUESTION FOR CONTACT (2, if any, #3 and so on.)

ACTION REQUESTED OF CONTACT    ACTION TAKEN
$\overline{62}$ $\overline{63}$ $\overline{64}$ $\overline{65}$  1. **LOAN OF BOOKS**     **NO**

$\overline{66}$ $\overline{67}$ $\overline{68}$ $\overline{69}$  2. **ENFORCE LAW**     **NOT YET**

3.

4.

KEYER (NOT LOGGERS): GO ON TO DECK 2; DUPLICATE COLUMNS 1-4 AND 10-15; PLACE A 2 IN COLUMN 5

16-19  4. (FOR EACH CONTACT ASK) Do you think you had some effect on (official)'s position?

(1 = effect  2 = neutral  3 = no effect)

FIRST CONTACT (1) 2 3  SECOND CONTACT (1) 2 3  THIRD CONTACT 1 2 3  FOURTH CONTACT 1 2 3

20-23  5. (FOR EACH CONTACT ASK) Were you satisfied with what (official/group) did? (1 = satisfied 2 = mixed
3 = unsatisfied)
FIRST CONTACT 1 2 (3)  SECOND CONTACT 1 2 3  THIRD CONTACT 1 2 3  FOURTH CONTACT 1 2 3

(FOR THE FOLLOWING QUESTIONS YOU SHOULD HAVE A LIST OF SCHOOL BOARD MEMBERS, AND BE ABLE TO READ THEIR NAMES TO THE RESPONDENT IF NECESSARY. CODE ALL ANSWERS TO THE FOLLOWING FOUR QUESTIONS ON THE LIST BELOW)

6. Which members of the board would you say agree with you about this issue? **A, B, C**

7. Which members of the board would you say disagree with you about this issue? **D**

8. What position has the Superintendent of the district taken? **NONE**

9. (IF OTHER OFFICIALS WERE CONTACTED ASK) What is the position of (other official)?

| | 24 | 25 | 26 | 27 | 28 | 29 | 30 | 31 | 32 | 33 | 34 | 35 | 36 | 37 | 38 | 39 | 40 | 41 | 42 |
|---|---|---|---|---|---|---|---|---|---|---|---|---|---|---|---|---|---|---|---|
| | A | B | C | D | E | F | G | H | I | J | K | L | M | N | SUPT. | OTHER 1 | OTHER 2 | OTHER 3 | OTHER 4 |
| AGREE | 1 | 1 | 1 | 1 | 1 | 1 | 1 | 1 | 1 | 1 | 1 | 1 | 1 | 1 | 1 | 1 | 1 | 1 | 1 |
| OPPOSE | 2 | 2 | 2 | 2 | 2 | 2 | 2 | 2 | 2 | 2 | 2 | 2 | 2 | 2 | 2 | 2 | 2 | 2 | 2 |
| NO POSITION | 3 | 3 | 3 | 3 | 3 | 3 | 3 | 3 | 3 | 3 | 3 | 3 | 3 | 3 | 3 | 3 | 3 | 3 | 3 |

10. Are you planning to underake any additonal activities in realtion to this matter?

43  1. NO (Why is that?)
2. (YES) (What are you planning to do?) **WILL STAY WITH IT UNTIL PRIVATE SCHOOL STUDENTS ARE LOANED BOOKS**

(DO NOT ASK THE RESPONDENT, BUT IF POSSIBLE CODE HIS/HER SEX, RACE, THEN ASK FOR THE OCCUPATION OF THE RESPONDENT HOUSEHOLDS)

44
45  **M** SEX    **CAUCASIAN** RACE    **SELF-EMPLOYED** OCCUPATION

TO BE CODED BY CASEA

FORM #4--SCREENING QUESTIONNAIRE FOR SUPERINTENDENT
OR BOARD MEMBERS

Sequence # of <u>first</u> report

Date of Interview *0̸9̸2̸4̸7̸4̸*  Your Name  *A. LOGGER*

Person Interviewed  *SUPERINTENDENT X*

‾1‾ ‾2‾ ‾3‾ ‾4‾ ‾5‾

‾ ‾ X X
‾6‾ ‾7‾ ‾8‾ ‾9‾

INSTRUCTIONS: ASK THE FOLLOWING QUESTIONS OF THE RESPONDENT IN ORDER TO OBTAIN
A COUNT OF THE NUMBER OF CONSTITUENCY CONTACTS RESPONDENT HAD SINCE YOU LAST
INTERVIEWED HIM. AFTER ASKING THE QUESTIONS ON THIS FORM, FILL OUT ONE CONVER-
SATION REPORT FOR EACH CONSTITUENCY CONTACT. IF A GROUP OF PERSONS CONTACTED THE
RESPONDENT, THIS COUNTS AS ONE CONTACT. IF SOME OF THE CONVERSATIONS WERE
CONFIDENTIAL USE CODE NAMES FOR THE CONSTITUENT RATHER THAN THE ACTUAL NAMES.

‾10‾ ‾11‾ ‾12‾ ‾31‾ ‾14‾ ‾15‾

___ (BLANK) ___ ___ ___
‾16‾ ‾17‾ ‾18‾ ‾19‾ ‾20‾ ‾21‾

‾22‾ ‾23‾ ‾24‾ ‾25‾ ‾26‾ ‾27‾

‾28‾ ‾29‾ ‾30‾ ‾31‾ ‾32‾ ‾33‾

‾34-35‾

1. (IF NEEDED) As you know, the purpose of this interview is
to help us monitor the types of suggestions, problems, demands,
or complaints that persons in the community have brought to you
or contacted you about during the past week. We also are interested in constituents who have contacted you just to express
their opinion on some aspect of the educational system.

    First, have any citizens from the district talked with you
this week about <u>SCHOOL FINANCES</u>? (IF NEEDED): By this
general topic we would include such things as budgetary increases,
allocations to different programs, and so on.

No = 00
(Yes) How many persons contacted you?  *10-12*

NOTES:

‾36-37‾

2. What about the <u>educational programs</u>? Have any constituents
contacted you this week about the curriculum, course <u>requirements</u>,
the <u>quality</u> of the program or the teaching?

No = 00
(Yes) How many?  *2*

‾38-39‾

3. The next set of topics concern <u>minority groups</u> and their
problems. (IF NEEDED): Have any constituents contacted you
about integration, bussing, women's rights, or other similar
items?

No = 00
(Yes) How many?  *1*

‾40-41‾

4. Were you contacted by any of the districts constituents
this week about <u>citizen participation</u> in educational matters?
(IF NEEDED) This could include such topics as local control
of schools, decentralization, decision-making policies of
the schools or the district, access to educational leaders,
and so on.

(No)= 00
Yes. How many contacts? _____

‾42-43‾

5. Did any constituents contact you this week about <u>student</u>
rights, responsibilities, behavior or topics related to this?

No = 00
(Yes) How many?  *1*

‾44-45‾

6. Other than conversations already covered, have any persons
from the community contacted you to express approval or disapproval or to provide suggestions about educational policies,
personnel, or any other matters of immediate concern to the
educational system?

No = 00
(Yes) How many? *SEVERAL*

Sequence # of <u>last</u> report

‾46‾ ‾47‾ ‾48‾ ‾49‾ ‾50‾

INSTRUCTIONS: FOR EACH CONTACT WITH A CONSTITUENT, FILL OUT ONE OF THE <u>CONVERSATION</u>
<u>REPORTS</u>. IF A SINGLE EXCHANGE COVERED MORE THAN ONE TOPIC, FILL OUT ONE FORM FOR
EACH TOPIC COVERED.

REMEMBER THAT THIS INFORMATION IS ENTIRELY CONFIDENTIAL. MAIL THESE FORMS TO CASEA
IMMEDIATELY AFTER COMPLETING THE INTERVIEW. DO NOT COPY THE FORM. DO NOT SHOW THEM
TO ANYONE. DO NOT DISCLOSE THESE CONTENTS TO ANYONE.

FORM #5=CONVERSATION REPORT: INTERVIEW GUIDE FOR
SUPERINTENDENT OR BOARD MEMBERS

TO BE CODED BY CASEA

Date of Interview _092474_    Your Name _A. LOGGER_

| 1 | 2 | 3 | 4 | | 5 |

Person Interviewed _SUPERINTENDENT_ (Was person interviewed the source or the

_C S X X_
6  7  8  9

recipient of a demand? _RECIPIENT_

| 10 | 11 | 12 | 13 | 14 | 15 |

INSTRUCTIONS: Fill out the following form for each of the contacts respondent had with constituents since you last interviewed him/her. If a single exchange covered more than one topic, fill out one form for each. If a single exchange covered more than one aspect of the same topic, or a subtopic, fill out one form for each aspect if needed.

| 16 | 17 | 18 | 19 | 20 | 21 |

| 22 | 23 | 24 | 25 | 26 | 27 |

(FOR THE FIRST CONSTITUENCY CONTACT, START WITH QUESTION 1. FOR EACH SUCCEEDING CONTACT, BEGIN WITH QUESTION 1a).

| 28 | 29 | 30 | 31 | 32 | 33 |

1. I have a few questions now about each conversation. I need to know who you talked with, what the topic of conversation was, and what his/her position is on the topic. This information will be kept entirely confidential. Let's begin with the first conversation on (topic).   _SCHOOL FINANCE_

    1a. Who talked with you about (topic) and what did he/she want? (RECORD COMMENTS BELOW AND CODE).

Constituent _MRS. ARTICULATE_    Representing _LOCAL SCHOOL P.T.A._

34-35

_____ (No. of Constituents Present)

TYPE OF STATEMENT (CODE ONE)

| TOPIC AND POSITION (SPECIFY FULLY) |
| --- |

_LUNCH PERIOD SHOULD BE_

36-37

①. Favor
02. Oppose
03. Req. Info.
04. Supply Info.

_LENGTHENED TO 55 MINUTES_

38    2. Do you agree or disagree with (name) about (topic)?

    1. Agree    2. Neutral    3. Disagree    7. N.A.    8. Refused  ⑨. Don't Know

39    3. Did the conversation have some effect, a small effect, or no effect on your position?

    ①. Some    2. Small    3. None    7. N.A.    8. Refused    9. Don't Know

40    4. Do you think the conversation had some effect, a small effect, or no effect on his/her position?

    1. Some   ②. Small    3. None    7. N.A.    8. Refused    9. Don't Know

    5. Did (name) want you to take some specific action yourself, or did he/she want the board to take action, or what? (SPECIFY ACTION REQUESTED AND CODE)

41-42
43-44
45-46

01. Action by Board      05. Requested Information
②. Action by Supt.      06. Other Action (specify)
03. Action by Board Member   97. Not applicable
04. Action by Administrator   98. Refused
                      99. Don't Know

(IF ACTION WAS REQUESTED, ASK):

    6. What has been done about the request?

47-48
49-50
51-52

01. Action taken as requested   04. Nothing yet
02. Action Refused          05. Others (specify) _____
③ Request Pending        97. N.A.
                       98. Refused
                       99. Don't Know

(IF THERE WERE A SERIES OF CONTACTS INVOLVING THE SAME ISSUE, ASK):

53    7. Are there any of the other persons who contacted you about this same issue for whom the answers to the questions would be identical to the ones for (name)? If you would tell me who these persons were and what groups they represented, we can avoid filling out a separate form for each. (RECORD NAMES, GROUPS AND TOTALS)   _NONE_

tee meetings, including public hearings. The other attended and recorded the meetings of the superintendent's administrative cabinet or staff. Interviewing of superintendents, board members, and constituents was also divided. Interview subjects were assigned to each observer, who was then responsible for all interview contacts with this individual. The board meeting observer was usually responsible for interviewing the superintendent and constituents who appeared before the school board. The cabinet meeting logger usually interviewed most of the school board members. Thus, we assigned responsibility for recording meetings so that each observer would become familiar with the long-term issues and decisions peculiar to that forum. Similarly, constituents who spoke at school board meetings and cabinet meetings were interviewed consistently by the same observer to ensure reliability and consistency.

The typical school board meeting log consisted of 100 to 300 coded forms, each of which recorded two public statements. And, as we shall see, the typical school district yielded more than twelve interviews concerning private communications every week. The total Demand-Response Log file consists of approximately forty thousand card images of data.

## Summary

Our first departure from past research on educational decision-making was to collect data on both events and perceptions over a long period of time. Our second departure was to make the communication the central focus of our study. Social scientists typically concentrate on the behavior modification component of policy-making. Given this interest, the decision or choice quite naturally becomes the unit of analysis. Unfortunately, this approach neglects the fact that much public business is dispatched without any attempt at closure: frequently "the decision" simply does not exist. It is entirely possible that a substantial proportion of the demands placed upon school districts can be satisfied without the modification of behavior or policies or a decision (for example, demands may require no more than the dissemination of readily available information). We believe that to focus exclusively on major decisions can be misleading because it ignores the overwhelming majority of routine public business.

The Demand-Response Log is designed to collect information on both the "articulated constituent preferences" and "behavior of government officials" components of the organizing concepts presented in figure 1.1. The unarticulated preferences of constituents and government officials are measured by survey research.

The balance of this book will discuss the interrelations between the survey, and Demand-Response Log components of our research.

# Notes

1. Our methodology was heavily influenced by Benjamin Walter (1963) and by David Kovenock (1967).
2. All school districts are identified by pseudonyms.
3. Our original sample of 12 districts had 4 hierarchical, 4 bargaining, 3 polyarchal, and 1 market designation. Two polyarchal districts dropped out and one polyarchal district was substituted.
4. The number of respondents in each survey group is summarized below.

| District | Public | School Officials | Community Elite |
|---|---|---|---|
| Coldren Corners | 198 | 15 | 39 |
| Barwig Park | 164 | 14 | 37 |
| Nelsonville | 144 | 19 | 19 |
| Leeville | 103 | 15 | 10 |
| Kentington | 218 | 18 | 10 |
| Macktown | 140 | 22 | 7 |
| Ballard City | 122 | 9 | 0 |
| Drummond Falls | 168 | 16 | 33 |
| Hartshorne Hts. | 177 | 16 | 10 |
| Grahamdale | 177 | 14 | 11 |
| Stumont | 120 | 11 | 19 |

# 3
# Unarticulated Preferences of Experts and Laymen

In this chapter we present the results of our survey research. We attempted to ascertain the unarticulated attitudes and preferences of three distinct populations in each school district: the public attentive to and interested in school district matters (hereafter called the public); active members of the community who could be identified as participants in public school district meetings (hereafter called the community elite); and school board members, superintendents, and other central school district administrators (hereafter called school officials). Our interest is both in describing the responses of each group and in examining the similarities and differences between the groups.

The chapter is organized by the substance of survey questions. We present findings on attitudes and preferences concerning most important problems, program expenditures, program approval, performance satisfaction, major issues, and efficacy. For each set of questions we will attempt to characterize the preferences of the three survey populations and to assess the extent to which preferences vary across school districts. We will also present a rigorous analysis to assess whose unarticulated attitudes and preferences school officials best represent for each set of questions. The chapter will conclude with an analysis of aggregate preference representativeness. The general survey questionnaire which was administered in all school districts is presented as an appendix to this chapter.

## Agenda Attitudes and Preferences

Our survey questionnaire had one open-ended question. We asked respondents to describe in their own words the most important problems facing the public schools in their community that school officials try to take care of. (Question 13 in the appendix to this chapter.) We coded a maximum of four answers from each survey respondent. Tables 3.1 and 3.2 summarize the responses from our public respondents and from school officials in our 11 school districts.[1]

Table 3.1 presents for each school district the three most frequent responses from the public concerning the most important problems facing the school districts in declining order of frequency. In Leeville, there is a tie for the third most frequently named problem. Thus, for that district alone, four most important problems are reported.

From the point of view of the general public, two issues dominate the first rank. Those issues are: students (primarily disciplinary problems) and finance. In only one district does neither of these two issues emerge as the most important.

43

TABLE 3.1

MOST IMPORTANT ISSUES FROM GENERAL PUBLIC SURVEY
Decreasing Order of Magnitude

| Coldren Corners | Finance | Students | Curriculum | |
|---|---|---|---|---|
| Barwig Park | Finance | Students | | |
| Nelsonville | Finance | Students | Curriculum | |
| Leeville | Students | Finance | Curriculum | Teachers |
| Kentington | Students | Teachers | Curriculum | |
| Macktown | Students | Discrimination | Finance | |
| Ballard City | Finance | Teachers | Students | |
| Drummond Falls | Finance | Curriculum | Students | |
| Hartshorne Hts. | Students | Discrimination | Curriculum | |
| Grahamdale | Students | Teachers | Curriculum | |
| Stumont | Discrimination | Students | Teachers | |

TABLE 3.2

MOST IMPORTANT ISSUES FROM
SCHOOL OFFICIAL SURVEYS
Decreasing Order of Magnitude

| Coldren Corners | Finance | District Operation | |
|---|---|---|---|
| Barwig Park | Finance | District Operation | |
| Nelsonville | Students | | |
| Leeville | Finance | Curriculum | District Operation |
| Kentington | Curriculum | Finance | |
| Macktown | District Operation | | |
| Ballard City | Finance | | |
| Drummond Falls | Finance | Teachers | |
| Hartshorne Hts. | Students | Finance | |
| Grahamdale | --No Consensus-- | | |
| Stumont | Finance | | |

Scattered throughout the remaining ranks are the problems of teachers, curriculum, and, on occasion, discrimination. It seems clear, therefore, that the public's central concerns are finance and student-related problems.

In choosing the most important problems named by school officials for table 3.2, a different procedure was employed. Due to the low number of school official respondents and the frequency with which one or two issues are named by nearly all, we chose not to present the three most frequently named problems as we did for the general public surveys. For an issue to be classified as most important for school officials, at least 40 percent of the respondents must name the issue as most important. The 40 percent criterion was not chosen independently of the data. Our analysis of the responses indicated that 40 percent was a prominent cut-off level.

The concern of the public over students and finance is shared, to some extent, by school officials (table 3.2). In eight districts these two problems are listed as most important. In one district there is no consensus, and in the other two, district operation and curriculum are regarded as most important. These two tables indicate that the public and school officials are in substantial agreement about the most important problems.

Since a different number of most important problems may be presented in tables 3.1 and 3.2 for each district, it is difficult to ascertain quantitatively the representativeness of school officials' unarticulated attitudes and preferences. Nevertheless, we offer the following index. The number of most important issues in the school official table gives the maximum number of issue agreements between experts and laymen for that district. A simple proportion of agreements to total possible agreements indicates that for Macktown and Stumont, scores of zero obtain. Hartshorne Hts., Barwig Park, Coldren Corners, Drummond Falls, and Kentington have agreement scores of 50. The agreement score for Leeville is 67, and the scores for Ballard City and Nelsonville are 100. Since there are no most important problems named by school officials in Grahamdale, no index of agreement is possible. This crude quantitative index suggests that experts and laymen exhibit high levels of agreement concerning the most important problems. This overall level of agreement is even more impressive when one considers that these responses are open-ended. Thus, school officials' unarticulated attitudes and preferences concerning the proper agenda for school districts are fairly representative of the public's unarticulated agenda preferences.

## Preference Aggregation

How does one identify the preferred policy of a group, given a range of preferences? There are two prominent choices: one may designate the plurality position as the group preference, or one may integrate all responses to identify an "average" position as the group preference. Each approach has advantages and disadvantages. The primary advantage of the plurality approach is that the designation rule mirrors the choice process available to public officials. Public officials must select one of a range of policy options. A budget, for example, is either increased, decreased, or held constant. It is not possible to compromise between purchasing a school bus and not purchasing a school bus by buying 55 percent of a bus. The weakness of this approach is that it ignores the preferences of those outside the plurality. Obviously, the smaller the plurality the greater the problem.

Given three choices, such as spend more, spend the same, spend less, it is possible to accept a plurality position which is opposed by 66 percent of the group.

The averaging approach, typically operationalized by assigning ordinal values to weight the proportion favoring each position, has the complementary strengths and weaknesses. On the one hand, the preference designation integrates all responses. On the other hand, the average preference may be the first choice of few or none of the group.

Given our interest in decision-making, representation, and responsiveness, the plurality aggregation rule is preferable for the major portion of the analysis. We view the averaging procedure as a useful complement to our plurality scale analysis. Since the overlap between the two approaches in our data is so great we shall present the plurality analysis in detail. We will compare average and plurality designations in order to explore the extent to which plurality preferences represent the distribution of preferences in each school district.

## Congruence

As Luttbeg notes, attitude congruence is one of several indicators of successful representation (Luttbeg, 1974). As discussed in chapter 1, we will not employ attitude similarities or congruence as direct evidence of responsiveness because of our process orientation to responsiveness. Responsiveness must include a component of governmental *behavior*. Attitudinal congruence may be a cause of responsive government, but such congruence is not a sufficient definition of responsiveness. We should underline that our survey questions go beyond general attitudes at the local level. They also tap a wide range of program preferences at the local, state, and federal levels.

The focus of our congruence analysis is the query: whose unarticulated preferences are best represented by those of school officials? We will present school official-public and school official-elite congruence scores, for each of five sets of questions, using both the modal and average analysis. Our congruence scores range from 0 to 100, with 0 representing absolute disagreement, and 100 representing perfect agreement. For the modal designations, congruence is the percentage of agreements. For the average scores, congruence is (100 minus the difference between scores).

## Program Expenditure

We now turn to a series of survey questions which deal with preferred priorities of expenditures. Respondents were given a list of 17 school services and programs, and were asked to indicate whether they preferred that money be decreased, remain the same, or increased in the next year or two for each. (Appendix questions 1a–1q.) Table 3.3 presents the modal response from the community surveys. Over all districts, the public prefers to increase spending in an average of 5 areas of expenditure. The range is from a low of 3 in Macktown and Coldren Corners to a high of 7 in Ballard City.

The fact that the public prefers to increase expenditures in only 5 of 17 possible school services and programs is hardly surprising. It has long been

TABLE 3.3

PROGRAM EXPENDITURE PREFERENCES:  PUBLIC

| Area | Coldren Corners | Barwig Park | Nelsonville | Leeville | Kentington | Macktown | Ballard City | Drummond Falls | Hartshorne Hts. | Grahamdale | Stumont |
|---|---|---|---|---|---|---|---|---|---|---|---|
| Basic Skills | I | I | I | S | I | I | I | I | I | I | I |
| Boys' Athletics | S | S | S | S | S | S | S | S | S | S | S |
| Girls' Athletics | S | S | S | S | S | S | S | S | S | S | S |
| Extracurricular | D | S | S | S | S | S | S | S | S | S | S |
| Special Education | I | I | I | I | I | I | I | I | I | I | I |
| Gifted Education | S | S | I | I | I | S-I | I | I | I | I | I |
| Buildings | S | I | S | I | S | S | I | S | S | S | I |
| Kindergartens | D | S | S | S | S | S | S | S | S | I | S-I |
| Adult Education | S | S | S | S | S | S | S | S | S | S | S |
| Lunches | S | S | S | S | S | S | S | S | S | S | S |
| Transportation | S | S | S | S | S | S | S | S | S | S | D |
| Vocational Education | I | I | I | I | I | I | I | I | I | I | I |
| College Preparation | S | S | S | S | S | S | S | S | S | I | S |
| Drivers' Education | S | S | S | S | S | S | S | S | S | S | S |
| Health Services | S | S | S | S | S | S | I | S | S | S | S |
| Guidance & Counseling | S | S | I | I | I | S | I | S | S | S | S |
| Administration | D | S | S | S | S | S | S | D | S | S | S |

I - Increase

S - Same

D - Decrease

assumed that the public does not support increased expenditures for education, or indeed, for any public service. There are, however, relatively few examples of public preferences for decrease of expenditures. Decrease was the modal preference only 5 times in all districts. Clearly, the public prefers that expenditures be neither decreased nor increased, but that they remain the same.

These data are inconsistent with a picture of generalized taxpayer revolt against educational expenditures. The few examples of modal preference for decreased expenditures are scattered over districts and programs. On the other hand, the programs which generate preferences for increased expenditures are popular in virtually all districts. Clearly, public preferences are selective.

In all 11 districts, the public prefers to increase expenditures for vocational education. The same can be said for special education for children with learning problems. Increased expenditures for basic skills are desired in 10 of 11 districts. Increased expenditures for special programs for gifted children are preferred in 8 districts. It is clear, therefore, that certain school programs are popular throughout our sample, and are not district-specific. There are two programs which do appear to be somewhat district-specific, improving school buildings and facilities, and guidance and counseling for students. These two programs solicit support for expenditure increases in four districts.

The public, then, while preferring to hold the line on expenditures, is willing to authorize increases for areas which appear to be of unusual concern. Those programs of greatest concern are either remedial or are geared toward acquisition of basic skills.

The elite are somewhat more willing to spend money than is our public sample. It is hardly unique to find that those who are more active are likely to be more supportive of an institution which attracts their participation.[2] Overall, the elite prefer to increase spending in approximately 7 of 17 issue areas (table 3.4). There are several areas which generate more support among the elite than among the general public. Girls' athletics and kindergartens are examples. Similarly, some areas—most notably vocational education—are more favored by the public than by the elite. While it is fair to generalize that elites are more supportive of expenditure increases than are members of the general public, it is important to note that elites favor increases for different programs in different districts.

The public supports expenditure increases in a few areas which are fairly constant across districts. The elite support expenditure increases more often but less consistently. School officials (table 3.5) are even more supportive of expenditure increases and are more consistent. As was the case with the other groups, basic skills and vocational education are extraordinarily popular. However, girls' athletics, which received no support among the public, and modest support among the elite, receives nearly unanimous support among American school officials. This item is of special significance because of U.S. federal spending mandates which dictate expenditure increases. The public does not want to increase expenditures, the elite is divided, and school officials favor increased expenditures.

School officials' support for increased expenditures can be documented by the fact that a majority of district modal preferences are for expenditure increases in seven areas (basic skills, girls' athletics, special education for gifted children, special education for children with learning problems, buildings and facilities, vocational education, and guidance). For two others, kindergartens and health services, increases are favored in five districts. In contrast, elite support in a

TABLE 3.4

PROGRAM EXPENDITURE PREFERENCES:  ELITE

| Area | Coldren Corners | Burwig Park | Nelsonville | Leeville | Kentington | Macktown | Ballard City | Drummond Falls | Hartshorne Hts. | Grahamdale | Stumont |
|---|---|---|---|---|---|---|---|---|---|---|---|
| Basic Skills | I | I | I | I | I | I | | I | I | I | I |
| Boys' Athletics | S | S | S | D-S | S | S | | S | S | S | S |
| Girls' Athletics | I | I | S | I | I | I | | S | S | I | S |
| Extracurricular | S | S | S | S | S | S | | S | S | S | S |
| Special Education | I | I | I | I | I | I | | I | I | I | I |
| Gifted Education | I | S | I | S | S | I-S | | I | I | I | I |
| Buildings | S | I | S-I | I | S | S | | I | I | S-I | S |
| Kindergartens | I | S | S | S | I | I-S | | I | I | I | I |
| Adult Education | S | S | S | S | S | S | | I | S | I | S |
| Lunches | S | S | S | S | I | I-S | | I | S | S | S |
| Transportation | D | S | S | S | S | S | | I | S | S | S |
| Vocational Education | I | I | I | S | I | S | | S-I | I | I | I |
| College Preparation | S | S | S | S | S | S | | S | S | I | S |
| Drivers' Education | S | S | S | S | S | S | | S | S | S | S |
| Health Services | S | S | S | S | S | I | | S | I | I | I |
| Guidance & Counseling | S | I | I | S | I | I | | S | I-S | S-I | I |
| Administration | D | S | S | D-S | D | D | | D | S | I | D |

I - Increase

S - Same

D - Decrease

TABLE 3.5

PROGRAM EXPENDITURE PREFERENCES: OFFICIALS

| Area | Coldren Corners | Barwig Park | Nelsonville | Leeville | Kentington | Macktown | Ballard City | Drummond Falls | Hartshorne Hts. | Grahamdale | Stumont |
|---|---|---|---|---|---|---|---|---|---|---|---|
| Basic Skills | I | I | I | I | S | I | I | I | I | I | I |
| Boys' Athletics | S | S | S | S | S | S | I | S | S | S | S |
| Girls' Athletics | I | I | I | I | S | I | I | I | I | I | I |
| Extracurricular | S | S | S | S | S | S | S-I | S | S | S | S |
| Special Education | I | S | I | I | I | S-I | I | S | I | I | I |
| Gifted Education | S-I | S | I | I | I | I | I | I | I | I | I |
| Buildings | S | I | I | I | S | S | I | I | I | I | I |
| Kindergartens | S | S | I | S | S | I | I | S | S | I | I |
| Adult Education | S | S | S | S | S | I | I | S | S | I | S |
| Lunches | S | S | S | S | S | S | S | S | S | S | S |
| Transportation | D | S | S | S | S | S | S-I | S | S | S | S |
| Vocational Education | I | I | I | I | I | I | I | I | I | I | I |
| College Preparation | S | S | S | S | S | S | I | S | S | S-I | S |
| Drivers' Education | D | S | S | S | S | S | I | S | S | S | S |
| Health Services | S | S | S | S | S | I | I | S | I | I | I |
| Guidance & Counseling | S | I | I | S | S-I | I | I | S | I | I | S-I |
| Administration | S | S | S | S | S | S | D-I | D-S | S | S-I | S |

I - Increase

S - Same

D - Decrease

majority of districts is generated for five expenditure items (basic skills, special education for children with learning problems, special education for gifted children, kindergartens, and vocational education), and for four items by the public (basic skills, special education for children with learning problems, special education for gifted children, and vocational education). The more active the sample, the greater the support for increasing expenditures.

Another way of looking at the division of opinion between support for increased spending, support for spending at the same level, and support for spending at a lower level, is that support for the current level of spending indicates general overall satisfaction. A preference for increased spending levels may indicate dissatisfaction with the *status quo*. Therefore, interpreting a general preference for increased spending as supportive of the school district's efforts in a given area is problematic. The most striking finding of the Program Expenditure tables is not so much patterns of preferences within districts, but patterns of preferences across districts. There is a pool of preferences and expectations that is more common to class of respondent then to school district.

Average preferences are quite similar to modal public preferences on program expenditure responses. Only 6 percent of the public preference designations change from the modal designation to an average designation. These shifts are random across subject areas. The public is quite firm in its opinion that funding for basic skills, special programs for children with learning disabilities, and vocational education should be increased. Similarly, programs for boys' athletics, girls' athletics, extracurricular activities, kindergartens, adult education, school lunches, college preparatory programs, driver educational programs, and administration should be kept at the same funding level to meet public preferences.

For elite respondents, designations vary from the modal to the average designations in 18 percent of the cases. All subject areas seem to be affected with the exception of basic skills and special programs for children with learning disabilities. For these two programs there are no differences. It is interesting to note that variance in response occurs both from *status quo* to change and vice versa.

School officials' average preferences also reflect modal preferences. Only 9 percent of designations shift, and they appear to be scattered randomly throughout the districts. Unlike other groups, almost all of the differences in modal and average preferences for school officials are from preference for the same level of spending to preference for either increased or decreased level of expenditures. For example, school officials' plurality position concerning transportation is to maintain the same level of expenditures in the districts. In four districts the average preference is different; in three the average preference is for decreasing expenditures. The remaining differences appear to be scattered fairly randomly across both school districts and substance areas.

The same picture emerges from the modal and the average analyses. The public preference is for holding the line on spending. Elites and school officials lean more towards an increase of spending in most areas.

The analysis of attitudinal congruence in table 3.6 confirms that school officials represent the unarticulated preferences of elites more than the public. For both modal and average analyses school official-elite congruence is greater than school official-public congruence in seven of ten districts. In only one district, Kentington, is school official-public congruence greater on both scales. Further

TABLE 3.6

PROGRAM EXPENDITURE ATTITUDE CONGRUENCE

| District | Modal School Officials | | Average School Officials | |
|---|---|---|---|---|
| | Public | Elite | Public | Elite |
| Coldren Corners | 65 | 82 | 87 | 89 |
| Barwig Park | 82 | 94 | 91 | 93 |
| Nelsonville | 82 | 88 | 87 | 89 |
| Leeville | 82 | 88 | 89 | 89 |
| Kentington | 94 | 65 | 93 | 85 |
| Macktown | 65 | 82 | 84 | 89 |
| Ballard City | 65 | -- | 80 | -- |
| Drummond Falls | 82 | 65 | 88 | 89 |
| Hartshorne Hts. | 82 | 88 | 89 | 90 |
| Grahamdale | 71 | 100 | 82 | 87 |
| Stumont | 82 | 82 | 91 | 87 |
| Mean | 77 | 83 | 87 | 89 |

scrutiny of the table indicates, however, that only according to modal preference aggregation are school officials' attitudes significantly more representative of elites. Nevertheless, in two out of three cases school officials reflect elite attitudes more than public attitudes.

## Program Approval

The survey questionnaire contained a series of questions in which respondents were asked to rate their approval of ongoing and possible programs in school districts (appendix questions 4a–4j). For each one of these program areas, the respondent was asked to indicate approval, disapproval, or neutrality. These questions tap broader educational attitudes and preferences which do not necessarily involve scarce resources.

The questions are phrased in such a way that responses can be placed along a classic liberal-conservative continuum. For example, the liberal point of view

TABLE 3.7

PROGRAM APPROVAL: PUBLIC

| Area | Coldren Corners | Harwig Park | Nelsonville | Leeville | Kentington | Macktown | Ballard City | Drummond Falls | Hartshorne Hts. | Grahamdale | Stumont |
|---|---|---|---|---|---|---|---|---|---|---|---|
| Sex Ed.-Secondary | A | A | A | A | A | A | A | A | A | A | A |
| Sex Ed.-Elementary | A | A | A | A | A | A | A | A | A | A | D |
| Student Freedom | D | D | D | D | D | D | D | D | D | D | D |
| Student Dress | A | A | A | A | A | D | A | A | A | A | A |
| Student Choice | A | A | A | A | A | A | A | A | A | D | A |
| Expel Troublemaker | A | A | A | A | A | A | A | A | A | A | A |
| Corporal Punishment | A | A | D | D | A | A | A | A | A | A | A |
| I.Q. Tests | D | A | D | A | D | D | A | D | A | D | A |
| Modern Methods | A | A | A | A | A | A | A | A | A | AD | A |
| Ban Books | D | D | D | D | D | D | D | D | D | D | A |

A = Approve

D = Disapprove

favors sex education, maximum individual student choice, and modern instructional methods and opposes corporal punishment, expelling troublemakers, using I.Q. tests to track students, and banning books by unpopular authors. Tables 3.7, 3.8, and 3.9 present the modal responses of our three groups of respondents.

Public opinion on program approval shows a pattern similar to what we found for program expenditure. In nine program areas, there is universal or near universal agreement across school districts. Sex education in secondary schools, sex education in elementary schools, expelling troublemakers, corporal punishment, and the use of modern teaching methods are approved in all or virtually all the school districts. The practice of banning books and allowing maximum student freedom is disapproved in all, or virtually all, the school districts. The single program which does not gain near unanimity across districts is the use of I.Q. tests to place students.

The public takes both liberal and conservative positions on the program approval questions. The liberal position is taken on sex education in both elementary

TABLE 3.8

PROGRAM APPROVAL:   ELITE

| Area | Coldren Corners | Burwig Park | Nelsonville | Leeville | Kentington | Macktown | Ballard City | Drummond Falls | Hartshorne Hts. | Grahamdale | Stumont |
|---|---|---|---|---|---|---|---|---|---|---|---|
| Sex Ed.-Secondary | A | A | A | A | A | A | | A | A | A | A |
| Sex Ed.-Elementary | A | A | AD | AN | A | A | | A | A | A | A |
| Student Freedom | D | D | D | D | D | A | | D | D | D | D |
| Student Dress | D | A | D | AD | D | D | | D | D | A | A |
| Student Choice | A | A | A | AD | D | A | | A | A | D | A |
| Expel Troublemaker | AD | A | A | A | D | A | | A | A | A | A |
| Corporal Punishment | D | AD | D | D | A | A | | A | A | A | A |
| I.Q. Tests | D | D | D | D | D | AD | | D | D | D | A |
| Modern Methods | A | A | A | A | AD | A | | N | A | A | A |
| Ban Books | D | D | D | D | D | D | | D | D | D | D |

A = Approve

D = Disapprove

N - Neutral

and secondary schools, on student choice, on modern methods of instruction, and banning books. However, on student freedom, student dress, expelling troublemakers, and corporal punishment, a conservative position is taken. A conservative position is taken on programs which bear directly on student personal behavior. This reflects the public concern documented in a previous section with student discipline as a most important problem.[3] With regard to instruction programs, public opinion tends to be liberal. The attentive public apparently discriminates between curriculum and student behavior.

Most districts are fairly evenly divided between conservative and liberal positions. There are three exceptions. In Stumont, the modal choice is the conservative position for seven of ten programs. In Macktown and Nelsonville, the modal choice is the liberal position for seven programs. Thus, the position of public opinion on the liberal-conservative continuum is specific to programs and districts.

The elite responses, as was the case with their program expenditure ques-

TABLE 3.9

PROGRAM APPROVAL: OFFICIALS

| Area | Coldren Corners | Barwig Park | Nelsonville | Leeville | Kentington | Macktown | Ballard City | Drummond Falls | Hartshorne Hts. | Grahamdale | Stumont |
|---|---|---|---|---|---|---|---|---|---|---|---|
| Sex Ed.-Secondary | A | A | A | A | A | A | A | A | A | A | A |
| Sex Ed.-Elementary | A | AD | A | A | A | A | A | A | A | A | A |
| Student Freedom | A | D | A | A | D | A | D | AD | D | A | D |
| Student Dress | D | A | D | AD | N | D | DN | D | A | D | A |
| Student Choice | A | A | A | A | A | A | A | A | A | A | A |
| Expel Troublemaker | D | A | AD | A | A | D | AD | AND | A | D | A |
| Corporal Punishment | D | A | D | D | D | D | D | D | D | D | A |
| I.Q. Tests | D | A | D | D | D | D | D | D | D | D | D |
| Modern Methods | A | D | A | A | A | A | A | A | A | A | A |
| Ban Books | D | D | D | D | D | D | D | D | D | D | D |

A = Approve

D = Disapprove

N = Neutral

tions, are slightly more mixed than those of the public. Elites are liberal on sex education, modern methods of instruction, and banning books. They match public conservative opinions on student freedom and expelling troublemakers. Unlike the public, elites are liberal in their rejection of I.Q. tests. Elite opinion is slightly liberal concerning student choice and student dress, slightly conservative concerning corporal punishment.

In each district the elites are more liberal than are the publics. The most conservative elites are those of Stumont (the location of the most conservative public) and Grahamdale. The most liberal elite is in Coldren Corners. Thus, only in one district do public and elite preferences deviate in tandem from the larger norm.

School officials' opinions are even more liberal than those of the elite. For all programs in all districts, school officials either take an overwhelmingly liberal position or opinion is mixed. There are no programs which generate a conservative plurality. It is interesting to note that the areas in which school officials take mixed positions are those which deal with student rights and discipline. Instead of taking a conservative position, as do the public, and to a lesser extent, members of the elite, school officials are more divided in their opinion. Apparently, liberal attitudes yield to ambivalence as attention is turned to day-to-day problems. Nevertheless, in ten of eleven districts, school official opinion is more liberal than both elite and public. The single exception is Barwig Park. In that district school officials are the most conservative of the three groups.

Modal analysis indicates a comparative conservatism on the part of the public. The average aggregation analysis indicates much more neutrality. The overwhelming majority of our public sample are not neutral concerning program approval issues. Rather, opinion on these issues is frequently polarized. Thus, averaging combines extreme preferences to neutrality. Clearly, averaging masks the texture of opinion diversity in this case.

Community elites' average opinions are more reflective of their modal opinions. Only 38 percent of their choices change to neutrality in the average aggregation. The imbalance of elite opinion is most apparent in three issue areas: approval of sex education in elementary and secondary schools and disapproval of banning books. Furthermore, the elite hold liberal opinions on these issues. This is additional evidence that the elite are more liberal than the public.

School official opinion is the most skewed. Only 18 percent of the designations shift to neutrality in the averaging analysis. Significantly, most shifting is from conservative modal positions on student freedom and expelling troublemakers to neutral average positions. School officials are more liberal than elites, who are more liberal than members of the public. Among school officials, there are six program areas in which the overall average score is classified as liberal; for the elites there are two, and for the public, there is one.[4] The closer one gets to the decision-making center, the more liberal are opinions on program approval.

It is possible to generalize from table 3.10 that school officials' program approval responses are more representative of elites than of the less active public. For the modal aggregation the finding must be qualified by the fact that school officials are equally representative of the public and elites in six districts. For the average aggregation there is significantly greater school official-elite congruence in seven school districts. And, as was the case for the program expenditure queries, school officials in Kentington (the Canadian district) exhibit greater congruence with their public.

## Performance Satisfaction

We asked a series of nine questions to ascertain satisfaction with current facilities, programs and personnel (appendix questions 14a–14i). Respondents were asked whether they were satisfied, neutral, or dissatisfied with school buildings, courses, discipline, teaching quality, teaching methods, race relations, principals, the school board and the superintendent. The modal responses of our three sample groups are presented in tables 3.11, 3.12, and 3.13.

The public is rarely neutral. Of the items under consideration, there is consensual satisfaction concerning school buildings and principals. There is consensual dissatisfaction concerning discipline. There is no public opinion shared across

TABLE 3.10

PROGRAM APPROVAL ATTITUDE CONGRUENCE

| District | Modal School Officials | | Average School Officials | |
|---|---|---|---|---|
|  | Public | Elite | Public | Elite |
| Coldren Corners | 60 | 90 | 64 | 76 |
| Barwig Park | 90 | 90 | 88 | 80 |
| Nelsonville | 80 | 90 | 80 | 86 |
| Leeville | 90 | 90 | 81 | 86 |
| Kentington | 80 | 60 | 89 | 80 |
| Macktown | 80 | 80 | 66 | 85 |
| Ballard City | 70 | –– | 82 | –– |
| Drummond Falls | 90 | 90 | 76 | 80 |
| Hartshorne Hts. | 80 | 80 | 85 | 85 |
| Grahamdale | 50 | 50 | 65 | 72 |
| Stumont | 70 | 90 | 82 | 87 |
| Mean | 76 | 81 | 78 | 82 |

districts on the other six satisfaction items. Unlike the earlier questions, attitudes on performance satisfaction seem idiosyncratic to individual districts.

In Kentington, Coldren Corners, and Nelsonville, the public is quite satisfied. For these districts, the public is dissatisfied with only one area—discipline—but then, all district publics are dissatisfied with the state of disciplinary programs. Of the eleven districts, four have extremely satisfied publics, and one has an extremely dissatisfied public. In the remaining six districts, there is satisfaction with some performance areas, and dissatisfaction with other performance areas. The dissatisfaction in these six districts centers on teaching, teachers, school boards, and superintendents.

The modal elite satisfaction designations indicate that the overall level of satisfaction is quite close to that of the public. Elites are also quite satisfied with buildings, principals, and courses. Elites mirror public dissatisfaction with discipline. However, some elite district-wide satisfaction does not match public opinion. The Kentington public is among the most satisfied; the Kentington elite is among the most dissatisfied. The Hartshorne Hts. public is satisfied in only four

TABLE 3.11

PERFORMANCE SATISFACTION: PUBLIC

| Area | Coldren Corners | Barwig Park | Nelsonville | Leeville | Kentington | Macktown | Ballard City | Drummond Falls | Hartshorne Hts. | Grahamdale | Stumont |
|---|---|---|---|---|---|---|---|---|---|---|---|
| School Buildings | S | S | S | S | S | S | S | S | S | S | S |
| Courses | S | S | S | S | S | S | D | S-D | S | D | S |
| Discipline | D | D | D | D | D | D | D | D | D | D | D |
| Teaching Quality | S | S | S | D | S | S | D | D | D | D | D |
| Teaching Methods | S | S | S | D | S | D | D | D | D | D | D |
| Race Relations | S | D | S | S | S | D | D | D | D | S | D |
| Principals | S | S | S | S | S | S | N | N | S | S | S |
| School Board | S | S | S | D | S | S | D | D | N | D | D |
| Superintendent | S | S | S | S-D | S-N | S | D | N | D | N | N |

S = Satisfied

D = Dissatisfied

N = Neutral

areas; the Hartshorne Hts. elite is dissatisfied in only one area. In five districts, elites are less satisfied than publics. In four districts elites are more satisfied than publics. Thus, the overall similarity of public and elite satisfaction masks the fact that public and elite satisfaction vary within school districts.

School officials differ markedly from the public and from the elite. They are satisfied across performance areas in all but one school district. Only 10 percent of their modal designations are dissatisfied or neutral. The officials who govern schools are substantially more satisfied than are those who are governed by their decisions. This finding is typical of governmental officials.[5] The greatest dissatisfaction is with discipline; nevertheless, officials in seven districts report modal satisfaction with discipline. The most dissatisfied school officials are in Ballard City, which is also the district with the most dissatisfied public. School officials in the other districts are satisfied regardless of the opinion of publics and elites.

As was the case with program approval, the average designations of public opinion are more neutral than are the modal designations. Sixty-one percent change from either satisfaction or dissatisfaction to neutrality when averaging is

TABLE 3.12

PERFORMANCE SATISFACTION: ELITE

| Area | Coldren Corners | Barwig Park | Nelsonville | Leeville | Kentington | Macktown | Ballard City | Drummond Falls | Hartshorne Hts. | Grahamdale | Stumont |
|---|---|---|---|---|---|---|---|---|---|---|---|
| School Buildings | S | D | S | S | S | S | | S | S | S | S |
| Courses | S | S | S | S | D | S | | S | S | D | S-D |
| Discipline | D | D | D | D | D | D | | D | D | D | D |
| Teaching Quality | S | S-D | D | S | D | S | | S | S | D | D |
| Teaching Methods | S | S | D | S | D | S | | S | S | S | D |
| Race Relations | S | D | S | S | N | S | | S | S | S | D |
| Principals | S | S | S | S | S | S | | S | S | D | D |
| School Board | S | S | S | D | D | S | | D | S | D | D |
| Superintendent | S | S | S | D | D | S | | D | S | D | D |

S = Satisfied

D = Dissatisfied

N = Neutral

employed. Generally speaking, members of the public hold bimodal opinions concerning performance satisfaction, which are averaged to neutrality. There are two exceptions. School buildings win modal and average satisfaction, and discipline is the object of modal and average public dissatisfaction in every district.

Elite average opinion also exhibits greater neutrality. Fifty percent shift to neutrality when opinions are aggregated by averaging. Strong elite dissatisfaction is maintained over districts in only one performance area: discipline. For the other program areas, there is substantial shifting to neutrality.

School officials' average performance satisfaction opinions are quite consistent with modal opinions. Of the few designations which differ, the changes are generally from satisfaction or dissatisfaction to neutrality. Nevertheless, school officials are quite satisfied with school district performance by average as well as modal opinion aggregation.

When we examine the congruence between the attitudes of our three groups, it is clear that once again school official attitudes are somewhat more reflective of elite, rather than public, opinion. (See table 3.14.) The underrepresentation of

# TABLE 3.13

## PERFORMANCE SATISFACTION:  OFFICIAL

| Area | Coldren Corners | Barwig Park | Nelsonville | Leeville | Kentington | Macktown | Ballard City | Drummond Falls | Hartshorne Hts. | Grahamdale | Stumont |
|---|---|---|---|---|---|---|---|---|---|---|---|
| School Buildings | S | D | S | D | S | S | D | S | S | S | S |
| Courses | S | S | S | S | S | S | S | S | S | S | S |
| Discipline | S | S | S | S | D | S | D | S | D | S | D |
| Teaching Quality | S | S | S | S | D | S | D | S | S | S | S |
| Teaching Methods | S | S | S | S | S | S | S-D | S | S | S | S |
| Race Relations | S | S | S | S | N | S | D | S | S | S | S |
| Principals | S | S | S | S | S | S | D | S | S | S | S |
| School Board | S | S | S | D | S | S | N-D | S | S | S | D |
| Superintendent | S | S | S | S | S | S | N | S | S | S | S |

S = Satisfied

D = Dissatisfied

N = Neutral

# TABLE 3.14

## PROGRAM SATISFACTION ATTITUDE CONGRUENCE

| District | Modal School Officials | | Average School Officials | |
|---|---|---|---|---|
| | Public | Elite | Public | Elite |
| Coldren Corners | 89 | 89 | 76 | 81 |
| Barwig Park | 67 | 78 | 67 | 61 |
| Nelsonville | 89 | 67 | 82 | 80 |
| Leeville | 56 | 67 | 67 | 75 |
| Kentington | 78 | 56 | 87 | 79 |
| Macktown | 67 | 89 | 63 | 78 |
| Ballard City | 56 | -- | 88 | -- |
| Drummond Falls | 22 | 67 | 64 | 89 |
| Hartshorne Hts. | 44 | 100 | 72 | 90 |
| Grahamdale | 33 | 33 | 65 | 68 |
| Stumont | 56 | 56 | 89 | 83 |
| Mean | 60 | 70 | 75 | 78 |

public attitudes is not great, but the direction is consistent, whether modal or averaging methods of measurement are used. Again, in Kentington, school officials are more representative of public than elite opinion.

## Controversial Issues

Modal responses from the three sample groups to a series of questions about controversial issues are presented in tables 3.15, 3.16, and 3.17. The survey questionnaire contained ten questions concerning contemporary management problems (appendix questions 2, 3, 5–12). Since the possible responses to these questions are not uniform, we have classified responses according to conservative, moderate, or liberal content. We designated as liberal those responses which favored increased spending, school tax increases, teachers' unions, teachers' right to strike, increased teachers' salaries, greater teacher influence in school governance, busing to achieve racial balance, courses in minority culture and history, integration, and affirmative action programs.

TABLE 3.15

ISSUES:   PUBLIC

| Area | Coldren Corners | Barwig Park | Nelsonville | Leeville | Kentington | Macktown | Ballard City | Drummond Falls | Hartshorne Hts. | Grahamdale | Stumont |
|---|---|---|---|---|---|---|---|---|---|---|---|
| Spending | C | M | M | C | M | M | M | C | M–L | L | M |
| Tax Increase | C | C | L | C | L | C | C | C | L | L | C |
| Teachers' Unions | C | C | C | L | L | C | L | L | L | C | L |
| Teachers' Strikes | C | C | L | C | C | C | L | L | C | C | C |
| Teachers' Salary | M | M | M | M | M | M | M | M | M | L | M |
| Teachers' Influence | L | L | L | L | L | L | L | L | L | L | L |
| Busing | C | C | C | C | C | C | C | C | C | C | C |
| Minority Courses | L | L | L | L | L | L | L | L | L | L | L |
| Integration | L | L | L | L | L | L | L | L | L | L | C |
| Hiring Minorities | L | L | L | L | L | L | L | L | C | L | L |

L = Liberal

M = Moderate

C = Conservative

TABLE 3.16

ISSUES: ELITE

| Area | Coldren Corners | Barwig Park | Nelsonville | Leeville | Kentington | Macktown | Ballard City | Drummond Falls | Hartshorne Hts. | Grahamdale | Stumont |
|---|---|---|---|---|---|---|---|---|---|---|---|
| Spending | M | L | M | M | L-C | M | | M | L | L | M-L |
| Tax Increase | L | L | L | L | L | L | | L | L | L | C |
| Teachers' Unions | L | C | C | L | L | L | | L | L | L-C | C |
| Teachers' Strikes | L | C | C | L | C | L | | L | L | C | C |
| Teachers' Salary | M | M | M | M-C | M | M | | M | M | M | M |
| Teachers' Influence | L | L | L | L | L | L | | L | L | L | L |
| Busing | M | C | C | M-C | M-C | M | | M | C | C | M |
| Minority Courses | L | L | L | L | L | L | | L | L | L | L |
| Integration | L | L | L | L | L | L | | L | L | L | L |
| Hiring Minorities | L | L | L | L | L | L | | L | L | L | L |

L = Liberal

M = Moderate

C = Conservative

Public opinion is consistent across districts on three of four racial questions. For minority courses, integration and affirmative action programs, the public in every school district except Stumont is liberal. However, in every school district, the modal response to the question on busing is conservative. Thus, the public in each school district favors various special programs and procedures for racial and ethnic minorities, yet denies that busing is an appropriate strategy to achieve these ends. Our public respondents mirror national surveys, which report substantial opposition to busing.

The public is consistent across districts on only one of the questions about the proper role of teachers. It takes a consistently liberal position on the question of whether or not teachers should be given increased influence in school governance. Responses on teachers' strikes were conservative for eight districts and liberal for three. Responses on teachers' unionization, tax increases, and expenditure levels drew a much more divided response.

We would expect the elite to be somewhat more liberal on these issues, as has been the case in our previous analysis, and as is generally suggested by most theories of public opinion and political participation. Such is the case. There is a

TABLE 3.17

ISSUES: OFFICIALS

| Area | Coldren Corners | Barwig Park | Nelsonville | Leeville | Kentington | Macktown | Ballard City | Drummond Falls | Hartshorne Hts. | Grahamdale | Stumont |
|---|---|---|---|---|---|---|---|---|---|---|---|
| Spending | M | L | L | M | M | M | L | M | L | L | L |
| Tax Increase | L | L | L | L | L | L | L | L | L | L | L |
| Teachers' Unions | L | C | L | L | L–C | L | L–C | L | L | L–C | L |
| Teachers' Strikes | C | C | C | C | C | L–C | C | C | C | C | C |
| Teachers' Salary | M | M | L | M | M | M | L | M | M | L | M |
| Teachers' Influence | L | C | L | L | C | L | L | C | L | L | L |
| Busing | M | M | C | M | M | L | L–M | M | M | M | M |
| Minority Courses | L | L | L | L | L | L | L | L | L | L | L |
| Integration | L | L | L | L | L | L | L | L | L | L | L |
| Hiring Minorities | L | L | L | L | C | L | L | L | L | L | L |

L = Liberal

M = Moderate

C = Conservative

liberal preference in six of the ten issue areas: tax increases, teacher unions, teacher influence, minority courses, integration, and hiring minorities. For no issue area is there a conservative consensus across districts. As was the case for the public, elites take a liberal position on three of the four minority issues and on the issue of giving teachers greater influence in the schools. They are more liberal than the public on the questions of tax increases and teacher unionization. Most significantly, on the busing question, the public took the conservative position in each school district, whereas elites chose the conservative option in only four. The greater liberalism of the elite is also illustrated by the fact that in five districts at least seven issue designations were liberal.

School officials are marginally more liberal than the elite. They would be significantly more liberal were they not solidly conservative on the question of teachers' strikes. Since school officials resist teachers' strikes vigorously, this conservatism is to be expected. Teachers' strikes is the single issue on which school officials dramatically part company from the elite and the public. On all other issues they are more liberal. For example, on the question of busing, we noted a conservative response from the public, a conservative-to-moderate response from the elite, and a moderate response from the school officials. On balance, therefore, school officials are the most liberal of our groups, with the conspicuous exception of their conservatism on teachers' strikes.

Once again, the average aggregation of public preferences averages extreme positions to moderate designations. Nearly half of the conservative and liberal modal designations became moderate average designations. Of the ten issue areas only three exhibit substantial consistency in the two aggregation procedures. Liberalism is maintained for increasing teacher influence and approving integration; conservatism is maintained for opposing busing.

For elites issue preferences too, averaging yields more moderate designations. However, only 17 percent of the designations differ in modal and average analyses, and the differences are randomly distributed over issue areas and school districts. For school officials 21 percent of designations differ in modal and average analyses. However, these differences do not change the overall finding that school officials are more liberal than elites, who are more liberal than the public.

The familiar pattern of school official attitudes being more representative of elites holds also for controversial issues (table 3.18). Irrespective of aggregation procedure, elites are closer in attitude to school officials than is the public. Again, Kentington is a nonconforming district. In short, the congruence analysis reflects

TABLE 3.18

ISSUE ATTITUDE CONGRUENCE

| District | Modal School Officials | | Average School Officials | |
|---|---|---|---|---|
| | Public | Elite | Public | Elite |
| Coldren Corners | 60 | 90 | 76 | 88 |
| Barwig Park | 60 | 80 | 76 | 87 |
| Nelsonville | 60 | 70 | 83 | 83 |
| Leeville | 70 | 90 | 72 | 77 |
| Kentington | 70 | 70 | 89 | 83 |
| Macktown | 70 | 90 | 74 | 90 |
| Ballard City | 50 | -- | 77 | -- |
| Drummond Falls | 50 | 80 | 71 | 84 |
| Hartshorne Hts. | 80 | 80 | 81 | 83 |
| Grahamdale | 90 | 80 | 76 | 84 |
| Stumont | 60 | 80 | 73 | 83 |
| Mean | 65 | 81 | 77 | 84 |

TABLE 3.19

EFFICACY: PUBLIC

| Area | Coldren Corners | Barwig Park | Nelsonville. | Leeville | Kentington | Macktown | Ballard City | Drummond Falls | Hartshorne Hts. | Grahamdale | Stumont |
|---|---|---|---|---|---|---|---|---|---|---|---|
| Attn. to People | L | M | M | M | M | M | L | M | M-L | L | M |
| Attn. to Problem | M | M | H | M | H | M | M | M | M | M | M |
| Citizen Influence | L | L | H | L | H | L | L | L | L | L | L |
| Board Elections | H-L | H | L | L | H-L | H | L | L | H | L | L |
| Budget Elections | L | H | L | L | L | L | L | L | L | L | L |

H = High

M = Medium

L = Low

the relative position of publics, elites, and school officials as the liberal-conservative continuum. School officials are more representative of elites because elites are more liberal than the public.

## Efficacy

Our survey instrument had five questions on efficacy (appendix questions 15–19). Although we will argue later that constituent attitudes toward government are an important component of responsiveness, we present our findings on efficacy here as well. In this section we present the current findings about the three groups for the purpose of describing the milieu of the districts.

It has become commonplace to observe that Americans feel helpless; that their perceived ability to influence complex government decisions is so low as to raise questions about the health of the American democracy. On the other hand, it is also alleged that school districts are the last bastion of public influence, and they are, at least symbolically, close to "the people." How do the people feel? Irrespective of the actual distribution of influence, an efficacious public is one indication of a healthy milieu. The modal designations are presented in tables 3.19, 3.20, and 3.21. Responses are grouped into high, medium, and low categories.

Overall, public responses indicate low efficacy. School district governance is not exempt from the national trend. More than half of the designations are low. However, two questions attract nearly universally low designations: citizen influ-

TABLE 3.20

EFFICACY:  ELITE

| Area | Coldren Corners | Barwig Park | Nelsonville | Leeville | Kentington | Macktown | Ballard City | Drummond Falls | Hartshorne Hts. | Grahamdale | Stumont |
|---|---|---|---|---|---|---|---|---|---|---|---|
| Attn. to People | H | M | H | M | M | M | | L | M | M | M |
| Attn. to Problem | H | H | H | M | M | H | | M | H | M | H |
| Citizen Influence | H | H | H | H | H | H | | H | H | H | L |
| Board Elections | H | H | H | H | L | H | | H | H-L | L | H-L |
| Budget Elections | L | H | L | H-L | H-L | H | | H | H | L | L |

H = High

M = Medium

L = Low

ence in school governance, and the ability of budget elections to provide account-ability. Citizens feel helpless; budget elections do not provide the presumed ac-countability. There is no school district in which high efficacy is indicated for more than two questions.

The modal responses of the elite indicate that they are more efficacious than the public. This parallels our earlier finding that the elite are more satisfied. Elites report greatest efficacy on the question concerning citizen influence about which the public was least efficacious. There is no consistently low response to any question; hence elites' higher efficacy is unmarred. In all districts save one, elites are more efficacious than the public. The exception is Kentington, the single district in which school officials are consistently closer to the public than to the elite.

School officials are the most efficacious of the three groups. Like most state and local officials, they "feel that governmental services and many other key institutions are doing a more effective job than the public is prepared to be-lieve." [6]

Of 55 school official designations, 50 are high; 5 are low. Three of the 5 low efficacy responses are in regard to budget elections and occur in districts without

TABLE 3.21

EFFICACY:   SCHOOL OFFICIALS

| Area | Coldren Corners | Barwig Park | Nelsonville | Leeville | Kentington | Macktown | Ballard City | Drummond Falls | Hartshorne Hts. | Grahamdale | Stumont |
|---|---|---|---|---|---|---|---|---|---|---|---|
| Attn. to People | H | H | H | H | H | H | L | H | H | H | H |
| Attn. to Problem | H | H | H | H | H | H | H | H | H | H | H |
| Citizen Influence | H | H | H | H | H | H | H | H | H | H | H |
| Board Elections | H | H | H | H | H | H | H | H | L | H | H |
| Budget Elections | H | H | H | H | L | H | L | H | H | H | L |

H = High

M = Medium

L = Low

such elections on a regular basis. Hence, the question is inappropriate. Excluding these responses, then, school officials are exceptionally efficacious.

It is important to underline that we did not ask school officials to comment on their own sense of efficacy. Rather, we asked them to provide perceptions of district-wide (that is lay) efficacy. In every district, school officials' level of efficacy is higher than elites' and publics'. For seven districts, high efficacy is the modal school official response to all questions. The *highest* level of public efficacy is the *lowest* level of school official efficacy. Such gross misperception, however, is certainly not unique to school officials. All government officials misperceive the level of lay isolation.

As was the case in other areas, aggregating attitudes by averaging presents a picture of greater moderation in all three samples. For members of the public, averaging increases efficacy across virtually all districts and question areas. The same is generally true of elites. However, elites do *not* appear more sanguine about the responsiveness of school administrators. Not only are school officials most efficacious; they are also most consistent for the two aggregation techniques. Our earlier conclusion is inescapable. School officials believe they are highly responsive; the public does not agree. The public believes itself to be helpless; school officials do not agree.

Although this phenomenon is typical of all governmental systems, it should

TABLE 3.22

EFFICACY ATTITUDE CONGRUENCE

| District | Modal School Officials | | Average School Officials | |
|---|---|---|---|---|
| | Public | Elite | Public | Elite |
| Coldren Corners | 20 | 80 | 62 | 83 |
| Barwig Park | 40 | 80 | 67 | 80 |
| Nelsonville | 40 | 80 | 52 | 69 |
| Leeville | 0 | 60 | 58 | 79 |
| Kentington | 80 | 40 | 72 | 65 |
| Macktown | 20 | 80 | 57 | 82 |
| Ballard City | 40 | -- | 81 | -- |
| Drummond Falls | 0 | 60 | 57 | 76 |
| Hartshorne Hts. | 0 | 80 | 69 | 81 |
| Grahamdale | 0 | 20 | 58 | 61 |
| Stumont | 20 | 60 | 64 | 67 |
| Mean | 24 | 64 | 63 | 74 |

not be dismissed as trivial. Institutional linkages do not contribute to an efficacious public. Elections, the traditional mechanism of accountability (Boyd, 1976), are not regarded as valuable by laymen. The greatest feelings of efficacy are generated as a consequence of personal interaction—bringing a problem (personally) to the attention of the board. Personal interaction appears more significant than institutional linkages.

School officials are clearly more representative of elites than public with regard to efficacy, with the now conspicuous exception of Kentington, our Canadian district (table 3.22).

## Representation in Perspective

Table 3.23 summarizes the analysis of attitude congruence and representation. Clearly, school officials' attitudes are more representative of elites than of publics. Kentington is a singular exception. For the Canadian district alone, the school official-public linkage is stronger. While in many cases the difference between school official-elite congruence, and school official-public congruence is slight, the overall pattern is remarkably strong.

The reason that elites' attitudes are closer to school officials' is that elite opinion is nearly always midway between public and school official opinion. The responses to program expenditure, program approval, and controversial issues questions can be arranged on a liberal-conservative continuum. Similarly, the responses to performance satisfaction and efficacy questions can be arranged on a continuum of school district support. Tables 3.24 and 3.25 present position orderings on the five disaggregated groups of questions and aggregate liberalism and aggregate support scales.

Tables 3.24 and 3.25 document that the PEO ordering occurs in 53 percent of modal analysis cases and 71 percent of average analysis cases. For both tech-

TABLE 3.23

WHOSE ATTITUDES DO SCHOOL OFFICIALS BEST REPRESENT?

| District | Modal | | | | | Average | | | | |
|---|---|---|---|---|---|---|---|---|---|---|
| | Expenditures | Approval | Satisfaction | Issue | Efficacy | Expenditures | Approval | Satisfaction | Issue | Efficacy |
| Coldren Corners | E | E | T | E | E | E | E | E | E | E |
| Barwig Park | E | T | E | E | E | E | P | P | E | E |
| Nelsonville | E | E | P | E | E | E | E | P | T | E |
| Leeville | E | T | E | E | E | T | E | E | E | E |
| Kentington | P | P | P | T | P | P | P | P | P | P |
| Macktown | E | T | E | E | E | E | E | E | E | E |
| Ballard City | | | | | | | | | | |
| Drummond Falls | P | T | E | E | E | E | E | E | E | E |
| Hartshorne Hts. | E | T | E | T | E | E | T | E | E | E |
| Grahamdale | E | T | T | P | E | E | E | E | E | E |
| Stumont | T | E | T | E | E | P | E | P | E | E |
| Mean | E | E | E | E | E | E | E | E | E | E |

P = Public

E = Elite

T = Tie

TABLE 3.24

MODAL ORDERINGS

| | Liberalism | | | | Support | | |
|---|---|---|---|---|---|---|---|
| District | Program Expenditure | Program Approval | Controversial Issues | Aggregate Liberalism | Performance Satisfaction | Efficacy | Aggregate Support |
| Coldren Corners | POE | PEO | POE | POE | PE-O | PEO | PEO |
| Barwig Park | POE | OPE | PO-E | PO-E | EPO | PEO | PE-O |
| Nelsonville | PEO | PEO | EPO | EPO | EPO | POE | EPO |
| Leeville | EPO | PEO | POE | PEO | PEO | PEO | PEO |
| Kentington | OPE | PEO | OPE | OPE | EOP | EPO | E-PO |
| Macktown | PEO | PEO | P-EO | PEO | PEO | PEO | PEO |
| Ballard City | -- | -- | -- | -- | -- | -- | -- |
| Drummond Falls | POE | PEO | PO-E | POE | PEO | PEO | PEO |
| Hartshorne Hts. | PEO | P-EO | POE | P-EO | P-EO | P-EO | P-EO |
| Grahamdale | P-EO | PEO | PE-O | PEO | EPO | PEO | PEO |
| Stumont | PEO | PEO | PEO | PEO | EPO | PEO | P-EO |
| Mean | PEO | PEO | POE | PEO | PEO | PEO | PEO |

P = Public
E = Elite
O = School Officials
-   indicates preceding or following pair tied

TABLE 3.25

AVERAGE ORDERINGS

| District | Liberalism | | | | Support | | |
| --- | --- | --- | --- | --- | --- | --- | --- |
| | Program Expenditure | Program Approval | Contro-versial Issues | Aggregate Liberalism | Performance Satisfaction | Efficacy | Aggregate Support |
| Coldren Corners | POE | PEO | PEO | PEO | PEO | PEO | PEO |
| Barwig Park | PEO | OPE | PEO | POE | EPO | PEO | PEO |
| Nelsonville | PEO | PEO | EPO | PEO | EPO | PEO | PE-O |
| Leeville | EPO | PEO | PEO | PEO | PEO | PEO | PEO |
| Kentington | OPE | EPO | OPE | PO-E | EPO | PEO | EPO |
| Macktown | PEO | PEO | PEO | PEO | PEO | PEO | PEO |
| Ballard City | -- | -- | -- | -- | -- | -- | -- |
| Drummond Falls | PEO | PEO | PEO | PEO | PEO | PEO | PEO |
| Hartshorne Hts. | PEO | PEO | POE | POE | PEO | PEO | PEO |
| Grahamdale | PEO | PEO | PEO | PEO | PEO | PEO | PEO |
| Stumont | EPO | PEO | EPO | EPO | EPO | PEO | EPO |
| Mean | PEO | PEO | PEO | PEO | PEO | PEO | PEO |

P = Public
E = Elite
O = School Officials
- indicates following or preceding pair tied

niques of aggregation the PEO ordering holds in more than six districts only for efficacy, aggregate support, and program approval. The mean ordering, however, is PEO for all scales except nominal controversial issues.

While the PEO ordering occurs more frequently than any other ordering, it dominates only selected scales and selected districts. Rarely are publics more liberal or more supportive than school officials. Nearly all departures from the PEO ordering are caused by elites who are more liberal-supportive than school officials. Nevertheless, it is the case that elite opinion is most often between school official and public opinion. As a result, school officials' unarticulated attitudes and preferences are more representative of the more active elites in their district than of the attentive public.

## Notes

1. Due to the low numbers of questionnaires returned by community elites and their range of responses, we do not present data on most important problems as reported by community elites. Hereafter, district order in tables follows rank of student enrollment from lowest to highest.
2. See, for example, Zeigler and Tucker (1978), chapter 2.
3. This is also consistent with national opinion surveys conducted by George Gallup which highlight discipline as a major school issue. See the *Gallup Opinion Index*, No. 135 (October 1976), pp. 14–26, for example.
4. This finding is consistent with an extensive body of literature which compares elite to mass opinion. See Dye and Zeigler (1978) for a summary.
5. See *Confidence and Concern: Citizens View American Government, A Survey of Public Attitudes* by the Subcommittee on Intergovernmental Relations of the Committee on Government Operations, United States Senate, 93d Congress, 1st Session, 1973, pp. 42–43.
6. *Ibid.*, p. 39.

## Appendix: Survey Questionnaire

1. A lot of people these days are concerned about the cost of education. Listed below are a number of school services and programs; please indicate whether you think the amount of money the schools in your community spend should decrease, remain the same, or increase, in the next year or two.
   a. Teaching basic skills—the 3 Rs
      (1) Decrease spending
      (2) Remain the same
      (3) Increase spending
      (8) No opinion
      (9) No response
   b. Boys' athletics
      (Same as a)
   c. Girls' athletics
      (Same as a)
   d. Extracurricular activities
      (Same as a)
   e. Special education for children with learning problems
      (Same as a)
   f. Special programs for gifted children
      (Same as a)
   g. Improving school buildings and facilities
      (Same as a)
   h. Kindergartens and preschool programs
      (Same as a)
   i. Adult education
      (Same as a)
   j. School lunches
      (Same as a)

   k. Transportation to and from school
     (Same as a)
   l. Vocational training
     (Same as a)
   m. College preparatory programs
     (Same as a)
   n. Driver education
     (Same as a)
   o. Health services in schools
     (Same as a)
   p. Guidance and counseling for students
     (Same as a)
   q. Administration and supervision
     (Same as a)

2. On the whole, do you think that the public schools in your community are spending too much money, about the right amount of money, or not enough money?
   (1) Too much
   (2) About right
   (3) Not enough
   (8) No opinion
   (9) No response

3. At the present time, if you were asked to vote on a school budget that included a tax increase, would you probably vote for the budget or against the budget?
   (1) For the budget
   (2) Against the budget
   (8) Don't know
   (9) No response

4. Listed below are a number of educational policies. Please indicate whether you personally approve or disapprove of these policies, and how strongly you feel about your opinion.
   a. Sex education in the secondary schools
     (1) Strongly approve
     (2) Mildly approve
     (3) Neutral
     (4) Mildly disapprove
     (5) Strongly disapprove
     (9) No response
   b. Sex education in the elementary schools
     (Same as a)
   c. Allowing students more freedom in school
     (Same as a)
   d. Strict rules governing student dress and grooming
     (Same as a)
   e. Allowing secondary school students to choose their own program of study
     (Same as a)
   f. Expelling troublemakers from school
     (Same as a)
   g. Permitting teachers to use corporal punishment
     (Same as a)
   h. Using I.Q. test scores to assign students to classes
     (Same as a)
   i. Replacing old-fashioned teaching methods with more modern methods
     (Same as a)
   j. Banning books by atheists and socialists from school libraries
     (Same as a)

5. Generally speaking, do you approve or disapprove of teachers joining unions?
   (1) Approve
   (2) Disapprove
   (8) No opinion
   (9) No response

6. Do you approve or disapprove of laws making it illegal for teachers to go on strike?
   (Same as 5)

7. Do you think that teacher salaries in your community are too low, about right or too high?
   (1) Too low
   (2) About right
   (3) Too high
   (8) No opinion
   (9) No response
8. Would you favor or oppose giving teachers more of a say about school district policies in your community?
   (1) Favor
   (2) Oppose
   (8) No opinion
   (9) No response
9. Which of the following statements best expresses your own opinion about busing students in order to bring about racial balance in the schools?
   (1) School officials should not hesitate to use busing to bring about racial balance in the schools
   (2) Busing should be used only as a last resort
   (3) Busing should never be used to bring about racial balance
   (8) No opinion
   (9) No response
10. Would you favor or oppose special courses in the secondary schools dealing with the history and culture of minority groups?
    (1) Favor
    (2) Oppose
    (8) No opinion
    (9) No response
11. Which of the following statements best expresses your opinion about race relations in the schools?
    (1) Separate but equal schools are better for both black and white students
    (2) Integration is better for black students but not for white students
    (3) Integration is better for white students but not for black students
    (4) Integration is better for both black and white students
    (8) No opinion
    (9) No response
12. Do you think that school officials in your community should make a special effort to hire qualified members of minority groups as teachers and administrators?
    (1) Yes
    (2) No
    (8) No opinion
    (9) No response
13. At the present time, what do you consider the most important problems facing the public schools in your community that school officials try to take care of? (Please describe each problem in a few words.)
14. How satisfied are you with the public schools in your community? Here is a list of some of the things many people are concerned about. We'd like to know what you're satisfied with and what you're dissatisfied with.
    a. School buildings and facilities
       (1) Very satisfied
       (2) Somewhat satisfied
       (3) Neutral
       (4) Somewhat dissatisfied
       (5) Very dissatisfied
       (9) No response
    b. The courses and educational programs provided in the schools
       (Same as a)
    c. Discipline in the schools
       (Same as a)
    d. The quality of teaching
       (Same as a)

    e. The teaching methods
      (Same as a)
    f. Race relations in the schools
      (Same as a)
    g. The principals and assistant principals
      (Same as a)
    h. The school board
      (Same as a)
    i. The superintendent of schools
      (Same as a)

15. Generally speaking, how much attention would you say school officials pay to what people like yourself think about the schools?
    (1) Quite a lot
    (2) Some, but not a great deal
    (3) Hardly any
    (4) No opinion
    (9) No response

16. If a group of citizens like yourself brought a problem to the attention of the school board, what do you think the school board would probably do?
    (1) Try to do something about the problem
    (2) Listen but not do anything about the problem
    (3) Refuse to listen
    (8) No opinion
    (9) No response

17. Some people feel that there is very little the average citizen can do to influence the way schools are run. Other people feel that there is a great deal the average citizen can do. What's your opinion?
    (1) There is very little the average citizen can do
    (2) There is a great deal the average citizen can do
    (8) I have no opinion
    (9) No response

18. Do you think school board elections make the school board pay attention to what the public wants, or do you think school board elections are pretty much a waste of time?
    (1) School board elections make the school board pay attention to what the public wants
    (2) School board elections are pretty much a waste of time
    (8) No opinion
    (9) No response

19. Do you think school budget elections give voters a real say in how much money the schools spend, or do you think school budget elections don't really make much difference?
    (1) School budget elections give voters a real say in how much money the schools spend
    (2) School budget elections don't really make much difference
    (8) No opinion
    (9) No response

20. Generally speaking, how much attention do you pay to what's going on in the public schools in your community?
    (1) Quite a bit
    (2) Some, but not a great deal
    (3) Hardly any
    (9) No response

21. Listed below are a number of school activities. Please indicate which things on the list you have done, and which things on the list you have not had a chance to do, within the past year.
    a. Visited a public school
      (1) Have
      (2) Have not
      (9) No response
    b. Belonged to a PTA or similar group
      (Same as a)
    c. Talked with a teacher about school matters
      (Same as a)

    d. Talked with a principal or an assistant principal about school matters
       (Same as a)
    e. Contacted a school board member about a school matter
       (Same as a)
    f. Attended a school board meeting
       (Same as a)
    g. Contacted the superintendent of schools about a school matter
       (Same as a)
    h. Voted in a school board election
       (Same as a)
    i. Voted in a school budget election
       (Same as a)

22. Do you have any children in the public schools?
    (1) Yes
    (2) No
    (9) No response

23. Do you have any children who attend private or parochial schools?
    (1) Yes
    (2) No
    (9) No response

24. What is your approximate age?
    (1) 18–29
    (2) 30–39
    (3) 40–49
    (4) 50–59
    (5) 60–69
    (6) 70 or over
    (9) No response

25. How far did your own formal schooling go? (Please check only one category.)
    (1) Never attended school
    (2) Grade school only
    (3) Some high school
    (4) Graduated high school
    (5) Some college
    (6) Graduated college
    (9) No response

26. What do you expect your immediate family's approximate income before taxes to be this year?
    (1) Under $5,000
    (2) $5,000–9,999
    (3) $10,000–14,999
    (4) $15,000–$24,999
    (5) $25,000 or over
    (9) No response

27. Do you own your own home, or do you rent?
    (1) Own
    (2) Rent
    (3) Other
    (9) No response

28. What is your sex?
    (1) Female
    (2) Male
    (9) No response

29. What is your racial-ethnic background?
    (1) Black
    (2) White
    (3) Asian
    (4) Latin American, Mexican, or Puerto Rican
    (5) American Indian
    (6) Other
    (9) No response

# 4
# School Board Meetings: A Selective View

In the next two chapters we present information on behavior at public school board meetings in the 11 school districts which participated in the Responsiveness Project. The present chapter offers a selective view of school board meetings drawn from local news media coverage of school districts and from our Demand-Response Log. To provide a background and an introduction to the milieu of the school districts, we present a narrative of major events as reported by local news media. From the Demand-Response Logs we present descriptive narratives of school board meetings which stimulated (1) greatest overall demand articulation, and (2) greatest public demand articulation. Thus, we shall present the "major events" in each district as selected by news media and level of activity at school board meetings.

Our goals here are both descriptive and analytic. The primary descriptive goal is to provide a substantive explication of the major issues confronted by the school districts. The districts vary widely in both the nature and frequency of nonroutine decision-making. The primary analytic goal is to assess the extent to which focusing on major events presents an accurate or distorted view of school district governance. In this chapter we shall gauge how well the issues of the "most important" meetings reflect the "most important" issues of the academic year. The perspective and methodology to be employed are those of the traditional case study. In the next chapter the focus will be on comprehensive data, that is, all behaviors at all school board meetings. Thus, it will also be possible to gauge the extent to which key events are representative of the sum of school district governance.

It is in the observation of such "critical events" that one should expect maximum lay participation. It is unrealistic to expect continuous lay participation. If there is to be any such participation—if the battle between experts and laymen is to be joined—it should be during the discussion of nonroutine issues.

Our selective view of school board meetings will be organized as follows: (1) media accounts of the entire year, (2) the single meeting during which most demands were made, (3) the single meeting at which most public demands were made. An assessment of linkages between the selective view of the media and the substance of individual meetings will follow.

**Key Events and Meetings**

## COLDREN CORNERS

### OVERVIEW

There were several controversial issues in Coldren Corners which stimulated considerable constituent input and significant concern on the part of school officials. The 1974–75 academic year began in the midst of a crisis of confidence in two areas—kindergartens and school finance.

In a recent session, the state legislature had initiated a program of financial support for local kindergarten programs. In the words of one Coldren Corners school board member, the legislature had issued "a clear legislative mandate" for the establishment of public school kindergartens throughout the state. The new district superintendent made kindergartens one of his highest priorities and included the new program in the 1974–75 school district budget. School board members, some of whom had been elected on a pro-kindergarten platform, agreed with the superintendent and included kindergartens as part of the 1974–75 tax levy that was submitted to the voters in May 1974.

The May tax levy failed. A second election in July brought an even larger defeat of the levy. Opponents pointed to the inclusion of the kindergarten program as the major cause of voter rejection. The main issue was not whether a public kindergarten program should be started in Coldren Corners, but over the proper role of the public in making the decision. In the past, kindergartens had been submitted to voters separately from the school levy—and had been rejected every time. Opponents claimed that the school board was attempting to circumvent the democratic process by denying public review at the polls.

Thus, attention was focused on the third levy election in September as our observation period began. Interested citizens had formed organizations on both sides of the question and were campaigning both for and against the levy. The September levy amount was approximately $1 million less than the May amount, due to revised revenue and cost estimates and some minor budget reductions. The September levy was approved by the voters, but this led to even more controversy.

The levy had passed by a majority of 13 votes. A recount was called for by levy opponents. After a series of discovered mistakes and new tallies, including one error of 144 votes, the final margin was established as a 14-vote majority in favor of the September levy. A complaint by levy foes led to a court decision upholding the levy election. An appeal of that decision was still pending at the end of the observation period.

Opponents of the kindergarten levy decision circulated recall petitions against the five board members subject to recall. The major charge was loss of confidence and dissatisfaction with school board members, due to their lack of responsiveness to community desires. More specifically, the handling of the kindergarten decision was contrary to the historic wishes of voters.

In the November elections, 75 percent of the eligible voters voted on the recall measure, and all five board members were retained, with a 60 percent favorable vote. Two important innovations toward school responsiveness emerged from these events. First, the school board decided to broadcast its public meetings over the district-owned FM radio station. Second, public participation in the school budgetary process would be encouraged earlier in and throughout the decision-making cycle.

In March 1975, the superintendent's office made public the results of standardized tests of ability in reading and mathematics skills administered earlier in the year. The tests indicated that the pupils' performance was generally near national norms. The consensus of teachers, adminstrators, board members, and vocal community members was that that was not good enough. The high aggregate socioeconomic status of Coldren Corners residents plus the presumed high quality of district programs led to higher expectations. School board members called for a renewed emphasis on basic skills, and two schools proposed establishing a basic skills emphasis as an alternative school program. One board member proposed that reading instruction in elementary schools should be increased at the expense of the fine arts. A district-wide program to teach students how to take standardized tests was started. School officials were nearly unanimous in their opinion that past test results must be "turned around."

Coldren Corners was one of only two districts in the state to make test scores public. The superintendent's reason for releasing the results was to stimulate school employees and parents in order to make the school district more accountable to the taxpayers. The most vocal responses were from the professional academic community. Some school principals expressed surprise at the low level of community reaction they received. Apparently, the release of test scores was more effective in stimulating the school community than the larger community.

## MEETING WITH MOST TOTAL DEMANDS

The meeting with the largest number of demands was a "work session," not a regular legislative meeting. Nine percent of all demands made at school board meetings were articulated at this one meeting. Only six members of the public attended. There were four topics on the agenda: budget-making process, budget committee procedures, school board meeting procedures, and citizen participation.

The only vote taken was a decision to reconsider the matter of citizen participation on the budget committee at a later work session when applicants would be interviewed. Two members of the public participated in the discussion, both school district supporters. One was a former budget committee member, a regular meeting attender whose avocation is the school district. The other was chairman of a citizen group supporting school levies.

The matter of school board meeting procedures was not discussed. The primary concern of the participants was citizen participation in the budget process and the makeup and role of the budget committee. A secondary concern was to insure voter approval of the annual levy.

Thus, the Coldren Corners school board meeting with greatest demand articulation was concerned with one of several key issues facing the district. However, public attendance and participation were extremely low at that meeting. School officials were the articulators at the most demanding school board meeting.

## MEETING WITH MOST PUBLIC DEMANDS

Fourteen percent of public demands were made at a single Coldren Corners school board meeting. That meeting was not the meeting with most total demands. Members of the public articulated demands on four separate issues at the meeting.

The president of the local Education Association asked that personnel be allowed to withhold information from a district directory if such information were to be available to the public. A citizen speaking as an individual urged the board and superintendent not to make the information available to the public.

Another citizen argued that a proposal to establish a student-teacher ratio was a curriculum decision which the board should consider at length. After the board voted 4–3 to review and then accept or modify the superintendent's recommendation on the matter, the chairman of the district's budget committee suggested procedures for review.

A spokesman for a neighborhood organization presented a report on the future of a local school. Finally, an individual urged the board to adopt a specific plan for implementing an environmental education program. Group sources accounted for three of eight demand statements.

Only one of the issues which stimulated lay demands at their most demanding school board meeting was identified as a major issue in the larger narrative. Neither the meeting with most demands nor the meeting with most public demands reflects well the main items on the Coldren Corners policy agenda during the observation period. The more restrictive and less restrictive case study approaches differ significantly.

## BARWIG PARK

### OVERVIEW

The academic year in Barwig Park began in the midst of a controversy and ended in the midst of another. Both controversies centered around the new superintendent of schools and the school board.

The first issue began in mid-September when the school board unanimously voted to elevate the acting superintendent to the position of superintendent. The ensuing controversy centered around two facts: first, the superintendent did not hold a doctoral degree; second, of the numerous candidates and ten finalists for the position, none were brought to Barwig Park for an interview.

The second controversy involved finance of new construction. The normal process for capital financing includes a referendum. However, voters had not responded favorably to referenda in the past. Since 1951, only 4 of 13 school referenda attempts had been successful. Consequently, the superintendent and school board chose a different route. They first applied for planning and construction grants from a state agency. This method, however, also required a referendum. To avoid a referendum, the superintendent and a unanimous board chose to apply to another state agency, which required only city council approval.

This action provoked negative reactions from two losers in a recent school board election and a city councilman. They argued that the board had not only chosen to circumvent voters but that it had proceeded without public input or support. The board and superintendent argued that this alternative was the only viable one. The superintendent stated, "It's our constitutional duty to provide education. There is not a constitutional right to a referendum."

The funding request was approved by the state and was passed on to the Barwig Park City Council where the measure stalled. By the end of our data collection period, no resolution to the controversy had been found.

Other issues developed which were important in Barwig Park. In November the school board passed a resolution on the protection and privacy of students' files. The resolution stated that parents, legal guardians, and all students over the age of 18 had the right to inspect their official records. It also stipulated that school officials could not release records without the student's permission.

Another continuing issue was the quality of education. The superintendent promised to return to a basic curriculum and raise student achievement levels. The school board decided to reinstate achievement testing for the 1975–76 academic year in order to provide high school counselors with better data for placing students in the most suitable classes. The superintendent also suggested publicly that corporal punishment was sometimes necessary as a disciplinary measure.

A final issue involved the method of electing school board members. Two of three candidates for the school board proposed ward-based elections. Proponents claimed that this would make school officials more responsive to their constituents. No change occurred during the 1974–75 academic year.

## MEETING WITH MOST TOTAL DEMANDS

The meeting of greatest total demands had only minimal lay participation and no lay demand articulation. It was by far the longest meeting of the year in terms of the total number of statements by all participants. Ten percent of demands made during the observation period were voiced at this meeting.

Most of the agenda was taken up with purchases, personnel matters, student discipline (probation and expulsion cases), and information reports on curriculum. An extensive discussion was conducted on revising the official board policy on evaluation of certificated personnel, but no action was taken. Other agenda items were disposed of by unanimous votes. The board authorized a pilot project in aesthetic education at the elementary level, approved as a pilot project a proposal for improving instruction in mathematics and reading in inner-city elementary school, approved tuition-free summer school, accepted a proposed policy on compulsory school attendance at a first reading, and appointed architects to prepare preliminary cost estimates to establish budgets scheduled for Phase I of the Long Range Building Program. This last item involved the major controversy in the district: the board and superintendent's determination to pursue a long-range building program without public approval. Thus, the agenda was extensive and included consideration of major issues at the meeting with most demands in Barwig Park. However, the role of laymen at this meeting was that of spectator, not of participant.

## MEETING WITH MOST PUBLIC DEMANDS

The board meeting which drew the greatest number of public demands in Barwig Park also drew the greatest attendance. Our observer estimated the audience at more than 80 persons, and noted that "some people couldn't get in because the meeting room was full.'' Only five demands were articulated by laymen at this meeting—yet these five demands were nearly all those articulated by laymen during the academic year.

Two group representatives, one from AAUW, one from ACLU, spoke on a proposed new student rights policy. They wanted clarification of the proposal and strengthening of student rights. This topic accounted for two of the five demands by the public. The other three demands were made in the last part of the meeting, earmarked for ''Presentations by Audience on Non-Agenda Items.'' The observer noted: ''This was the important part of the meeting—the boardroom was filled to capacity—mainly by teachers and other school officials who were concerned over the change in the evaluation of reading skills programs.'' The three speakers were against the proposed plan for establishing reading grades. They wanted individualized reading instruction. One was the president of the Barwig Park Education Association, who presented a petition by teachers; one was a spokesman for the League of Women Voters; the third was an ''unaffiliated'' individual. Group sources accounted for four of five demand statements.

If one were to characterize events in Barwig Park from observation of meetings with lay demand articulation alone, an unrepresentative picture would result. This is the case for no other reason than that lay demand-articulation is extremely rare in Barwig Park. Laymen were stimulated to voice demands concerning one of several major issues at their most demanding meeting. Similarly, the meeting with most total demands addressed only part of the district policy agenda. The one element constant, however, in all selective views of major events is that laymen did not express their policy preferences at public school board meetings.

# NELSONVILLE

## OVERVIEW

There were two relatively controversial issues that created considerable debate in Nelsonville. The first concerned busing—but not busing to achieve racial balance. In September parents began complaining about the inadequacy of the school transportation system. Parents voiced concern that their children had to walk considerable distances to school. Icy roads during winter made this dangerous as well as inconvenient. Complaints of ''half-filled buses driving past children'' were also common. By February, the state legislature became involved in the problem. Three state legislators participated in a demonstration walk of the distance that some children had to walk to one school. The problem was being considered by both the school board and the state legislature, but no decisions were made. Complaints grew infrequent after winter.

A second issue also stimulated public involvement. Due to declining enrollments and continuing economic problems, the district faced the need for consolidation of schools. Since consolidation would mean not only closing some neighborhood schools but also transporting some students to more distant schools, many parents took an interest in the issue. Parental protests occurred during a series of public hearings initiated by the school board in February at different locations throughout the city. At these hearings it became clear that the public opposed all school closures. In legislative session, the board voted to: (1)

close several junior high and elementary schools, (2) consolidate the ninth grade with high schools, and (3) reorganize the remaining junior high schools. This action was in conformity with the administrative proposal advanced prior to the public hearings. The decision closed the issue in the district.

## MEETING WITH MOST TOTAL DEMANDS

The most demanding meeting was routine in substance. Six votes were taken concerning approval of minutes, personnel, purchases, maintenance, student travel requests, and two job reclassifications. All but the latter were unanimous. Other items on the agenda were housekeeping matters: a report on letters and communications received by the superintendent and a scheduled financial report on several accounts.

Four other reports on policy matters "brought forth lengthy discussions," according to school board minutes. They were: a staff recommendation to sell a school which the district leases but also maintains, requests for full-day parent-teacher conferences, testing results, and the tentative calendar for school year 1975–76. Thus, the school board meeting with the most demands dealt largely with routine matters.

## MEETING WITH MOST PUBLIC DEMANDS

The meeting of greatest public demands was a special meeting on the problem of school closures and district reorganization. Eighteen demand statements were made by laymen on this issue—nearly half of lay demands made during the academic year. All were made by "unaffiliated" individuals speaking in opposition to some element of the closure plan, or suggesting ways to open up decision-making and expand sources of information on the issue. The subsequent hearings on the school closure issue garnered most of the other public demands articulated. Thus, in Nelsonville, public participation and demand articulation centered on one of the major problems confronted by the school district. In contrast, the single most demand-laden school board meeting focused mainly on routine housekeeping matters.

# LEEVILLE

## OVERVIEW

The actions of other public officials were the source of the major problems and controversies which came before the Leeville school board. Heated communitywide pressure was brought to bear on the board only on a school budget issue, but this public outcry was part of a more general "taxpayers' revolt" stimulated by statewide court-ordered property reevaluation.

At the beginning of the school year, the long-standing issue of constructing a new high school was thought to be resolved. Under state law, school capital expenditures must be approved by the city council. Under threat of loss of district accreditation, the city council authorized the capital expenditure. The issue was reopened early in 1975 when the new governor ordered a freeze on state approval of building projects. The future of the new high school was clouded not only by uncertainty about whether the school could be excluded from the state freeze, but also by a city council decision in March to order a moratorium on all "unnecessary" construction.

The council's freeze was the result of the public outcry for cuts in city spending that erupted after new property valuations were issued in February. The mayor, by office chairman of both the school board and the city council, renewed his vocal and long-standing opposton to the new school. Two weeks after it voted the freeze, the city council excluded the new school from the moratorium.

The school board was responsible for implementing several new programs mandated by state law: breakfasts for low-income children, equal opportunity education, special education for children with special learning needs, and bilingual education. The substance of these programs was not controversial, but the board's attempts to carry out the legislative mandates brought it into conflict with interest groups.

The board established out-of-school locations for the breakfast program in community centers, but a statewide citizens' group charged that offsite locations were in violation of the law. The issue was settled in December, when a lack of volunteers forced the closure of two out-of-school sites, and the board voted to move the program into school buildings.

Special education was not a controversial issue in itself. However, a neighborhood school organization protested the location of a site for the program at their school because it would displace physical education classes to inadequate facilities. In January, the board voted to transfer the site to another school.

The most serious controversy erupted over the handling of state funds. The city manager applied all the state appropriation to lower the city tax rate. The school board charged that this was a violation of the law. They argued that $715,000 should have been credited to the school budget. The superintendent contended that this "mishandling" of funds was the reason for the deficit in the current school budget. School officials were supported by a variety of local and statewide citizens' and teachers' organizations and the state education commission on this issue.

The school board refused to compromise on the allocation of the funds. The state attorney general filed suit against the city on behalf of the State Department of Education. State officials characterized the lawsuit as a "good faith controversy" to obtain a judicial interpretation. A state reimbursement for special education was credited to the school district to offset the budget deficit while the dispute was being litigated.

Racial and sexual equity was an issue in Leeville during the data collection period. In April, reports by a school district committee and the teachers' union charged discrimination against women in administrative appointments and labeled textbooks sexist and racist.

The board was confronted with demands for sexual equality in school athletics from students, teachers, coaches, parents, and the local chapter of NOW. The board expressed its desire to achieve equity in athletics but did not resolve the problem during our study.

In September, a local civil rights group presented a list of demands to the school board calling for removal of racism from the curriculum, hiring of more minority teachers, establishment of a Third World Studies program, elimination of standard tests for program placement, and involvement of community groups in implementing these demands. The board created a special subcommittee that, along with an existing advisory council, would meet with the group. However, the group declined, because "no working relationship had been defined." Representatives of the group continued to attend board meetings and articulated their demands. Despite this activity, racism was not a focus of board action.

The board attempted to deal with the problem of under-enrolled schools by consolidating small neighborhood schools. Parents protested against the proposed closing and succeeded in winning a one-year reprieve. In March, the board established a citizens' committee to study the problem of declining enrollment "with an eye toward recommending the closing or consolidation of elementary schools." The board made explicit its intent to keep this panel "outside the political arena" and deliberately appointed members who had no "special interests in preserving neighborhood schools" and no job involvement in the school system.

A controversy arose over proposed budget reductions. The mayor, an outspoken critic of city and school spending, called for cutting 100 teaching positions; the teachers' union opposed eliminating more than 40. Citizens demanded that the board cut administrative positions and not teachers. The board first voted to eliminate 60 teaching positions, then reconsidered and cut 100, then reversed itself again and settled finally on 75. Although the mayor spearheaded personal attacks on the superintendent on the question of administrative reductions, the board did not eliminate any administrative positions.

## MEETING WITH MOST TOTAL DEMANDS

The meeting was concerned with four problems: kindergarten consolidation, establishment of a school breakfast program, demands by a Committee Against Racism (CAR) for a public forum, and implementation of a new state law mandating textbook loans to parochial students. Members of the public participated in discussion on the first three of these items, particularly the kindergarten problem. The main issue was when consolidation should take place. Enrollment projections had proved to be inaccurate for a number of schools, resulting in under-enrolled kindergarten classes. Board members had raised the possibility of reorganizing kindergarten classes and releasing teachers during a previous meeting. The administration's recommendation was to defer adoption of a consolidation plan until May, which would be implemented the following school year.

An estimated eighty people were in attendance, including, according to a newspaper account, "About 50 parents of kindergarten aged children [who] asked that their children's classes not be disrupted during the school year." Several parents addressed the board, others participated more spontaneously during the discussion—calling out, clapping and cheering. The board approved the administration's recommendation by a 5–2 vote; ancillary motions—such as reaffirming minimum class size guidelines, eliminating long-term kindergarten substitute teacher positions—also passed by split votes.

Members of the public also spoke on setting up a state-mandated breakfast program for low-income children. The board deferred action by referring the matter back to the administration "for more details"—again, by a split vote. Similar action was taken on another state-mandated program—textbook loans to parochial students. A motion directing the administration to present recommendations at the next meeting for implementing the program was passed by a split vote (4–2).

The admininistration's reply to the petition presented by the CAR in September was referred to the district's Black Advisory Council. A special subcommittee of three members was named to work with CAR by unanimous votes. The CAR spokesmen objected strenuously to these actions, demanding to be heard by, and to deal with, the school board as a whole.

The balance of the agenda, on which the public did not speak, was disposed of by unanimous actions: to notify the city manager and the city council that the board was willing to continue to work with them on the plans for the construction of a new high school; to instruct the board negotiator to meet with the city's labor counsel; to approve the implementation of a blood donor drive in the high schools by a teen-age organization concerned with city problems; to accept a recently drawn manual for the custodial services; to approve funds for purchase of safety equipment in vocational classes; to approve requests for salary increases of non-represented groups from existing budget; and to approve numerous personnel actions.

The Leeville school board meeting with the greatest number of demands was not the meeting with greatest lay demands. Nevertheless, lay participation at the meeting was considerable. The most demanding meeting disposed of both major and routine items. Interestingly, the major items were temporarily resolved by deciding to defer action. Apparently laymen were satisfied by the decisions to decide later.

## MEETING WITH MOST PUBLIC DEMANDS

The meeting which had the greatest number of statements and demands by the public was a special meeting to review the budget and funding. The local newspaper estimated attendance at 1,600 to 1,800 people. Over one-fifth of lay demands made during the academic year were articulated at this meeting. For the most part, the public expressed, often vehemently, opposition to board policies and budget decisions, the administration (particularly the superintendent), and increased city taxes. Most demands were expressed by individuals who did not claim to represent organized groups.

Thus, a selective view of public demand articulation in Leeville would be one of considerable public outcry against district policy on an extremely salient issue. It is of no small significance that those demands were heard, not at a regular decision-making session, but at a special meeting called presumably to hear lay dissatisfaction.

# KENTINGTON

## OVERVIEW

The Kentington School District experienced a number of conflicts during the 1974–75 academic year. Each issue ultimately involved the action and interaction of constituents, school district officials, and the education ministry of the provincial government.

The first significant issue involved the janitors of the Kentington schools. In mid-September and in December of 1974, the janitors refused to service the schools in the evenings. Their action was a protest against the board's failure to conduct a rating of schools to equalize janitorial work loads and to live up to the work load policy of 2,500 square feet per man hour, which was established after the first protest action. The December protest was ended when the provincial labor relations board determined that the janitors were engaging in unfair practices.

The Public Employees' Union and the Kentington school board entered negotiations in September to resolve differences between the parties. The union demanded raises for the janitors from $4.42 to $7.12 per hour. The chairman of the Kentington school board, responded to the demand by calling it "overwhelming, inflationary, and cynical." Negotiations between the two sides broke down, and the union went on strike in February.

The strike virtually closed the schools. The school board tried to open the schools for one hour each day for students to pick up homework assignments, but pressure from disgruntled students and parents finally forced the board to open some of the schools for half of each day. This latter action drew considerable criticism from the union and from the president of the Kentington Teachers' Association. The constituents in the school district carried their protests to the provincial legislature, where they attempted to persuade the education minister to reopen the schools. She refused to act on their request, suggesting that the strike negotiations made the problems "purely a labor dispute."

Finally, the school board went to the provincial Supreme Court to seek an injunction limiting the number of pickets at the schools. In March the court placed severe limitations on the number and hours of picketers at the schools. It maintained that "the interruption of education was doing irreparable harm to the young scholars." A tentative agreement between the janitors and the school board was finally reached, and the janitors returned to work in April.

The second issue concerned negotiations between teachers and the school board on the terms of the 1975 contracts. The Kentington school board joined 67 other boards in the province in urging provincewide negotiations. The teachers in Kentington favored the current system of local bargaining. When efforts to find a compromise failed, the provincial education minister introduced a bill in the legislature to break the deadlock. The effect of the bill was to force local boards to deal separately with teachers in their districts. The law was passed, much to the dismay of the Kentington board, which considered the action too favorable to the teachers. In early December, the teachers and board members both ratified a 1975 contract which gave the teachers an average 16.3 percent pay raise.

Constituent input concerning the contract negotiations and the teachers' demands was varied. Some citizens felt strongly that the teachers deserved whatever pay increases they could get. Others suggested that the minority of a few thousand teachers had undemocratically betrayed the wishes of the majority of Kentingtonians who had elected the board members.

A third issue involved differences in opinion about philosophies of education, curriculum, and discipline. A range of constituent opinion was expressed on each issue. Kentington has a variety of schools, ranging from very structured to academically unstructured. Thus, citizens opposing one or the other type of school are occasionally critical of problems which occur in those schools. Input regarding curriculum changes ranged from requests for more religious training to demands for complete curricular reform.

The proponents of reform were particularly irate when several innovative educators were fired in the Kentington area and when the provincial education minister fired the director and entire staff of her Department of Research and Development. The staff had been charged with the responsibility of reforming the educational processes and substance in the province.

## MEETING WITH MOST TOTAL DEMANDS

As measured by the number of statements the most demanding meeting was also the longest board meeting of the year. The board undertook a large amount of business: 54 votes were taken, only 4 of which were nonunanimous (and one of these was a humorous dissent). The only people in the audience were administrative staff and the press.

The long list of motions on which votes were taken was a consequence of the board's procedure in disposing of recommendations in the reports of its subcommittees and of the superintendent. Blanket or consent agendas were not used; each recommendation was voted on separately. The board: moved to receive and file correspondence; received board election results; installed new board members; approved staff changes; approved a student report policy; requested a report on special education and alternative classes; discussed a traffic safety problem; authorized two special elective courses; authorized formal support for federal funding for French (bilingual) program in primary grades; recommended to the provincial education minister that she name a man to work with the already-named female sex discrimination consultant; forwarded a copy of a report on the district's Industrial Education program to the sex discrimination consultant; directed the Instruction-Curriculum Committee to develop a program for a particular school; referred report on Outdoor Education to the Instruction-Curriculum Committee; requested reports on locally developed elective courses; approved final cost of an addition to a school; directed that thermostats be lowered in all district buildings to conserve energy; formalized ceding of land to the district by a municipality; directed a special request to the provincial department of education to approve funding for a community school; amended board by-laws regarding conduct of board meetings; recommended to the provincial school board association that kindergarten and grade 1 admissions criteria set forth in the Public Schools Act be changed; approved a monthly finance report; adopted a policy on equipment replacement; approved sale of school supply kits; adjusted a financial arrangement with a community association for funding a community school project; requested the provincial department of education to expedite approval of a proposed management system for construction of a new school; approved a proposal to appeal to businesses to implement the metric system to reinforce metric education in the schools; requested report on the district's scholarship system; and requested the teachers' association to offer a reaction to the report of a Task Force on Teaching.

In Kentington the day of greatest demands was not the day of greatest conflict. Most of the topics of discussion were routine, housekeeping matters. It is not surprising, therefore, that there was no lay participation. The day of most demands was not the day the public was most stimulated to attend and speak.

## MEETING WITH MOST PUBLIC DEMAND

The meeting of most public demands centered on a major issue: the labor dispute between the board and the school custodians' union. The custodians had struck, and school aides and secretarial staff had been honoring the picket lines. The day before this board meeting, a court order placed severe limits on picketing of schools. There were two board meetings on the same day: the regularly scheduled one, and a special meeting held immediately afterwards to consider current negotiations with custodians and hours of school operation (which were severely curtailed during the strike). The nine demand statements by the public (nearly half the number articulated all year) all occurred at the regular meeting, and all concerned the custodians' strike.

A parents' group had organized in reaction to the strike, and had been active and visible at both the board and provincial level, seeking to operate the schools full-time and to end the strike. The president of this group demanded summer school to make up work and that something be done to prevent the situation from happening again. She asserted that the responsibility was with the board and not at the provincial level.

A spokesman for a parents' group told the board that they wanted their children back in school, that the situation had been especially hard on parents who had to cope with strike hardships and pay taxes too. These comments met with applause. She suggested that the schools be closed entirely until the labor dispute was finally resolved. A spokesman for another parents' group espoused full-time operation, and expressed the opinion that the board's reasons for virtually closing the schools were "fatuous," not very compelling. Group spokesmen accounted for all demand statements made at the meeting.

The selective views of Kentington school board meetings differ substantially. The narrative summary suggests considerable controversy and public input. The meeting of greatest public demand articulation contained a significant public outcry on a major issue. However, the meeting of greatest total demand articulation was concerned with routine matters and was conducted with virtually no public input or audience.

# MACKTOWN

## OVERVIEW

The major problem faced by the Macktown School District in 1974–75 was lack of money. The source of this problem was the repeal in November of the state sales tax on food and prescription drugs which resulted in a 10 percent loss of revenue for the district. Concern was voiced by numerous school officials, including the superintendent, who feared that the district could lose as much as $3.2 million.

A highly publicized incident involved the suspension in March of two high school teachers for insubordination. One was later charged with assault for attacking an assistant superintendent. The teacher later announced that he would be a candidate for the school board. The litigation was not resolved during the data collection period.

The district focused on educational programs during the academic year. A reading program for the elementary schools utilizing reading specialists, prepackaged reading programs, and other such aids reportedly improved the reading skills of students over the last three years. A program for students having difficulties in mathematics, involving the use of electronic calculators, was also reported successful. General achievement tests indicated improvement in these areas. Another compensatory effort, the free lunch program, was expanded to include more students.

The Macktown School District became "fully integrated" (i.e., there were no all-white schools in the district) as of fall 1974. Some schools continued to have very small nonwhite enrollments, which stimulated legal action initiated prior to 1974. The district maintained that HEW integration guidelines had been followed. In December, a federal appeals court ruled that there was insufficient evidence to indicate that the Macktown schools were illegally segregated. Although minority advocates were unconvinced, school officials interpreted the legal decision as approval of their racial policies.

## MEETING WITH MOST TOTAL DEMANDS

The meeting focused on routine items: action on housekeeping and personnel matters and purchases; a request by the superintendent that a committee be set up to evaluate the district's Affirmative Action program and make recommendations for improvement; presentation of the first of a planned series of program reviews of individual schools by superintendent-appointed lay committees. Program proposals were presented in reports by three committees of the board. The finance committee report discussed routine bookkeeping matters, a recommendation to invest in short-term local commercial paper, replacement of the automobile fleet, and a pilot program to curb vandalism. The Community Relations Committee reported on a Neighborhood Council proposal for a multiethnic center at a local school; a project proposal by a private and a junior college for mobilizing community resources for senior citizen education programs. The Education Committee reported on an exchange program with Costa Rica; a proposal for a creative arts center; summer school programs; textbook adoptions; and a proposal for dance in residence programs at two sites. The most demanding meeting in Macktown reflects the general tranquility and low public participation experienced throughout the year.

## MEETING WITH MOST PUBLIC DEMANDS

Three lay demands were voiced at the meeting with greatest lay demand articulation. The three were about ¼ of the total lay demands made at meetings during the observation period. A spokesman for the Macktown Education Association made all three demands. One was a request that announcements of school cancellations because of weather indicate whether or not teachers were to report. The second was an objection to the way state assessment tests "were used . . . as evaluation." He also urged caution against "letting the state have a say about what is taught in individual classrooms."

Unlike the other school districts the three selective views of major events at Macktown school board meetings present a consistent picture. In this district the routine character of the meeting with most total demands is shared by the meeting with most public demands and with the larger school board agenda.

## BALLARD CITY

### OVERVIEW

A variety of problems plagued the Ballard City School District during the 1974–75 academic year. Many of the problems are common to urban school districts—lack of adequate financing, vandalism and violence, demands by teachers for better pay and more favorable working conditions. Other problems are more unique, such as the loss of federal funds for noncompliance with civil rights requirements, and the threatened resignation of the superintendent of schools.

The opening weeks of the academic year were marred by violence in the schools. Within the first month, 18 teachers had been assaulted and numerous fights, robberies, and racial altercations had been reported. These violent acts took place in schools that were already being patrolled by security officers. As a result, attendance at the troubled schools declined, and teachers, who had gone on strike the previous year, threatened to strike again.

A task force comprised of police officials, teachers, administrators, and community relations spokesmen was organized in early September. In October, the task force decided that principals should be able to conduct either random or continuous searches of student lockers for illegal drugs or weapons. However, the assaults continued. Finally, in November, the task force promulgated a 14-page policy to prevent violence in the schools. The document's major provisions were:

1) Principals will sign complaints against anyone on school property without authority.
2) A principal may sign a complaint against anyone interfering with persons on the way to or from school property or anyone disturbing a class or school-sponsored activity.
3) The district will participate in prosecution of serious crimes, physical assaults on school employees or students, use or sale of illegal drugs, or thefts of school property.
4) In emergency situations, the police have a legal right to take direct action in schools, even though their presence has not been requested.

A number of contending forces including the superintendent, the school board, and the teachers' union closed ranks and took a unified stand against disorder in the schools.

Another problem concerned teacher contract negotiations. During 1973–74, teachers staged the first teachers' strike in the city's history. The experiences of that strike, and the difficulties that surrounded it, added significance to negotiations. Among the items submitted by the teachers was a request for a two-year contract with a 15 percent raise each year, plus quarterly cost of living adjustments. This request was submitted at a time when the board president estimated that the district would be $11 million short of needed revenues.

In early April, union leadership called for a vote to decide whether to strike again. The district had proposed a 5 percent across-the-board pay increase as its final offer; at this point, the teachers were asking a 9.5 percent across-the-board increase. The union's executive board voted unanimously to reject the district's offer and urged the teachers to strike. The teachers, however, also rejected the call to strike. They agreed to the first public contract negotiations in the history of the district. Within two days the opposing sides resolved five of nine contract disputes. The teachers voted against the advice of their union leadership, and accepted the contract offer from the Board of Education.

A third problem was finance. As noted, the board president estimated an $11 million budget deficit. This estimate was made prior to the development of two additional difficulties. First, a statewide interest group filed a suit challenging the legality of city collection of sales tax for schools. Second, the Department of Health, Education, and Welfare threatened to suspend any further federal funds because of alleged noncompliance with civil rights requirements.

One of the most persistent and perplexing problems facing the district has been its relations with HEW. The district had received an Emergency School Aid Act grant to finance desegregation efforts. To qualify for the grant, the district agreed to comply with federal requirements involving integration of administrators, equity in special education programs, and student transfer policy. In late January, HEW informed the district that it was in noncompliance.

The superintendent initially denied the charge. Then he suggested that HEW and the district simply disagreed on the interpretation of the term "compliance." The school board was split on the issue of compliance. Faced with the alternative of loss of federal funds, the district chose to comply with HEW's suggested alternatives. A temporary settlement was reached in February.

The student transfer issue arose again when HEW ordered the district to retransfer students to the schools according to residence zones. The students had been transferred out of residence zones earlier in the year. A local judge temporarily enjoined the district from retransferring the students. The district was being ordered to do two conflicting things by different agencies of government. To add to the difficulties, HEW told the district to file a petition to block the temporary injunction. When the district refused, the ESAA funds were again frozen. Litigation was in progress as data collection concluded.

The last major problem confronting the district was conflict between the superintendent of schools and the school board. The superintendent announced his decision to seek another job in late February, just as the teachers' contract negotiations were beginning. In July 1974, the board had voted 6–1 to give him a one-year contract extension (to July 1976) and an 8 percent raise. The superintendent publicly criticized the school board for not offering him the support and assistance he deemed necessary. He specifically charged that some board members considered him just another employee and that they had undermined his authority. He also complained that the board had sent him to the negotiating table against the teachers during the previous year's contract talks against his advice and without a coherent strategy.

School board members suggested that they were split 5–4 in favor of terminating the superintendent. Both the superintendent and the board hired attorneys to represent them. The superintendent began to interview for other positions and left the district at the end of the academic year.

## Meeting with Most Total Demands

The meeting with most demands was a marathon that began at 3:00 P.M., recessed at 6:25 P.M., reconvened at 9:50 P.M., and finally adjourned at 3:16 A.M. In the afternoon session, the board presented athletic awards to high school teams, and several proposed library policies were presented for a second reading. The board formally established the duties of the secretary of the board, an action that involved two split votes and one unanimous vote.

One lay spokesman represented two public groups. On behalf of an educational civic group, she urged the board to continue cosponsorship of a program at a private hospital which provided medical care for needy children. The board chairman requested a report on the program from the superintendent. Speaking for the educational civic group, the layman requested a school policy establishing increased accountability for board assignment of special education children. As spokesman for a task force on violence, she requested that films "depicting violence" not be shown under school auspices, and that detailed records, accessible to the public, be kept on all film showings. The board voted 8–1 to arrange for board and parental viewing of films.

The major goal of the meeting was to adopt a comprehensive plan for administrative reorganization. At the afternoon session, a spokesman for the Ballard City School Administrator's Association registered objections to part of the plan. Adoption of the plan involved 13 votes, only two of which were unanimous. The reorganization plan was labeled the superintendent's plan. Part of the plan, creating broad departments, had been approved earlier in the year. Assignment of administrators to departments and specified lines of authority had already been revised and tabled since mid-October. The board was divided in its support of the superintendent's plan; those who wanted to modify the plan were in the majority. The rest of the agenda dealt with routine personnel, purchasing, district operation matters, and information reports.

Thus, the most demanding meeting in Ballard City contained both routine and episodic issues. Administrative organization, a key controversial issue throughout the academic year, was the major agenda item.

## Meeting with Most Public Demands

The meeting at which the most lay demands were made was not the marathon meeting on administrative reorganization. The topic which stimulated the most lay input at their most demanding meeting was racial discrimination—a major issue for the Ballard City School District.

Eleven demand statements were made by two members of the Baptist Ministers' Union and the NAACP regional director, protesting discriminatory demotion of blacks and other minority employees in the wake of budget cutbacks. An extended discussion and argument between speakers and board members ensued.

Other lay demands at that meeting included procedural requests that agenda items be passed over until scheduled speakers arrived. A member of a Community Advisory Committee speaking on an ESAA grant proposal, and a spokesman for a school PTA recommending utilization of that school as a learning center for special education classes, accounted for two demands. All lay demands were made by individuals claiming group affiliations.

The meetings with greatest total and greatest public demands each reflect one of several controversial issues which occupied the Ballard City district. However, the smaller selective views do not indicate the overall range of issues which were important during the 1974–75 academic year.

# DRUMMOND FALLS

## OVERVIEW

School finance and associated problems were the dominant themes in the Drummond Falls School District during the 1974–75 academic year. Rejection of both a bond issue and the annual school tax levy by voters brought on a series of crises surrounding the necessity to reduce spending by 20 percent. The issues articulated during the election campaigns indicated that, while poor economic conditions were one cause of the bond and levy failures, an equally important reason was declining faith in the school board and administration.

In September the school board approved putting a $35.3 million bond issue on the November general election ballot—a reduction of $3.7 million from the superintendent's original recommendation. The issue was to provide funds for renovation and improvement of various facilities in the school district and for construction of a vocational training facility and a center for the handicapped. The bond issue soon became a source of controversy, with several normally supportive community groups (including the Chamber of Commerce and the Parent-Teacher-Student Association) not endorsing the issue.

Opponents of the bond issue cited economic arguments such as the weak state of the local economy and possible inflationary effects, but they also raised the larger question of the responsibility and accountability of the school district administration. They argued that the majority of bond funds were to be allocated to routine maintenance, which should be part of regular yearly budgets. They also said that there was ambiguity over which projects would be financed—district officials could reallocate bond funds without taxpayer approval. The charge was also made that school officials were asking for the bond issue mainly because state and local matching funds were available. Opponents saw the bond issue as an example of the school board approving the recommendation of administrators without sufficient independent information necessary to judge the merits of the request.

The bond issue was soundly defeated; only 40 percent voted for it, while a plurality of 60 percent was necessary for approval. The school board and administration turned their attention to the annual school tax levy election and considered the possibility of resubmitting the bond issue to the voters in February along with the levy. In view of the bond issue defeat, the district initiated a major campaign to seek community input on all areas of school finance. Telephone and mail surveys were undertaken, a series of special public meetings was held, and a television program with live responses to telephone questions was broadcast in an effort to learn about community desires and to educate the public about the problems of school finance.

In December, the administration and school board decided to abandon the bond issue and to propose a unique tax levy to the voters. The levy issue was offered as a layered proposal; a separate vote was to be taken on a $2.45 million deferred maintenance program. Although this request was lower than the previous year's approved levy, opposition quickly mounted against the proposal. For only the second time in history, the Chamber of Commerce did not support the February levy. Along with other critics, they made educational accountability a major campaign issue. They claimed that, although student enrollment had dropped from 99,000 to 68,000 in the past seven years, the district was maintaining a capacity for over 100,000 students. In the past seven years, the number of school employees had increased by 20 percent in spite of declining enrollments, and the yearly cost per pupil had risen from $775 to $1,900.

The February levy failed when it won less than 50 percent approval (60 percent was needed). School critics saw the result as a mandate for officials to reevaluate their programs. School officials saw the result as evidence of a communication failure. A second and final levy election was scheduled for April. It was decided to offer only the $53 million basic education proposal.

Some critics, including the Chamber of Commerce, voiced support of the second levy in view of the disastrous consequences of its failure. The school board predicted in March that over 1,600 positions would be eliminated if the second levy failed. The superintendent indicated that a 36 percent across-the-board cut in all budgets would follow a levy failure. In February and March the school board held 21 community meetings on the school budget. About 1,000 people attended overall.

The April levy measure also failed, winning 54 percent of the vote instead of the necessary 60 percent. This was the first time in history that a levy had been defeated in a second vote. School officials attributed the failure to a general property owners' revolt and the idea that state officials would act to avoid disaster should the levy fail. Defeat of the school proposal was evidence of considerable discontent, yet the school district proposal was supported by a majority of voters.

School officials turned to the task of informing over 1,700 employees of their termination. A proposal to retain employees on the basis of merit was rejected in favor of seniority as the basis of continuing employment. The criterion was modified in order to maintain minority group employees. Minority employees with about five years of service would be retained; other employees would be retained with a minimum of about nine years of service. The school board was also faced with the prospect of choosing 20 to 30 elementary schools to close.

The Drummond Falls Teachers' Association threatened a general strike and a lawsuit to challenge the district's reduction in force policy. A march to the state capitol was held in May. The governor called on the legislature to pass some program to provide a measure of relief to districts where levies had failed and said he would be extremely reluctant to sign appropriations measures until such a program was passed.

There was no resolution of any issues associated with the levy failure during the data collection period. We later learned that the superintendent was replaced prior to the 1975–76 academic year.

## MEETING WITH MOST TOTAL DEMANDS

Two meetings tied for having the most demands articulated. The first was a "committee of the whole" meeting held at a local high school. Approximately fifty people attended. Two matters were listed on the agenda for discussion: a vacancy in an associate superintendent position (which was not discussed), and the bond issue. The meeting was then to be open to "concerns and questions relative to school-related matters from the citizens of the local community." Discussion of the bond issue dominated the meeting and was informational rather than conflictual.

The other most demanding meeting was a regular legislative session. The business of this meeting was generally routine and noncontroversial. Audience size was estimated to be twenty-five. The 15 votes taken were unanimous.

The proposed bond issue was also discussed at this latter meeting. The chairman of an ad hoc citizen support committee spoke to the main point of opposition, which was concern about how the funds raised by the sale of bonds would be used. He recommended that the board make a formal statement of its priorities, and the board complied. The board aired its concern about the Chamber of Commerce's refusal to endorse the bond issue and discussed what might be done to regain the Chamber's traditional support.

The board discussed a rumor that desegregation efforts would bring about a boundary change. Several board members reiterated the district's commitment to voluntary desegregation, rather than desegregation by boundary changes.

The ordinary business of the meeting included: approving "for execution" a purchase contract for window glass; considering a church's request for district cooperation in developing its own off-street parking facilities by vacating an unimproved school site; appealing to the State Department of Public Instruction for an "exception" to license two vehicles for school bus operation; declaring overcrowding at a middle school to be an emergency (so that the bidding procedure for portable classrooms could be expedited); awarding purchase orders for various items to low bidders; certifying completion of work on two construction and maintenance projects; authorizing payrolls and bill payments; canceling several uncollectable debts to the district; approving the superintendent's personnel report; receiving a report from the board president on the State School Directors' Legislative Meeting; and hearing a presentation by a board member of a proposal to hire an outside management firm to audit nonacademic areas of administration and to analyze salaries of all school district jobs.

Thus, the most demanding meeting considered both routine and controversial episodic issues. Laymen voiced demands concerning the latter; school officials dominated discussion of the former.

## MEETING WITH MOST PUBLIC DEMANDS

The meeting was held in the midst of the finance crisis. Two budget levies had failed, and in reaction to proposed layoffs, a teachers' strike had threatened. A strike had been postponed only the day before. The observer estimated 200 people in attendance. All public demands concerned the consequences of the financial crisis.

The first topic was a proposal for operating the schools in spite of the levy failure. A board member suggested asking the state legislature to rescind the 180-day school year law and the continuing contract law. The attorney for the teachers' union demanded that teacher contracts not be abrogated or impaired. The board voted unanimously to table the proposal.

Community advisory committee representatives offered general support for the board and the superintendent and specific support for the proposal to petition the state legislature. Spokesmen from an ad hoc citizens' committee opposed the layoffs and urged the board to exhaust other legal and budgetary options, but also expressed general support for the board and extended an offer to help the board deal with the situation. At the end of the meeting, an unaffiliated individual told the board that they should follow the example of business and industry and "make do with what revenue you've got," educate the largest segment of children and cut compensatory education. Another citizen spoke against that approach. Another individual expressed the opinion that the state should fund the district 100 percent. Other public demand statements were pleas to continue specific programs in spite of the financial crisis.

For Drummond Falls the three selected views each highlight school finance as the dominating issue of the 1974–75 academic year. As is the case in almost all other districts, the board meeting with greatest demand articulation has a large component of demand statements on routine, housekeeping matters.

# HARTSHORNE HTS.

## OVERVIEW

During the 1974–75 academic year, the Hartshorne Hts. schools had to deal with a number of complex problems. Among the most important were: a dispute with the Department of Health, Education and Welfare; violence and vandalism in the schools; two issues having to do with school board members; and school finance.

The dispute with HEW began with a complaint made in 1973. A black interest group charged that the school district's policies on suspension and punishment were discriminatory. HEW was asked to investigate whether the district was in violation of the Federal Civil Rights Act. The district stood to lose $7 million in federal aid if it were found to be in violation. The school district at first cooperated with the investigation. However, a conflict arose over the use of the school's records of suspension cases. The school district stated that the privacy of records was being violated and ordered the system's records closed to HEW investigators.

A lawsuit was initiated by the Justice Department in November in order to force the school district to make its records available. At hearings in February, the court ordered the parties to work out guidelines which would allow HEW to continue its investigation. In May, a U.S. Senator held hearings on the matter. However, a solution was not forthcoming from either the Senate or the school district's discussion with HEW. In late May, the court ruled that the district must comply with HEW's requests to see the records.

Violence and vandalism are familiar problems in the Hartshorne Hts. schools. Policemen were stationed in some schools, and the district employed a special officer to coordinate its security programs. In January, the school board held special public hearings on discipline problems, which were very well attended. It was suggested at the hearings that closing school campuses to outsiders would help reduce violence and vandalism. Students argued at later meetings that open campuses were not a cause of the problems; rather, discipline problems were rooted in the students themselves. In early April the board decided to establish student advisory councils in each school to promote student involvement in solving the problems of discipline and security.

Two issues involving school board members became important. The first involved the question of how school board members should be chosen. The current procedure was for candidates to be nominated by an annual convention. The governor than appointed Hartshorne Hts. school board members, but he was not limited in choice to the nominees of the convention. Other school districts in the state elected school board members, and changing to an election system was proposed in Hartshorne Hts. Part of the stimulus came from the campaign of a candidate for the state senate who made school board elections a campaign issue.

The second question involving school board members was whether the student member of the board should have voting rights. Both the school board and the school board nominating convention have opposed giving student members full voting privileges. The state attorney general's office stated that there were no legal restrictions which prevent the student member from voting. However, state law allows for only seven voting members on the school board. Thus, unless the law were changed the student member could not have voting privileges unless he were appointed by the governor to fill a regular vacancy.

A conflict over school finance arose between the school board and the county council. After being approved by the school board, the school budget becomes part of the larger county budget, and is subject to amendment and revision by county officials. The school board presented a $112 million budget in January. At public budget hearings held by the board in January, the teachers' organization recommended a $120 million budget. In May, the county executive recommended to the county council that the school budget be cut to $103.2 million. At a county council meeting in May, both parents and teachers expressed support of full funding for the school budget, even if that meant an increase in property taxes. School officials expressed dismay over the situation, which was not resolved during the data collection period.

## MEETING WITH MOST TOTAL AND MOST PUBLIC DEMANDS

A single school board meeting had both the most total and the most public demands articulated. The agenda items on which the public spoke included: understaffing at an elementary school, changing guidelines for the Citizens' Advisory Council, school security and student involvement policy, restoring busing of children in an area said by parents to be unsafe, student travel to U.S.S.R., Bicentennial Committee report, and a Department Chairperson Implementation recommendation. Numerous topics were discussed without public participation: changes in secondary grading policy, proposal for a consultant's feasibility study on renovation of three downtown elementary schools, 1974 enrollment report, and appointment of an architect for construction of Hartshorne Hts. High School. With the exception of the architect appointment all board action was unanimous.

Most public demands dealt with understaffing at an elementary school. A spokesman for the school's parents and the chairman of a Citizens' Advisory Countil (CAC) objected to having several classes where one teacher was teaching two grades. No board action was taken. There was a consensus between board and spokesman that the school's parents would help campaign for more teachers for the school district as a whole.

The next largest portion of demands were from another CAC chairman in a report to the board on changing guidelines for CAC's. The demands were suggestions concerning the size, composition, and purpose of CAC's. The report was an informational item on the agenda, and required no board action. Demands were also made by students and parents on the topic of school violence and vandalism—a visible and continuing problem in the district. The demands were ideas on how communication among students could be used to reduce injury and loss.

Other demands concerned: a school travel club's request for permission for a trip to U.S.S.R., parents' request that children in an unsafe area continue to be bused, a report from a board-appointed Bicentennial Committee, and comments from a teachers' association spokesman to a school board staff report on "Department Chairperson Implementation." The first two requests were unanimously approved; the last two were informational items on the agenda not requiring board action.

Hartshorne Hts. is the only district in which a single board meeting accounts for the greatest number of public and total demands. The meeting addressed both routine and episodic issues. However, the leading controversial issues— discrimination, school board member selection, student violence, and finance— were not on the agenda of that meeting. A case study of the most demanding meeting in Hartshorne Hts. would not adequately portray the substance of key issues during the academic year.

# GRAHAMDALE

## OVERVIEW

For the most part, the Grahamdale School District went through a rather uneventful year. No issues that stimulated extraordinary public concern were raised. Prior to initiation of data collection in September, voters approved a $21.6 million bond issue. Although most of those monies were committed to projects underway, school officials viewed the vote as indicating public support of the district.

One potentially explosive issue was a sex education program being offered in high schools by health science students from the local university. However, the majority of citizen comments were mild. Board discussion was abbreviated. Because the program was only temporary, no action was taken, and the controversy died.

Another potential problem involved an allegation by the federal government that Title I money was being diverted from its original purpose. However, the district persuaded the federal government that it was following grant regulations. Consequently, there was little public awareness of a problem. It became a simple budgetary matter to be resolved by federal and local experts.

Late in the year a bill was passed by the state legislature that would allow high school students to drop out of school at the end of their tenth year. The bill was highly controversial among school officials. The bill was sponsored by a state legislator who was also a school administrator in Grahamdale.

Increasing vandalism and burglaries were serious problems. A portion of the September school bond issue was to be used for a district-wide surveillance program to help control this problem. Because of its high proportion of ethnic minority students, bilingual education was an ongoing issue in the Grahamdale school district. No attempt was made by either the public or school officials to seek some solution to the problem during 1974–75.

## Meeting with Most Total Demands

The meeting dealt largely with a number of housekeeping matters: adjusting inventories, granting utility easements, leasing building space, purchasing property, increasing budget allotments for federal programs, appointment of board counsel, school district appointment to the Metro Justice Commission, enrollment report, and report on substitute teacher rolls. There was only one nonunanimous vote—on the inventory adjustment.

Two relatively lengthy discussions accounted for nearly half the statements made. The first was a detailed presentation on a district-developed pilot program for individualized reading instruction. The report by the reading specialist was so involved that the observer made this marginal comment: "Board and audience perplexed, confused and/or bored with detailed presentation." Comments by the superintendent and school board indicated that the presentation was made to increase accountability to the board and public. Yet the style of presentation precluded lay response. Nevertheless, the superintendent expressed satisfaction with the report.

The controlled, overtechnical, carefully prepared, and polite presentation was strikingly contrasted by an unexpected confrontation with the teachers' union which occurred under the agenda heading, "Other matters which may come before the board." The union spokesman was welcomed by the board chairman, who indicated pleasure that the union president was not the speaker. The spokesman presented a complaint at the lack of administrative support for a faculty-student-developed pilot project at a junior high school. The board, through the chairman, refused to consider the matter. An angry argument ensued about proper procedures for a bargaining agent to bring grievances before the board. The chairman objected to the lack of "early warning" about the agenda item; charged it was misleadingly titled; and insisted that it be demonstrated that all administrative channels had been exhausted. The argument escalated to a shouting match between members of the audience (which included teachers) and the board and ended with the chairman gaveling the topic out of order.

## Meeting with Most Public Demands

Another school board meeting garnered the greatest number of demands made by laymen. Nearly half the demands articulated by the public during the academic year occurred at that meeting. All but one were made on a single agenda item: closure and boundary changes affecting four local schools. In addition to parents of affected students, demands were made by spokesmen of the Downtown Neighborhoods Association, an Urban Renewal Committee, and a bank. The other demand was a recommendation for sabbatical leaves presented by the teachers' association, which was unanimously approved by the school board.

The three selective views of school board meetings in Grahamdale contrast sharply. The meetings with most public and most total demands present pictures of sharp conflict. However, the overview presents a picture of tranquility. The heated exchanges at the two board meetings were anomalies. Neither the issues nor the conflicts of those meetings were sustained throughout the academic year.

# STUMONT

## OVERVIEW

The 1974–1975 school year saw a number of ongoing adminstrative and operational problems involving finance. The contract with district teachers was subject to renewal at the end of the academic year. The central issue in negotiations was teachers' demand for a sizable pay increase. At the same time, it was expected that state school funding might be reduced. The anticipated reduction would not only jeopardize a pay increase for teachers, it might well make it necessary to eliminate some administrative positions.

Early in the school year, there was considerable debate concerning the hour at which school began for elementary school children. The issue arose with a proposal to establish a uniform starting time for all elementary school chidlren. Stumont gave up uniform starting times in connection with integration in the early 1970's when a shortage of buses necessitated staggered starting times. A citizen group organized on the issue and protested directly to the school board in the fall of 1974. They objected to children leaving home in the early morning darkness, for fear of accidents and injuries. About one hundred and twenty citizens attended a January school board meeting when this topic of concern was discussed. At a February meeting the issue was resolved when the Board set later starting times for younger children. The citizen group appeared satisfied with the compromise.

During the course of the school year, the Stumont School Board had to replace three of its members who voluntarily resigned. Two members resigned to seek higher public office, and one resigned because board membership interfered with his professional responsibilities. No controversial disputes contributed to any of the resignations. New members were appointed by the school board. This was the third time in six months and the fifth time in five years that board members were replaced without an election. Only two of seven board members in Stumont were originally chosen by election.

Stumont is in the only county in its state that does not pay its school board. In a November meeting the City Council voted to pay school board members, but the mayor vetoed the measure. He stated he was willing to pay school board members a small honorarium only. The City Council Rules Committee requested the state legislature to enact legislation shifting the responsibility for setting school board salaries from the city council to the school board. No decision was rendered by the legislature on this issue during the data collection period.

Because of an increase in school vandalism, the school administration instituted an elaborate audio intrusion alarm system. As another antivandalism measure, guards in mobile homes were placed on some campuses. It was reported to the school board that vandalism decreased considerably on those campuses with the mobile homes.

## MEETING WITH MOST TOTAL DEMANDS

The meeting with most demands was the longest meeting of the year by two measures. First, the largest number of statements occurred, and second, it lasted from 8:00 P.M. to 1:20 A.M. Only four statements were made by members of the public. The substance of the meeting was routine: purchases, contracts, bids, site approval and acquisition, and so on.

The board voted unanimously to name the Stumont Teachers Union exclusive collective bargaining agent for teachers on the basis of the union's presentation of a petition signed by a majority of the system's teachers. The president of the Stumont Education Association objected and stated that his association would challenge the union to an election for representation.

The board voted 4–3 to readopt its present policy handbook so that all policies now in effect would continue in effect after January 1. The assistant city general counsel advised the board that there was still some question as to whether the school district was subject to the state administrative procedures act. If so, three public hearings would be required to make any policy changes after the first of the year.

The three board members who voted against the readoption of existing policies wanted revisions which had been drawn by the administrative staff during the previous few weeks. The staff revisions were not accepted, and these three voted against readoption of existing policies. This review and readoption was essentially a housekeeping matter to maintain continuity in the face of changes in the state law.

Nearly a dozen specific policies were discussed, including one that allowed parent and school groups to obtain interest-free loans from the school board to purchase items such as air-conditioners for classrooms and band and choral uniforms—a practice which, in conjunction with extracurricular fees, came under critical board scrutiny. This and collective bargaining were the only items on which members of the public spoke.

The board discussed sites for new educational facilities, including a tract for a new vocational high school. Two members objected to that site "because they said that the school system is locating all of its facilities in the suburbs rather than the central city."

A list of some of the other votes gives a flavor of the board decisions made at the meeting: approve contract with local television station, authorize workshop in community relations at building level, designate board members delegates to State School Board Association, acquire warehouse, approve payment for past unauthorized hiring of consultant, approve carpet purchase, renegotiate sugar purchase contract, accept bid for sale of school. The most demanding school board meeting was concerned with several of the major issues on the district agenda for the entire academic year.

## MEETING WITH MOST PUBLIC DEMANDS

Lay demand articulation in Stumont was so rare that four such demands at a single meeting accounted for ⅓ of lay demands made during the academic year. Of the four, three expressed opposition to a district proposal to establish a uniform starting time for all elementary children. One speaker was the president of a school's Dad's Club; the other two were spokesmen from a citizen group organized for the starting time issue. Our observer estimated attendance at one hundred twenty, and noted: "There's standing room only and precious little of that—think they're here mostly for school starting time issue." No decision was made at this meeting. The issue was resolved at the next meeting, a meeting which drew the greatest number of public statements. The board set staggered starting times—a resolution that apparently satisfied the citizens' organization.

The fourth demand was made by the business manager of the local public employees' union. It concerned recognition of the local as a bargaining unit. The union spokesman wanted the board to defer action to another meeting when public employees could attend and present their case. The board did act, however, and the action was not that requested by the union spokesman.

The selective views of most demanding school board meetings identify several of the major issues on the larger Stumont agenda. However, the selective views do not accurately portray the range of important issues dealt with during the 1974–75 academic year.

## Conclusions

In table 4.1 we present a brief summary of the major events described in the media-based narratives. The issues are arrayed in an impressionistic order of importance. An examination of the table indicates that finance occurs most fre-

TABLE 4.1

MOST IMPORTANT ISSUES IN DISTRICT NARRATIVES

| | |
|---|---|
| Coldren Corners | Curriculum, Finance, School Board, Students |
| Barwig Park | Administration, Finance, Students, Curriculum, School Board |
| Nelsonville | Student Services, Local Schools |
| Leeville | Finance, Local Schools, District Operations, Discrimination |
| Kentington | District Operation, Teachers, Curriculum |
| Macktown | Finance, Teachers |
| Ballard City | Students, Teachers, Finance, Discrimination, Administration |
| Drummond Falls | Finance, Teachers |
| Hartshorne Hts. | Discrimination, Students, School Board, Finance |
| Grahamdale | Curriculum, Discrimination, Students |
| Stumont | Teachers, District Operations, School Board, Students |

quently. The second most frequent topic is students, followed by teachers. The other topics are more or less idiosyncratic to particular districts.

At the risk of being redundant, it is important to repeat that these narratives highlight conflictual and potentially conflictual episodes. They are not comprehensive descriptions. However, we believe that they are representative of how the districts would appear to the casual, nonsystematic observer.

In many districts it would appear that there is substantial politicization. Events are described in which mayors and superintendents clash publicly, in which citizens' groups make demands which are responded to or ignored by school boards and superintendents, in which racial problems are discussed, in which federal intervention is imposed on local districts. In short, although there is variance, the picture is one of school districts in turmoil. Teachers' strikes, vandalism, school closings, financial disputes, intraelite argument are events which normally are associated by political scientists, journalists, and laymen with political conflict and the resolution of such conflict. The narratives make it apparent that opportunities for lay participation, and hence, opportunities for school district responsiveness to articulated lay preferences, exist.

Some episodes in the narratives involved public participation. For many of these the cycle of decision-making was incomplete. Issues were raised, groups articulated preferences, and school boards and superintendents considered alternatives. However, issues were frequently left unresolved, or at least were not resolved during the period of our observation. This is not to say that decisions were never made. The point is simply that closure is difficult when issues are complex, laymen become involved, or other governments intervene. Even a nine-month observation period was too short to observe the entire policy cycle from issue articulation to resolution on most episodes involving conflict.

The narratives point out that, while most of our districts employ similar formal organizational structures, there are some exceptions. The Hartshorne Hts. school board is appointed by the governor. The mayor of Leeville is, *ex officio,* the school board chairman. In these two districts there are unusual linkages between local, state, and school district government.

The major issues identified in the narratives correspond quite well to the topics identified by national news media as significant. School finance, for example, has been in the headlines for the last four or five years as being a major source of controversy in educational governance. Student discipline and basic skills are other issues of nationwide concern which are prominent in the narratives. Our sample of school districts is not large enough to confirm that the national news media identify significant issues by aggregating the events of individual school districts. We find it equally plausible to argue that local news media focus on issues of supposed national import when they occur because of the presumed scope of applicability. In later chapters we will explore how representative "significant episodes" are of the universe of issues considered by our school districts.

## The Public: An Arroyo

A key characteristic of public demands can be demonstrated by their distribution over time. Only a chemical trace of all demands are made by the public. At a "normal" board meeting, about three public (as opposed to about thirty-six "establishment") demands will be made.

TABLE 4.2

DISTRIBUTION OF DEMANDS:  OVERALL AND PUBLIC

| District | Mean Per Meeting | Public | N | Meeting With Greatest Demands | | |
|---|---|---|---|---|---|---|
| | | | | Public | % of Demands | Public |
| Coldren Corners | 43 | 3 | 84 | 10 | 9 | 14 |
| Barwig Park | 25 | * | 40 | 5 | 10 | 83 |
| Nelsonville | 16 | 2 | 52 | 18 | 17 | 46 |
| Leeville | 59 | 10 | 108 | 43 | 9 | 21 |
| Kentington | 46 | 1 | 126 | 9 | 9 | 47 |
| Macktown | 20 | 1 | 62 | 3 | 22 | 27 |
| Ballard City | 84 | 5 | 192 | 15 | 12 | 16 |
| Drummond Falls | 32 | 5 | 85** | 27 | 7 | 14 |
| Hartshorne Hts. | 34 | 7 | 87 | 31 | 16 | 28 |
| Grahamdale | 12 | 1 | 68 | 10 | 30 | 43 |
| Stumont | 53 | 1 | 113 | 4 | 21 | 33 |

\*    Less than 1%

\*\*   2 separate days

Additionally, establishment demands are reasonably stable in comparison to those of the public. They are less concentrated on a particular meeting day. Public demands are quite another matter. Not only are they sparse; they are also much more occasional, much less sustained. Thus, about ⅓ of all public demands for an entire year are made at the single meeting that attracts the greatest number of demands.

The point can be made clear by looking at the distribution of demands in Grahamdale, Coldren Corners, Kentington, and Barwig Park (table 4.2). In three of these districts, about half of all public demands were made at a single meeting; in the fourth, virtually all public demands were made at a single meeting. By contrast, the greatest concentration of establishment demands is less than the average of public demands. Thus, the public does not engage in a sustained interaction with the board.

Districts with a dispersion of demands (Coldren Corners and Drummond Falls) are also characterized by their infrequency. In only one district, Leeville,

TABLE 4.3

DAYS OF GREATEST PUBLIC DEMANDS

| District | Issue-Specific or Diffuse | Group-Individual-Dominated | Predominantly Supportive or Opposing | Remarks |
|---|---|---|---|---|
| Coldren Corners | Diffuse | Individual | Mixed | |
| Barwig Park | Diffuse | Group | Opposing | |
| Nelsonville | Specific | Individual | Opposing | Closure & consolidation--"Mass" meeting. |
| Leeville | Specific | Individual | Opposing | Budget, spec. meeting. |
| Kentington | Specific | Group | Opposing | Custodians' strike... In midst of crisis. |
| Macktown | Diffuse | Group | Opposing | 2 Teacher Assn. requests. |
| Ballard City | Specific | Group | Opposing | Black objection to demotions. |
| Drummond Falls | Specific | Group | Mixed | Levy failure... In midst of crisis. |
| Hartshorne Hts. | Diffuse | Group | Opposing | |
| Grahamdale | Specific | Group | Opposing | Boundary changes & closures, various schools. |
| Stumont | Specific | Group | Opposing | Major controversy-- School starting time. |

do demands appear to be sufficiently frequent and dispersed to justify regarding the public as more than occasional visitors. Public articulation of demands is consequently not part of the normal routine of school district governance.

We have seen that, in all but one district, meetings of greatest overall demand are not the meetings which attract the most public demands. The substance of these meetings is routine; housekeeping matters. Thus, even if the public were interested, they lack the expertise requisite for effective interaction with school officials at those meetings.

Table 4.3 summarizes the narratives of meetings with greatest public demands. In most cases, the day of public demands presents the school district with the greatest opportunity to be responsive to demands. It is true that in some districts, some constituents were asking school officials to intervene with a higher level of government. Nevertheless, in almost all cases, the opportunity for response existed. However, the opportunity was rarely exercised. In most cases, the board preferred to wait until expert reaction was forthcoming. The fact that in many cases the day of most demands occurred at nonlegislative sessions further suggests a conscious decision to segregate public inputs from decisions.

An appropriate way to describe school board meetings is not in terms of response to public demands, but rather in terms of insulation from public demands. Still, when the public does become aroused, the news media describe the district as "under crisis." This description appears to exist because, at such meetings, the dominant mode of expression is opposition to proposed policy—a mode which does not characterize typical public input.

This chapter has presented three selected views of important school board meeting issues. For the most part, the views are inconsistent. Summaries of important issues during the entire academic year drawn from news media suggest ongoing turmoil. Yet, the meetings at which most total demands are articulated are most often dominated by routine, housekeeping matters. Nearly all cases of most demanding meetings are examples of unusually productive school board sessions in which school officials are expressing demands among themselves.

Two points are particularly striking about meetings which stimulate the most lay demand articulation. First, they are not the meetings of greatest total demand articulation. Second, lay demand articulation rarely results in concrete action at the meeting. Demand articulation by laymen is not treated as a resource appropriate to decision-making. Rather, lay input is seen primarily as a form of agenda-setting. Lay demand articulation is typically met by a resolution to have experts report on appropriate actions to be taken at a later date.

# 5

# School Board Meetings: A Comprehensive View

The goal of this chapter is to describe the events which occur at public school board meetings. Although our Demand-Response Logs are designed to provide as comprehensive a description as possible of school board meetings, it is clearly untenable to present this material in full detail. Our analysis will focus on the influence exercised by experts and laymen. The data base of the previous chapter was selective reporting of subjectively defined important events. The data base of the present chapter is the universe of communications at school board meetings.

Whatever else may be said about school board meetings, they are forums of decision-making by legally elected and appointed public officials. Choices are made between alternatives, proposals are advanced and developed, debate is heard, and votes are taken. At such meetings, members of the public have an opportunity, if they choose to exercise it, to participate. Thus, public school board meetings provide a clear opportunity for interaction between experts and laymen. Moreover, because school board members are, in our terms, laymen, school board meetings will always consist of interactions between experts and laymen.

Our focus in describing communications and decisions made at public school board meetings will be on the comparative role played by experts and laymen. To repeat, we define laymen as those individuals who are not employed by the school district and who do not profess professional expertise with respect to school governance.

## Actors and Attendance

### ACTORS AT SCHOOL BOARD MEETINGS

The participants at school board meetings may be divided into the general categories of experts and laymen. Among experts are superintendents, staff experts, and line experts. Staff experts are associate superintendents and other cabinet level administrators whose administrative responsibilities are for the school district as a whole. Line experts include principals, teachers, lower level administrators, and other employees of the school district. Our subcategories of laymen include school board members, members of the public, and representatives of other governments. While it may be the case that members of the latter group are experts in their own right, representatives of other governments are not experts with respect to educational policy or administration.

108

Throughout this chapter, our focus will be upon the interaction between experts, whose resources are those associated with professionalism, and laymen, whose resources are those associated with participation and democracy. How often are these two sets of expectations in conflict? When these two sets of expectations and values are in conflict, whose are most likely to win?

How do the various participants, both expert and laymen, come to participate at school board meetings? We know much more about how administrators and board members are recruited than we do about how members of the lay public are induced to participate.

To be an administrator, one must first be a teacher. To survive as a teacher—or to become an administrator—one must learn to understand and accept occupational norms. The expected behavior for teachers—less so now, but certainly true when today's administrators were teachers—is quiescence, acceptance of authority, and conservatism (Corwin, 1966; Jennings and Zeigler, 1969). Those who cannot accept the norms drop out (Zeigler, 1967). Surviving long enough to become an administrator requires more than an employee orientation. In addition to "knowing one's place," male teachers (superintendents are nearly universally males) have to face the financial and psychological deprivations of exisiting in a highly feminized occupation. Ninety percent of all elementary teachers and about half of high school teachers are females. It is not surprising that only about 10 percent of the male teachers lasts longer than five years (Clark, 1964, pp. 734–769). The pool of eligibles is thus reduced considerably to those male teachers who, through keeping clear of controversy, are able to survive. As Carlson notes, sheer *perseverance* seems to be a contingency of the career path of the superintendent (1972, p. 9). It is, perhaps, here as a teacher, or more specifically, as a fraction of those administrators that survive, that future superintendents first develop their suspicion of lay control. In competition with parents for obedience of the child, teachers develop defensive reactions: opposition to paraprofessionals, resentment of parental interference, belief in certification and using methods courses. Surviving administrators, buffeted by the tensions of their jobs, tend to become more politically conservative, and develop an unusually high need for respect, an exaggerated concern for authority, and a personal rigidity and fear of risk taking behavior (Zeigler, 1967, p. 28; Brown, 1970, pp. 473–481).

Awareness of the occupational recruitment of administrators and specifically superintendents—coupled with their unusually high small-town representation and working-class origins—helps considerably in understanding their view of school governance. Given relatively humble origins, and the development of a defensive response to criticism, overcompensation is virtually guaranteed. Thus, the development of expertise as a resource comes naturally. Taken together, these various strands of the recruitment process add up to senior administrators perceiving their roles as "narrow and defensive" (Crain, 1968, p. 117). They are often intolerant of lay criticism and frequently unwilling to engage in dialogue with outsiders. Criticisms may be answered with either complete disagreement or with irrelevant replies loaded with trivial detail (Crain, 1968, p. 117). For superintendents, expertise is not only a resource, it is a way of life learned early, and it is necessary for psychic and occupational survival.

The major lay participants in school board meetings are, of course, school board members. When compared to the general public, board members have qualities that—rightly or wrongly—are more valued and esteemed in American society. Specifically, they are more male, white, middle-aged; longer residents of their communities; much better educated and have more prestigious occupations; are more Protestant, more devout, more Republican (Zeigler, *et al.*, 1974, p. 28). Although the fallacy of inferring attitudes and behaviors from the social origins and positions of public officials is by now well established, social characteristics are important because certain perspectives are inevitably underrepresented on governing bodies by virtue of the status bias of members.

The upper class bias of school boards is hardly unique; indeed, all governmental bodies exhibit such bias. Nor is it surprising that school boards attract a disproportionate share of people, who, along with their families, have been associated with education. What *is* unique is the isolation of the school board members from political involvement. Because governing schools is part of the political process, we might expect board members to spring disproportionately from politicized homes. Such is not the case (Zeigler, *et al.*, 1974, p. 29). Board members are no more likely than the general public to come from the homes more involved in public affairs. For all the usual findings about the political backgrounds of political elites, the pattern obviously does not apply to local elites in education. Thus, the recruiting process provides more evidence of a recurring theme of this discourse, the apolitical character of participants in educational governance.

The stong tendency of school boards to perpetuate themselves adds to their noncompetitive, nonpartisan nature. School board elections are only moderately competitive. Only about half of board members are elected in a contest with an incumbent (Zeigler, *et al.*, 1974, p. 38). Those who challenge incumbents are likely to stress ideological concerns and specific issues as opposed to such symbolic euphemisms as "better schools." Still, most board members can cite only one difference with their electoral opponents, and such differences are not likely to relate directly to educational programs.

In addition to self-perpetuation by default, there is deliberate self-perpetuation (Zeigler, *et al.*, 1974, pp. 33–34). If one adds the activity of the PTA (closely identified with the establishment), superintendents, and teachers to the recruitment by the board, about half of the members of the school boards are products of self-perpetuation. To a substantial degree, the pool of eligibles comes to be those people recognized by the local educational professionals and elites as potential board members.

## ATTENDANCE

All 11 school boards hold at least one regular legislative session each month to sit as deliberative, decision-making bodies. The meetings also serve as media of communication between the school board, school district employees, and members of the public. All actors are invited to attend and participate. In all districts formal arrangements and informal norms permit all to speak at public school board meetings. Thus, experts and laymen may be motivated to attend school board meetings for a variety of reasons. They may wish to acquire information, to observe the process of governance, or to participate in school board deliberation and decision-making.

As table 5.1 indicates, there is considerable range of attendance—both within and across districts. Kentington, for example, has extremely low attendance. In

TABLE 5.1

ATTENDANCE AT SCHOOL BOARD MEETINGS

| | | Meeting With Greatest Attendance | |
| District | Average Attendance | Attendance | % of Total Attendance |
| --- | --- | --- | --- |
| Coldren Corners | 37 | 250 | 32 |
| Barwig Park | 39 | 80 | 12 |
| Nelsonville | 141 | 998 | 37 |
| Leeville | 246 | 1600 | 32 |
| Kentington | 9 | 30 | 11 |
| Macktown | 44 | 75 | 12 |
| Ballard City | 48 | 200 | 22 |
| Drummond Falls | 90 | 400 | 12 |
| Hartshorne Hts. | 67 | 200 | 17 |
| Grahamdale | 42 | 350 | 44 |
| Stumont | 52 | 120 | 23 |

some districts an average of 100 or more attend school board meetings. In six districts, a single meeting produced more than $1/5$ of total attendance. Furthermore, those districts with the greatest average attendance—Leeville and Nelsonville—had disproportionate attendance at a single meeting. To some extent, each district had a few school board meetings which attracted unusually high attendance. Each district had at least one meeting which attracted double or more the average attendance. Because of this sizable—albeit inconsistent—attendance, it is reasonable to expect that participation in school board meetings will include actors other than school board members, superintendents, and staff administrators. The purpose of this chapter is to explore the extent to which each actor exercises the option to participate.

The previous chapter focused upon meetings with greatest total and greatest public demand articulation. We saw that there was little overlap between greatest overall and public demand articulation. We note here that there is little overlap between school board meetings which attract most demands and meetings which attract greatest attendance. Surprisingly, in only three districts are the meetings of greatest lay demands the meetings of greatest attendance. In short, there are ebbs and flows of attendance, lay demand articulation, and school official demand articulation which do not coincide.

## The Agenda of School Board Meetings

The agenda of school board meetings is comprised of all communications which occur at the meetings. The most basic unit of analysis is the statement.

TABLE 5.2

PURPOSE AND RESOLUTION OF DISCUSSIONS AT SCHOOL BOARD MEETINGS

| District | N of Discussions | Decision Intended | Decision Reached When Intended | Decision by Vote |
|---|---|---|---|---|
| Coldren Corners | 284 | 58% | 96% | 87% |
| Barwig Park | 333 | 96 | 58 | 86 |
| Nelsonville | 191 | 59 | 99 | 89 |
| Leeville | 343 | 97 | 94 | 90 |
| Kentington | 618 | 84 | 93 | 86 |
| Macktown | 179 | 64 | 99 | 97 |
| Ballard City | 609 | 67 | 95 | 85 |
| Drummond Falls | 488 | 47 | 93 | 84 |
| Hartshorne Hts. | 172 | 95 | 67 | 72 |
| Grahamdale | 388 | 60 | 94 | 73 |
| Stumont | 265 | 83 | 98 | 93 |
| Mean | | 74 | 90 | 86 |

Observations in our 11 school districts indicate that statements were only partially organized and bounded by formal parliamentary agendas. An ideal sequence such as topic introduction, discussion, and resolution rarely occurred. A more typical pattern was topic introduction, discussion on a *number* of related topics, and resolution of *some* of the issues raised. Thus, our concept of agenda leads us to work with data that are more comprehensive but less organized than those found in agenda documents and reconstructed minutes of meetings.[1] Our procedure was to record the substance of each statement and to aggregate statements on the same topic into units called "discussions."

The primary function of public school board meetings is decision-making. As table 5.2 summarizes, an average of nearly ¾ of discussions are intended to conclude with some sort of clear decision. As the wide range of proportions of discussions intended for decisions indicates, our school boards differ in the character of their public meetings. Two patterns emerge. Six boards combine decision-making and public hearing functions. One-third to over half the discussions in these districts are intended to disseminate information, to stimulate general discussion, to gauge popular preferences, or to achieve purposes other than an immediate decision. In five districts public hearing functions are served in fewer than 20 percent of discussions. Table 5.2 also shows that school boards successfully reach decisions when they are intended. The mean proportion is 90 percent. In all districts the majority of decisions are made by a formal vote. Board meetings are formal forums of decision.

The agenda of school board meetings can also be described in terms of the topics of discussion. Some school board meeting discussions are not concerned with the substance of educational governance. We designated interactions such as callings to order, pledges to the flag, introduction of notable students and community members, commemorative memorabilia outside the context of formal discussion, etc., as nonsubstantive in nature. An average of 17 percent of all discussions were deemed nonsubstantive. Nonsubstantive discussion appears to be independent of the extent to which discussions are intended to result in decisions. The balance of our analysis of school board meetings will include only those discussions which are substantive in nature.

Our typology of topics was developed from survey, interview, and observational data. The categories are defined in the appendix to this chapter. The distribution of discussion units among topics is presented in table 5.3. The table indicates that in 9 of 11 districts, district operation (maintenance, facilities, materials, and so forth) was the most frequently discussed topic. Thus, in most districts, the school board agenda is devoted largely to housekeeping matters. Con-

TABLE 5.3

DISTRIBUTION OF TOPICS DISCUSSED AT

SCHOOL BOARD MEETINGS (Percentage)

| District | Curriculum | Student Services | Students | Parents | Teachers | Administrators | Local Schools | School Board | Finance | Discrimination | Other Government | District Operation |
|---|---|---|---|---|---|---|---|---|---|---|---|---|
| Coldren Corners | 3% | 10% | 11% | 3% | 13% | 15% | 5% | 4% | 9% | 2% | 8% | 16% |
| Barwig Park | 19 | 11 | 30 | 4 | 5 | 6 | 0 | 2 | 7 | 0 | 5 | 12 |
| Nelsonville | 7 | 11 | 6 | 2 | 13 | 6 | 12 | 1 | 11 | 0 | 3 | 23 |
| Leeville | 3 | 14 | 5 | 2 | 15 | 15 | 4 | 9 | 11 | 1 | 4 | 15 |
| Kentington | 15 | 12 | 7 | 3 | 10 | 9 | 7 | 5 | 6 | 0 | 4 | 22 |
| Macktown | 1 | 12 | 8 | 6 | 14 | 7 | 6 | 2 | 6 | 2 | 8 | 22 |
| Ballard City | 7 | 9 | 5 | 1 | 15 | 20 | 5 | 9 | 4 | 1 | 7 | 17 |
| Drummond Falls | 5 | 7 | 5 | 1 | 13 | 7 | 9 | 3 | 22 | 1 | 5 | 23 |
| Hartshorne Hts. | 2 | 10 | 16 | 4 | 14 | 6 | 7 | 1 | 10 | 0 | 7 | 23 |
| Grahamdale | 9 | 6 | 6 | 0 | 11 | 4 | 4 | 5 | 7 | 0 | 4 | 43 |
| Stumont | 2 | 4 | 9 | 2 | 16 | 16 | 3 | 5 | 8 | 1 | 4 | 29 |

spicuously absent from these agendas are topics of educational governance which dominate popular and scholarly literature and the mass media. For example, discrimination (equality, busing, affirmative action) is never discussed in five districts, and is the topic of two percent or fewer of the discussions in the other six districts.

Also curious is the small proporation of discussions devoted to curriculum matters. After all, the curriculum is presumably the heart of the educational process. What is taught, how it is taught, and who will teach it are matters which are pondered by educators at considerable length. School boards do not ponder them—at least, not in public meetings. In only two of our districts does curriculum achieve second place among topics discussed.

Finally, school boards do not discuss finance extensively. Again, one would assume they do, since financial problems are allegedly of critical importance in American education. In one district, Drummond Falls, finance is discussed with relative frequency, largely due to the fact that three elections concerning school finance were held there during the observation period. In sum, those topics which attract the most professional and popular attention outside of school board meetings are rarely discussed at school board meetings. Other than a common concern with district operation, the topics most frequently discussed are largely idiosyncratic.

The issues which dominate the so-called national agenda of school governance are not reflected in the agendas of individual school boards. To what extent are the issues perceived as most prominent in individual districts reflected in the agendas of their respective school boards? Table 5.4 indicates the proportion of school board discussions devoted to topics which are prominent in each school district according to the surveys of constituents and school officials discussed in chapter 3, and the descriptive narrative overviews presented in chapter 4. We are comparing prominent agenda topics with three perceptions of prominent issues: perceptions of district residents and patrons, perceptions of district officials, and perceptions of the news media.

It is not surprising that the proportion of media-identified issues match board agendas more closely than do the citizen and school official perceptions. To a great extent, the media are merely reporting and summarizing discussions at school board meetings. It is surprising that a majority of school board discussions are occupied by matters which are not perceived as very important by either the news media, school officials, or the public. Perhaps most surprising is that the items seen by school officials as most important occupy, on the average, only 18 percent of school board agendas. Why do school officials dwell on housekeeping and trivial matters to the exclusion of matters they and others deem most important? The most plausible explanation is that they do not perceive school board meetings as appropriate forums in which to resolve or even discuss the most important matters in their district. School officials may well be devoting maximum time and effort to the important issues in their districts outside of school board meetings. Nevertheless, it is significant that the public meetings of the chief policy-making body in the school district spend so little time on the matters of greatest concern to both the school district and constituents.

The agendas of school board meetings can be described in terms of the intensity of discussions. We define intensity of each discussion unit in terms of the number of statements it contains. Table 5.5 presents the distribution of statements across topics. District operation is again the most prominent single topic. How-

TABLE 5.4

PROPORTION OF SCHOOL BOARD DISCUSSIONS
CONCERNED WITH IMPORTANT ISSUES

| District | Public Survey | School Official Survey | Narratives |
|----------|---------------|------------------------|------------|
| Coldren Corners | 23% | 25% | 27% |
| Barwig Park | 37 | 19 | 64 |
| Nelsonville | 24 | 6 | 23 |
| Leeville | 34 | 29 | 31 |
| Kentington | 32 | 21 | 47 |
| Macktown | 16 | 22 | 20 |
| Ballard City | 24 | 4 | 45 |
| Drummond Falls | 32 | 35 | 35 |
| Hartshorne Hts. | 18 | 26 | 37 |
| Grahamdale | 26 | * | 15 |
| Stumont | 26 | 8 | 59 |
| Mean | 27 | 20 | 37 |

* No consensus

ever, it is the leading topic in only five districts. While a large number of school board discussions are concerned with housekeeping matters, apparently many of those discussions are relatively short.

We commented earlier on the fact that topics discussed at school board meetings do not reflect the issues considered by constituents, school district officials, or the media to be most important. Our analysis of intensity of discussion (table 5.6) reinforces this conclusion. In no district does the proportion of statements concerned with "most important issues" (as defined by the public and school officials) equal half of all statements. Again, the agenda of school officials is least well met. In only two districts do the topics identified by the media as most important exceed half of all statements. There is no escaping the conclusion that public school board meetings are not primarily concerned with the most important issues facing the respective school districts.

TABLE 5.5

DISTRIBUTION OF STATEMENTS AT SCHOOL

BOARD MEETINGS, BY TOPIC

| District | N of Statements | Curriculum | Student Services | Students | Parents | Teachers | Administrators | Local Schools | School Board | Finance | Discrimination | Other Government | District Operation |
|---|---|---|---|---|---|---|---|---|---|---|---|---|---|
| Coldren Corners | 2999 | 5% | 11% | 16% | 2% | 9% | 13% | 5% | 3% | 20% | 1% | 6% | 10% |
| Barwig Park | 2262 | 20 | 10 | 26 | 2 | 7 | 4 | 0 | 1 | 13 | 0 | 3 | 13 |
| Nelsonville | 2291 | 5 | 13 | 10 | 2 | 3 | 5 | 26 | 0 | 8 | 0 | 3 | 24 |
| Leeville | 3106 | 2 | 16 | 7 | 3 | 9 | 12 | 5 | 13 | 8 | 0 | 4 | 21 |
| Kentington | 3704 | 16 | 11 | 8 | 4 | 9 | 7 | 10 | 5 | 4 | 0 | 4 | 23 |
| Macktown | 1197 | 1 | 10 | 11 | 4 | 10 | 5 | 9 | 2 | 13 | 1 | 11 | 25 |
| Ballard City | 4377 | 5 | 8 | 4 | 1 | 22 | 19 | 10 | 5 | 1 | 1 | 7 | 16 |
| Drummond Falls | 5836 | 5 | 5 | 6 | 2 | 11 | 4 | 10 | 1 | 33 | 2 | 5 | 18 |
| Hartshorne Hts. | 2183 | 5 | 20 | 25 | 5 | 7 | 3 | 7 | 0 | 11 | 0 | 5 | 12 |
| Grahamdale | 3489 | 10 | 5 | 11 | 0 | 10 | 2 | 8 | 6 | 8 | 0 | 2 | 35 |
| Stumont | 2552 | 3 | 4 | 8 | 9 | 12 | 15 | 2 | 7 | 10 | 0 | 4 | 25 |

TABLE 5.6

PROPORTION OF SCHOOL BOARD STATEMENTS
CONCERNED WITH IMPORTANT ISSUES

| District | Public Survey | School Official Survey | Narratives |
|----------|---------------|------------------------|------------|
| Coldren Corners | 41% | 30% | 44% |
| Barwig Park | 39 | 26 | 64 |
| Nelsonville | 23 | 10 | 39 |
| Leeville | 26 | 31 | 33 |
| Kentington | 33 | 20 | 48 |
| Macktown | 25 | 25 | 23 |
| Ballard City | 27 | 1 | 47 |
| Drummond Falls | 44 | 44 | 44 |
| Hartshorne Hts. | 30 | 36 | 36 |
| Grahamdale | 31 | * | 21 |
| Stumont | 20 | 10 | 52 |
| Mean | 31 | 23 | 41 |

* No consensus

Differences are evident between the distribution of discussion and intensity of discussion by topic in all 11 districts. How shall the topics which receive disproportionate attention be identified? A simple way of addressing this question would be to compare proportions of discussions and statements presented in tables 5.3 and 5.5. This method implies the expectation that each discussion of a topic will consist of the same number of statements. However, two other models are equally plausible. One alternative is that topics of frequent discussion will require fewer statements. The reasoning is that a certain amount of expository discussion is necessary whenever a new topic is introduced. As a topic is discussed again and again, the number of introductory statements decreases. The other alternative is that frequently discussed topics will generate more statements as they are discussed again and again. The reasoning is that frequently discussed topics relate to difficult and often controversial problems. The greater the number of discussions,

TABLE 5.7

REGRESSION OF STATEMENTS AND DISCUSSIONS

AT SCHOOL BOARD MEETINGS

| District | Intercept | Slope | $R^2$ |
|---|---|---|---|
| Coldren Corners | 1.72 | .81 | .46 |
| Barwig Park | .47 | .92 | .91 |
| Nelsonville | .87 | .88 | .60 |
| Leeville | .60 | .95 | .73 |
| Kentington | -.08 | 1.02 | .95 |
| Macktown | .60 | 1.01 | .78 |
| Ballard City | -.60 | 1.06 | .81 |
| Drummond Falls | -.87 | 1.11 | .82 |
| Hartshorne Hts. | 1.99 | .76 | .46 |
| Grahamdale | 1.53 | .79 | .94 |
| Stumont | 1.82 | .78 | .89 |

the greater the probability that more people will want to voice their opinions. As a result, the most frequent topics of discussion should be the most intensively discussed topics.

Linear regression is a statistical model which can be used to test the applicability of the three "models" of discussion intensity. The independent variable is the proportion of times a topic is discussed, and the dependent variable is the proportion of statements made on the topic. The equal share model predicts a slope close to 1.0 and an intercept term close to 0. The model of lower intensity of frequently discussed topics predicts a slope greater than 1.0 and a positive intercept term, which represents the more or less constant cost of introducing a topic. The model of greater intensity of frequently discussed topics predicts a slope of less than 1.0 and a negative intercept term.

The results of regression analyses for the 11 school districts summarized in table 5.7 indicate that each model is plausible. The equal share model applies quite well to the discussions and statements in Kentington. The higher intensity model seems to hold for Ballard City and Drummond Falls. In those two districts the topics which are discussed most frequently are also those which are discussed most intensively. The lower intensity model seems to hold for the other eight school districts: the topics which are discussed most frequently are discussed less intensively.

The extent of disproportionate discussion from that predicted by the appropriate model in each school district can be measured by the residual of actual proportion of statements from the prediction of the regression equation. These residuals are presented in table 5.8. In all districts except Kentington (the equal share model district), there is at least one topic for which the intensity of discus-

TABLE 5.8

DISPROPORTIONATE INTENSITY OF DISCUSSIONS AT SCHOOL BOARD MEETINGS

DEVIATION FROM PREDICTED PERCENTAGE

| District | Curriculum | Student Services | Students | Parents | Teachers | Administrators | Local Schools | School Board | Finance | Discrimination | Other Government | District Operation |
|---|---|---|---|---|---|---|---|---|---|---|---|---|
| Coldren Corners | .84 | 1.16 | 5.35 | -2.16 | -3.27 | .89 | -.78 | -1.97 | 10.97 | -2.35 | -2.21 | -4.70 |
| Barwig Park | 1.97 | -.64 | -2.19 | -2.20 | 1.91 | -2.02 | -.47 | -1.32 | 6.06 | .47 | -2.09 | 1.44 |
| Nelsonville | -2.07 | 2.39 | 3.82 | -.64 | -9.38 | -1.18 | 14.50 | -1.76 | -2.61 | .87 | .53 | -1.66 |
| Leeville | -1.44 | 2.14 | 1.66 | .50 | -5.80 | -2.80 | .61 | 3.88 | -3.02 | -1.55 | -.39 | 6.20 |
| Kentington | .78 | -1.16 | .94 | 1.02 | -1.12 | -2.10 | 2.94 | -.02 | -2.04 | .08 | .00 | .64 |
| Macktown | -.61 | -2.70 | 2.33 | -2.65 | -4.72 | -2.66 | 2.35 | -.62 | 6.35 | -1.62 | 2.33 | 2.21 |
| Ballard City | -1.83 | -.96 | -.71 | .54 | 6.67 | -1.64 | 5.29 | 3.96 | -2.65 | .54 | .17 | -1.45 |
| Drummond Falls | .30 | -1.92 | 1.30 | 1.76 | -2.60 | -2.92 | .85 | -1.47 | 9.38 | 1.76 | .30 | -6.73 |
| Hartshorne Hts. | 1.49 | 10.40 | 10.83 | -.03 | -5.05 | -3.56 | -.32 | -2.75 | 1.40 | -1.99 | -2.32 | -7.50 |
| Grahamdale | 1.32 | -1.30 | 4.70 | -1.53 | -.27 | -2.71 | 3.29 | .50 | .91 | -1.53 | -2.71 | .69 |
| Stumont | -.38 | -.94 | -.83 | 5.62 | -2.29 | .71 | -2.16 | 1.28 | 1.94 | -2.60 | -.94 | .58 |

119

TABLE 5.9

DISPROPORTIONALITY OF SCHOOL BOARD DISCUSSIONS
CONCERNED WITH IMPORTANT ISSUES

Mean Disproportionality Score

| District | Public Survey | School Official Survey | Narratives |
|---|---|---|---|
| Coldren Corners | 4.32 | 3.14 | 3.80 |
| Barwig Park | 1.94 | 3.75 | .50 |
| Nelsonville | - .29 | 3.82 | 8.45 |
| Leeville | -2.15 | .58 | .56 |
| Kentington | .20 | - .63 | .10 |
| Macktown | 2.35 | 2.21 | .82 |
| Ballard City | 1.10 | -2.65 | .44 |
| Drummond Falls | 3.66 | 3.39 | 3.39 |
| Hartshorne Hts. | 3.44 | 7.95 | 1.87 |
| Grahamdale | 1.92 | * | 2.14 |
| Stumont | -1.89 | 1.94 | - .30 |
| Mean | 1.33 | 2.35 | 1.98 |

* No consensus

sion differs by at least five percent from the prediction of the model. However, there are no strong patterns of topic overdiscussion or underdiscussion common to the 11 school districts. Finance is the most frequently overdiscussed topic; teachers is the most frequently underdiscussed topic. Each is disproportionate in only four school districts.

Are the topics which are disproportionately discussed in each district of particular importance? Table 5.9 matches the topics most important according to constituents, school officials, and communications media in each district with disproportionality of discussion intensity at school board meetings. Over all districts, the most intensive discussions occur on those topics regarded as important by school officials, as indicated by the mean disproportionality. The public's concerns are less intensively discussed. Surprisingly, the important issues identified by news media are subjects of disproportionate intensity in only one district.

Using the five percent criterion, there are only two examples of significant dispro-portionality: one for school officials and one for news media. Our earlier conclu-sion is corroborated by this analysis of disproportionate intensity. There is no gainsaying the conclusion that school board meetings are not forums which con-sider at length the "most important issues" by any definition.

## HOW SIMILAR ARE THE AGENDAS OF THE ELEVEN SCHOOL DISTRICTS?

Chapter 2 illustrates that our 11 districts are quite diverse in such attri-butes as size, wealth, racial and ethnic composition, and geographic location. Chapter 3 documented some diversity of attitudes and preferences. Chapter 4 indicated that districts faced different important issues. One of the presumed merits of local control of educational governance is the ability of school officials to concern themselves with the problems and issues in their own school districts.

TABLE 5.10

DIFFERENCE SCORES FOR DISCUSSIONS
SCHOOL BOARD MEETINGS

| District | Coldren Corners | Barwig Park | Nelsonville | Leeville | Kentington | Macktown | Ballard City | Drummond Falls | Hartshorne Hts. | Grahamdale | Stumont |
|---|---|---|---|---|---|---|---|---|---|---|---|
| Coldren Corners | -- | 36 | 25.5 | 13.5 | 22.5 | 19.5 | 21 | 25 | 16.5 | 34 | 18 |
| Barwig Park | | -- | 35.5 | 41 | 29.5 | 33.5 | 44.5 | 46 | 32.5 | 45 | 47 |
| Nelsonville | | | -- | 25 | 19 | 17 | 33.5 | 16.5 | 17 | 22.5 | 23.5 |
| Leeville | | | | -- | 20.5 | 23 | 14 | 25.5 | 26 | 34.5 | 19.5 |
| Kentington | | | | | -- | 17 | 24 | 28 | 22 | 23.5 | 25.5 |
| Macktown | | | | | | -- | 26 | 21.5 | 12 | 30.5 | 22.5 |
| Ballard City | | | | | | | -- | 27.5 | 29 | 32.5 | 22.5 |
| Drummond Falls | | | | | | | | -- | 20.5 | 28 | 26 |
| Hartshorne Hts. | | | | | | | | | -- | 31.5 | 24 |
| Grahamdale | | | | | | | | | | -- | 17 |
| Stumont | | | | | | | | | | | -- |
| Mean | 23 | 39 | 24 | 24 | 23 | 22 | 27 | 26 | 23 | 30 | 25 |

Grand Mean = 26

TABLE 5.11

DIFFERENCE SCORES FOR STATEMENTS

SCHOOL BOARD MEETINGS

| District | Coldren Corners | Barwig Park | Nelsonville | Leeville | Kentington | Macktown | Ballard City | Drummond Falls | Hartshorne Hts. | Grahamdale | Stumont |
|---|---|---|---|---|---|---|---|---|---|---|---|
| Coldren Corners | -- | 29 | 38.5 | 27.5 | 33 | 26.5 | 34 | 28.5 | 25.5 | 39 | 32 |
| Barwig Park | | -- | 42.5 | 42.5 | 32 | 40 | 52 | 41.5 | 21.5 | 39 | 49 |
| Nelsonville | | | -- | 30.5 | 26 | 29.5 | 40 | 36.5 | 33.5 | 31 | 37 |
| Leeville | | | | -- | 22.5 | 26 | 32.5 | 37 | 33 | 31.5 | 20.5 |
| Kentington | | | | | -- | 22.5 | 34.5 | 33.5 | 34.5 | 23 | 27 |
| Macktown | | | | | | -- | 35.5 | 27 | 30 | 25.5 | 25.5 |
| Ballard City | | | | | | | -- | 39 | 46.5 | 40 | 32 |
| Drummond Falls | | | | | | | | -- | 38 | 34.5 | 35.5 |
| Hartshorne Hts. | | | | | | | | | -- | 39.5 | 41.5 |
| Grahamdale | | | | | | | | | | -- | 23 |
| Stumont | | | | | | | | | | | -- |
| Mean | 31 | 39 | 35 | 30 | 29 | 29 | 39 | 35 | 34 | 33 | 32 |

Grand Mean = 33

We therefore might expect the distribution of discussions and discussion intensities among topics at school board meetings to vary considerably across districts. For example, a district with budgetary problems might concentrate on finance, districts engaging in contract negotiations with teachers might concentrate on teachers, and so forth.

On the other hand, the thesis of the so-called "nationalization of educational governance" has been repeatedly advanced by both scholars and practitioners (Guthrie, 1975; Zeigler, *et al.,* 1977b). This thesis would predict that—since so many of the concerns and issues facing local school districts originate at the national level of government—the agendas of school board meetings, irrespective of their location, would be similar.

How similar are the distributions of discussions and statements over topics in our 11 school districts? To investigate this question we calculated difference scores for discussion and statement distributions for each of the 55 unique dyads of school districts (tables 5.10 and 5.11). The difference scores range from 0, indicating identical distribution among 12 topic areas, to 100, indicating maximum dissimilarity.[2] This index is an approximation of the common proportion of the agendas of pairs of school districts' board meetings.

For distributions of discussions, about ¾ of the school board agenda is common across districts, as indicated by the overall mean difference score of 26. Only Barwig Park is conspicuously different from the other districts. The distributions of statements yield similar results. The overall mean difference score of 33 indicates that ⅔ of the school board agendas are common across districts. All 11 school districts' mean difference scores cluster around the grand mean. A possible explanation for the observed similarity is the great emphasis on the topic of district operation in all school districts. To measure the impact of district operation as the most frequent topic, we recalculated the difference scores excluding discussions of district operation. The results of that calculation were not appreciably different from the difference scores including district operation (grand mean of 30 for discussions and 34 for statements). Thus, irrespective of unique local conditions, the distribution of topics at school board meetings is remarkably similar.

## Agenda-Setting

Do school boards have similar agendas because, in spite of their diversity, they have similar problems to solve? If so, we should pay particular attention to the question of who sets the agenda. The actor who assumes this responsibility enjoys a substantial advantage: the opportunity to decide what will be decided upon. By so doing, the agenda-setter establishes not only the acceptable limits of debate, but also the participants in the debate (Schattschneider, 1960; Cobb and Elder, 1972). Issues are defined and acceptable policy alternatives are considered, but only after the definition of issues. The end product of agenda-setting is a formal commitment by a district to address itself to a particular problem.

Clearly, if action at the agenda-setting stage is not responsive, it is virtually impossible for a responsive policy to be enacted. Thus, agenda-setting is the opening round in the struggle for influence (determining to whose demands a response will be developed). If the issues are defined so as to exclude the interests of the major factions within a community, we can expect public participation to be low. The agenda can be narrowed to essentially technical or housekeeping matters of no interest to anyone except the most dedicated connoisseur of educational policy.

We have discovered that the issues of greatest concern to the public and school officials do not occupy a substantial portion of school board meeting agendas. Who is responsible? Clearly, the educational establishment is (table 5.12). The most dominant actors in agenda-setting are the superintendent and his staff administrators. Involvement by other actors is minimal. About ⅔ of all agenda items are introduced by centrally based administrators.

The dominance of agenda-setting by professionals is in keeping with the professional ethos of school administrators and boards. Handbooks prepared by state school board associations to guide board members are quite explicit about the agenda-setting responsibilities of the superintendent and his staff: "It is often said that the board makes policy and the superintendent administers it. This is not the way in which effective boards operate. In actual practice the superintendent

TABLE 5.12

AGENDA SETTING AT SCHOOL BOARD MEETINGS
Proportion of Discussions

| District | School Board | Supt. | Staff Experts | Line Experts | Public | Gov't. Officials |
|---|---|---|---|---|---|---|
| Coldren Corners | 22 % | 60 % | 11 % | 2 % | 5 % | 0 % |
| Barwig Park | 9 | 62 | 22 | 2 | 5 | 0 |
| Nelsonville | 18 | 73 | 1 | 0 | 7 | 1 |
| Leeville | 39 | 39 | 20 | * | 1 | 0 |
| Kentington | 57 | 18 | 12 | 9 | 4 | 0 |
| Macktown | 27 | 56 | 7 | 5 | 5 | 0 |
| Ballard City | 27 | 32 | 22 | 9 | 9 | * |
| Drummond Falls | 23 | 24 | 15 | 4 | 33 | * |
| Hartshorne Hts. | 9 | 41 | 43 | 2 | 5 | 0 |
| Grahamdale | 11 | 73 | 12 | 2 | 1 | 0 |
| Stumont | 18 | 35 | 42 | 3 | 2 | 1 |
| Mean | 24 | 47 | 19 | 3 | 7 | * |

* Less than 1%

generally indicates policy-making and provides the evidence on which the board makes decisions. . . . an agenda, or list of topics to be discussed, should be prepared by the superintendent and furnished to each board member. . . . in advance of the meeting." [3] Some references are made to the inclusion of the board chairman in setting the agenda, but the thrust is clear. Nor are school boards unique in allowing their agenda to be set for them. Most legislatures in state and local government, indeed, even the United States Congress, are "law declaring, rather than lawmaking bodies" (Chamberlain, 1936, p. 3).

The legislature rarely acts of its own volition. Proposals are made to it by parties interested, and it is for the legislature to afford a forum before which those measures can be debated [Chamberlain, 1936, p. 64].

Although the formal agenda is professionally dominated (Zeigler, *et al.*, 1974, p. 190), the opportunity exists for anyone to introduce topics not included in the formal agenda. The opportunity is, however, rarely utilized. Central administrators occupy a powerful gatekeeping position. They are in a position to establish an agenda which will minimize controversy and maximize routine decision-making. That is, superintendents and staff experts can set an agenda which, because it emphasizes technical problems, requires administrative resolution. As Boyd asserts: "There is reason to believe that many, perhaps even most, school administrators are inclined to be cautious in their policy initiations and reluctant to test the boundaries of their influence" (Boyd, 1976, p. 568). Whether or not administrators consciously load school board agendas with trivia, it is clear that the substance of those agendas does not reflect public and professional concerns.

Underlying this general description of professional dominance, there are subtle and substantial exceptions. In one district, Kentington, the rules of agenda-setting are unique: the board sets a majority of the agenda. In another district, Leeville, the board, although not setting the majority of the agenda, does participate on an equal basis with the superintendent (although not with the superintendent *and* staff). In two districts (Stumont and Hartshorne Hts.), the staff is somewhat more active than the superintendent in setting the agenda. In these cases, proposals come from the "expert's experts," i.e., professional bureaucrats whose careers are firmly rooted within the middle echelons of management. In Ballard City, there is somewhat of a balance in agenda-setting among board, superintendent, and staff. In five districts the superintendent alone sets the majority of the agenda (Barwig Park, Macktown, Nelsonville, Grahamdale, and Coldren Corners). Finally, in Drummond Falls, we find the sole example of active public participation in agenda-setting. Indeed, the public is responsible for more of the agenda than any other actor.

According to bargaining and polyarchal modes of decision-making, political influence (in this case agenda-setting) should follow lines of legal authority. The public elects a board to make policy; the board appoints a superintendent to administer policy. Thus, administration follows the mandate of legislators, who follow the instructions of their constituents. The major source of power is electoral support, and the norm of policy-making is responsiveness to public demands and preferences. This model suggests frequent participation in agenda-setting by school boards and other laymen. Yet, for school board meeting agendas, this is not the case.

The pattern of agenda-setting most closely approximates the hierarchical mode. According to the hierarchical view, the major source of power is information; the norm is deference to expertise. Problems are brought to the attention of the board by the experts: the superintendent and his staff. Laymen can *react* to the agenda, but rarely can they determine it.

The agenda-setting role of various actors can be further explored by examining the extent to which each sets the agenda for various topics considered by the board. Does the actor who dominates agenda-setting over all topics tend to initiate a majority of discussions for each topic? In the five districts for which the majority of agenda items are introduced by the superintendent, the tendency is for him also to introduce a majority of discussions on most topics. Similarly, in Kentington, where the school board initiates a majority of the total agenda, the board initiates a majority of discussions on most topics.

In Stumont no actor sets a majority of the total agenda, yet staff experts initiate a majority of discussions in most topic areas. In the remaining four districts no actor sets a majority of either the aggregate agenda or the agenda disaggregated by topics.

Is agenda-setting of certain topics dominated by the same actor across districts? Although superintendents are the most dominant agenda-setters, it is possible for other actors to specialize and dominate agenda-setting in specific topics. This, however, does not occur. Only superintendents appear as majority agenda-setters in a majority of districts. Of the 12 substantive topic areas, superintendents control most of the agenda in most districts for four topics: students, administrators, finance, and district operation. Thus, while all actors participate in agenda-setting, and all have some area which they "control," only the leading expert—the superintendent—exercises more than idiosyncratic agenda-setting authority. The only exception to this rule is, as we previously noted, the Canadian district.

This disaggregated analysis reconfirms the dominance of experts and the inferior strategic position of laymen. With one exception, the majority of statements are devoted to items introduced by experts. In districts where experts do not dominate, no one does. Laymen do not fill the void.

## Participation in School Board Meetings

Although by our definition agenda-setting can occur during meetings, it usually occurs prior to meetings. At the meeting itself, all potential actors have opportunity to participate in discussions, regardless of their role in agenda-setting.

Our definition of participation is once again made in terms of communication: a participant is one who speaks. Once a discussion has been initiated, virtually anyone can speak. Public participation, however, is frequently restricted both in terms of when members of the audience can speak and in terms of how long an individual may speak.

All school districts solicit lay public participation. Realistically speaking, public participation is limited to certain formal opportunities, at the pleasure of the board. Whereas the board, superintendent, and staff interact spontaneously, members of the public must be recognized before they are allowed to speak. Board-superintendent interaction is continuous and informal; public participation is segmented and structured.

As was the case with the agenda, it is possible to examine participation in two ways: distribution of participation and intensity of participation. In looking first at the distribution of participation (table 5.13) our unit of analysis is the discussion, and our query is "In what proportion of all discussion does a given actor speak?"

School board members spoke in virtually all discussions—hardly a startling finding. However, there was considerable variation in participation by other actors. The superintendent, substantially less active than the board, ranges in participation from a low of 18 percent in Barwig Park to a high of 59 percent in Grahamdale. Staff participation also varies considerably from Grahamdale's high of 63 percent to a low of 18 percent in Drummond Falls. Line experts displayed substantially less variation and were never as active as staff experts. Line experts (usually school principals) might be expected to provide information about the implementation of decisions and bring to the board's attention potential problems in the daily functioning of the school system. However, such input is not typical of board meetings.

Nor is public participation a prominent feature of board meetings. The public

TABLE 5.13

PARTICIPATION IN SCHOOL BOARD DISCUSSIONS
Percent of Discussions

| District | School Board | Supt. | Staff Experts | Line Experts | Public | Gov't. Officials |
|---|---|---|---|---|---|---|
| Coldren Corners | 97% | 71% | 31% | 11% | 31% | 1% |
| Barwig Park | 93 | 18 | 45 | 25 | 6 | 1 |
| Nelsonville | 100 | 45 | 28 | 17 | 20 | 2 |
| Leeville | 99 | 48 | 25 | 19 | 31 | * |
| Kentington | 94 | 24 | 28 | 16 | 6 | * |
| Macktown | 84 | 42 | 44 | 16 | 16 | 0 |
| Ballard City | 92 | 36 | 34 | 18 | 14 | 1 |
| Drummond Falls | 96 | 46 | 18 | 16 | 36 | * |
| Hartshorne Hts. | 91 | 53 | 38 | 17 | 42 | 1 |
| Grahamdale | 84 | 57 | 63 | 14 | 10 | 2 |
| Stumont | 98 | 32 | 27 | 19 | 9 | 2 |
| Mean | 93 | 43 | 35 | 17 | 20 | 1 |

* Less than 1%.

spoke on an average of 20 percent of all topics. However, public participation varies substantially among districts. It is virtually nonexistent in Barwig Park and Kentington, while in Hartshorne Hts., 42 percent of the discussions stimulate public comment. Unusually high public participation also occurred in Leeville, Coldren Corners and Drummond Falls. Thus, while the public can hardly be regarded as a major participant, there are exceptions.

However, the exceptions prove somewhat illusory when we shift our attention to the statement, rather than the topic, as the unit of analysis. The question now becomes "What proportion of all statements does a given actor make?" Here, the ranges of participation are less extreme. Again, the board does most of the talking; the administration does most of the listening; and the public is passive (table 5.14). Since 91 percent of all statements are made by members of the educational establishment, school board meetings may be characterized largely as discussions between board members and administration with a trivial amount of public participation.

The nature of public representation does little to assuage the feeling of "in house" discussions. In 9 of 11 districts, organized groups make a majority of

TABLE 5.14

STATEMENTS AT SCHOOL BOARD MEETINGS

Percent of Statements

| District | School Board | Supt. | Staff Experts | Line Experts | Public | Gov't. Officials |
|----------|--------------|-------|---------------|--------------|--------|------------------|
| Coldren Corners | 57% | 17% | 8% | 5% | 12% | 1% |
| Barwig Park | 61 | 8 | 20 | 9 | 2 | 0 |
| Nelsonville | 54 | 18 | 8 | 4 | 16 | * |
| Leeville | 61 | 12 | 7 | 6 | 14 | * |
| Kentington | 74 | 7 | 11 | 5 | 3 | * |
| Macktown | 50 | 14 | 25 | 5 | 5 | 0 |
| Ballard City | 70 | 8 | 10 | 6 | 5 | * |
| Drummond Falls | 66 | 10 | 7 | 5 | 13 | * |
| Hartshorne Hts. | 47 | 15 | 14 | 8 | 16 | * |
| Grahamdale | 48 | 10 | 28 | 6 | 6 | 1 |
| Stumont | 69 | 9 | 10 | 6 | 5 | 1 |
| Mean | 60 | 12 | 13 | 6 | 9 | * |

* Less than 1%

public statements; of these, 8 districts are characterized by having a majority of statements made by educational groups (table 5.15).

However, the voices of the public, although rarely heard, may rise to crescendo levels on certain topics. As we know, much of the agenda of board meetings is devoted to noncontroversial routine matters—matters which are unlikely to interest laymen. On those occasions when the board does discuss a topic of more general interest, does public participation increase?

When public statements are disaggregated by topics, it can be seen that they are concentrated in certain substantive areas. On the average, ⅓ of public statements occur on a single topic in each school district. However, each district's public has its own unique interest. No modal topic is common to more than three districts.

Public participation is, at best, modest. However, the diversity of topics attracting public attention does suggest that, even though professionals and experts control the agenda, the public finds ways to address a selective agenda.

Staff experts and line experts tend to speak more often about district operation, as one would expect. However, they are not well synchronized into the

TABLE 5.15

DISTRIBUTION OF STATEMENTS BY PUBLIC

(In Percentages)

| District | Educ. Group | Non-Educ. Group | Parent | Other Individ. |
|----------|-------------|-----------------|--------|----------------|
| Coldren Corners | 47% | 4% | 11% | 38% |
| Barwig Park | 33 | 33 | 4 | 31 |
| Nelsonville | 26 | 6 | 33 | 36 |
| Leeville | 24 | 11 | 14 | 51 |
| Kentington | 65 | 8 | 8 | 18 |
| Macktown | 75 | 14 | 0 | 11 |
| Ballard City | 51 | 22 | 10 | 17 |
| Drummond Falls | 51 | 6 | 11 | 32 |
| Hartshorne Hts. | 71 | * | 4 | 22 |
| Grahamdale | 60 | 16 | 15 | 9 |
| Stumont | 59 | 8 | 18 | 16 |

* Less than 1%

general flow of discussion. In most districts their modal topics are not those of the district as a whole.

Superintendents are conversational generalists. In 10 of 11 districts, the topic which attracts a plurality of superintendent statements is the most frequently discussed topic at school board meetings. Given their role in agenda-setting and discussion it is clear that superintendents are discussion and opinion leaders.

## Nature of Communication

In addition to quantity of participation at school board meetings, one should also be concerned with the quality of participation. We distinguish between communications characterized as substantive demands for specific action by the school board and simple informational exchanges. Political scientists and other students of public policy, heavily influenced by systems theory (Easton, 1957), place substantial reliance upon demands as a key ingredient in the policy formation process. Policy is portrayed as an output of a system. Systems transform demands into decisions or make policy. Demands occur when "individuals or groups, in response to real or perceived environmental conditions, act to affect public policy" (Dye, 1972, p. 19). Thus, without demands, there can be no deci-

TABLE 5.16

PERCENT OF VARIOUS TYPES OF STATEMENTS

AT SCHOOL BOARD MEETINGS

| District | Demands in Favor | Demands Opposed | Requests Information | Supplies Information |
|---|---|---|---|---|
| Coldren Corners | 22% | 3% | 25% | 49% |
| Barwig Park | 18 | * | 24 | 58 |
| Nelsonville | 11 | 3 | 18 | 67 |
| Leeville | 27 | 10 | 21 | 42 |
| Kentington | 30 | 6 | 17 | 47 |
| Macktown | 23 | 1 | 24 | 53 |
| Ballard City | 28 | 7 | 22 | 42 |
| Drummond Falls | 17 | 4 | 19 | 60 |
| Hartshorne Hts. | 21 | 5 | 20 | 53 |
| Grahamdale | 4 | 2 | 18 | 76 |
| Stumont | 20 | * | 20 | 59 |
| Mean | 20 | 4 | 19 | 55 |

* Less than 1%

sions. Systems theory assumes the existence of demands. Our foeus is upon the frequency and source of demands.

To investigate the qualitative nature of the discussion at school board meetings, we have utilized a four-category typology. Statements have been characterized as demands in favor of some action, demands opposed to some action, requests for information, and supplying of information. Table 5.16 provides a summary of the communications by type in each of the 11 districts.

As can be seen from the table, communications characterized as supplying information were most prominent in each of the districts. The mean proportion of statements supplying information over all districts is 55 percent. Statements characterized as requests for information and demands in favor were balanced as the next most prominent. The overall mean proportions are 20 percent for demands in favor and 19 percent for requests for information. Requests for information are more frequent than demands in favor for 6 districts, less frequent for 4 districts, and equally as frequent in 1 district. In all 11 districts, the lowest proportion of discrete communications was for those characterized as being demands opposed. The mean proportion of demands opposed is only 4 percent.

Earlier we saw that the primary function of school board meetings is decision-making and that school boards are highly successful in reaching decisions when they are intended. The data in table 5.16 inform us that school board meetings are rarely forums of direct conflict resolution. Decisions at school board meetings may, *ipso facto*, achieve resolution of conflict. However, school board meetings themselves are clearly not arenas of conflict articulation. The relative infrequency of demands opposed, and the aggregate 5 to 1 ratio of demands in favor to demands opposed suggest that school board meetings are quite harmonious sessions where speakers share opinions and preferences.

Just as different actors have different substantive interests, we might expect them to have different ways of communicating. Although we have characterized board meetings as largely informational, demands are made and decisions reached. We may expect that all participants vary their communication style according to their status. Those with the clearest monopoly of information—the experts—will use this mode of communication (that is, information exchange) more often than laymen. The superintendent, and especially his administrative

TABLE 5.17

SUPERINTENDENT STATEMENTS

| District | Demands In Favor | Demands Opposed | Requests Information | Supplies Information |
|---|---|---|---|---|
| Coldren Corners | 24% | *% | 5% | 72% |
| Barwig Park | * | 0 | 7 | 93 |
| Nelsonville | 6 | 1 | 5 | 88 |
| Leeville | 18 | 5 | 6 | 71 |
| Kentington | 11 | 5 | 5 | 79 |
| Macktown | 20 | * | 7 | 73 |
| Ballard City | 43 | 1 | 13 | 43 |
| Drummond Falls | 8 | 1 | 6 | 85 |
| Hartshorne Hts. | 20 | 6 | 4 | 70 |
| Grahamdale | 6 | * | 15 | 79 |
| Stumont | 3 | 0 | 7 | 90 |
| Mean | 15 | 2 | 7 | 75 |

* Less than 1%

staff, should view their role as information suppliers. Once they abandon this role, they invite loss of status as experts; loss of such status means sacrificing a crucial resource. This loss is, of course, serious for superintendents, whose vulnerability to an angry board, or an aroused public, is a source of anxiety. Clearly, the most advantageous role for administrators is that of neutral expert.

Superintendents, as expected, specialize in informational exchange. An average of 75 percent of their statements supply information (table 5.17). Staff experts specialize even more in supplying information. An average of 87 percent of their comments are information-supplying. Exceptions occur. In Ballard City, the superintendent and other administrators make an unusually high proportion of demand statements. We saw from the narrative that the Ballard City superintendent was engaged in an unsuccessful personal struggle to maintain his position. We observed in chapter 3 that both public and school officials reported unusually low levels of performance satisfaction. Their unusual reliance upon the demand mode of communication is further evidence that the expertise of administrators in

TABLE 5.18

SCHOOL BOARD STATEMENTS

| District | Demands In Favor | Demands Opposed | Requests Information | Supplies Information |
|----------|------------------|-----------------|----------------------|----------------------|
| Coldren Corners | 31% | 2% | 36% | 31% |
| Barwig Park | 29 | * | 37 | 34 |
| Nelsonville | 12 | 1 | 26 | 61 |
| Leeville | 33 | 12 | 26 | 29 |
| Kentington | 36 | 7 | 21 | 36 |
| Macktown | 28 | 1 | 41 | 30 |
| Ballard City | 29 | 7 | 28 | 36 |
| Drummond Falls | 19 | 3 | 25 | 53 |
| Hartshorne Hts. | 24 | 6 | 35 | 35 |
| Grahamdale | 4 | 1 | 27 | 68 |
| Stumont | 27 | * | 27 | 46 |
| Mean | 25 | 4 | 30 | 45 |

* Less than 1%

Ballard City was subject to challenge. Administrators did not assume the role of neutral expert because they were unable to do so.

This exception aside, superintendents and administrators supply information. Boards, laymen elected by laymen, do not perform this function as often as do administrators (table 5.18). Their dominant mode of communication is also information exchange. However, they are far more likely than superintendents and administrators to *request* information. Further, they assume more responsibility for demand-making. The Grahamdale board is a singular exception. An average of 29 percent of all board statements are demands. The role of the board then, is (in addition to supplying information) to ask questions and to articulate positive demands. The high ratio of positive to negative demands (an average of 6 to 1) suggests clearly that boards are not critical bodies.

It is important to reiterate that we are describing the behavior of school officials in public meetings. Such behavior is constrained by well-developed formal and informal norms. Foremost among such norms is "unity." Unity is articulated in educational administration texts, is emphasized in meetings of professional associations (the number of panels on "how to deal with split boards" attests to the perception of division of opinion as a problem), is articulated in the manuals provided to board members, and is encouraged in the formal and informal socialization of board members. Of greatest importance is unanimity in decision-making, especially voting decisions. Dissent should be minimized and should not be articulated once a majority position has been established.

There is a substantial belief that explicitly political (i.e., conflictual) legislative behavior is inappropriate; that the board meeting is less a decision-making arena then a public display. Hence, as one school board manual explains, "When a school board holds a meeting, both the board and its individual members are on display. The public, the press, and employees of the district will tend to judge the board and the district by the manner in which the board meetings are conducted and by the words and actions of individual members of the board. In other words, a school board meeting is to some extent a public performance of the board and the school staff." Another manual states, "Nothing is more damaging to a board—to its internal relations or its prestige with the public—than for a board member to quarrel publicly with a decision a board has made." [4]

School boards—in their public capacity—are quasi-legislative. Their public behavior is one of a presentation or performance. The action of the performance develops along clearly understood and predictable lines; each major actor, the board and superintendent, understands his assigned roles and performs as expected. The role of the superintendent is to provide expert advice. The role of the board is to accept that advice.[5]

How are boards advised to regard the public? Again, some guidance can be gained by excerpts from board members' handbooks: "Do not engage in debate with members of the audience. . . . local boards must . . . recognize that from time to time individuals and special interest groups will attempt to change or redirect the curricula for their own reasons and purposes. . . . allow public questions at specific and limited times during the meeting or at the close of the meeting." While it is not accurate to say that boards are advised to discourage the public, it is accurate to say that the public is viewed with suspicion.

Such suspicion may be warranted. On the one hand, the public—like all other participants—is largely involved in communication exchange (table 5.19). On the

TABLE 5.19

PUBLIC STATEMENTS

| District | Demands In Favor | Demands Opposed | Requests Information | Supplies Information |
|---|---|---|---|---|
| Coldren Corners | 21% | 8% | 23% | 48% |
| Barwig Park | 4 | 8 | 4 | 84 |
| Nelsonville | 4 | 7 | 15 | 74 |
| Leeville | 30 | 17 | 28 | 25 |
| Kentington | 18 | 5 | 11 | 65 |
| Macktown | 16 | 5 | 8 | 72 |
| Ballard City | 22 | 33 | 10 | 35 |
| Drummond Falls | 24 | 12 | 14 | 50 |
| Hartshorne Hts. | 30 | 6 | 20 | 44 |
| Granamdale | 12 | 20 | 9 | 60 |
| Stumont | 10 | 3 | 3 | 84 |
| Mean | 17 | 11 | 13 | 58 |

other hand, the public devotes a larger proportion of its statements to negative demands than does any other actor. In four districts, the public makes more negative than positive demands. However, these districts are also characterized by a low rate of public participation. Hence, viewed in aggregate terms, the amount of dissent provided by the public in these districts is minimal. Still, when dissent occurs, it is likely to come from the public.

Boards are advised to avoid making decisions based on the "demands of special interest groups," to remain free from "the dictates of special interest pressure groups," and to "refuse to surrender independent judgment to individuals or special interest groups." Yet the greater threat to harmony comes from unaffiliated individuals. Two-thirds of group statements supply information, and group originated demands are disproportionately positive. Individuals' proportion of negative demands is higher than that of any other actor. On the average, unaffiliated individuals make nearly as many negative as positive demands.

There is only one district in which groups make more negative than positive demands: Ballard City. There are five districts in which individuals make more negative than positive demands. Significantly, Ballard City's public input—both from groups and individuals—is negative. We note again that this district is

TABLE 5.20

PUBLIC STATEMENTS BY GROUP SPOKESMEN

| District | Demands In Favor | Demands Opposed | Requests Information | Supplies Information |
|---|---|---|---|---|
| Coldren Corners | 20% | 5% | 28% | 47% |
| Barwig Park | 6 | 6 | 3 | 85 |
| Nelsonville | 8 | 6 | 5 | 81 |
| Leeville | 26 | 19 | 25 | 30 |
| Kentington | 21 | 1 | 1 | 77 |
| Macktown | 14 | 4 | 1 | 81 |
| Ballard City | 23 | 33 | 6 | 38 |
| Drummond Falls | 23 | 7 | 7 | 63 |
| Hartshorne Hts. | 29 | 7 | 21 | 43 |
| Grahamdale | 14 | 14 | 4 | 68 |
| Stumont | 11 | 4 | 1 | 84 |
| Mean | 18 | 11 | 9 | 63 |

TABLE 5.21

PUBLIC STATEMENTS BY UNAFFILIATED INDIVIDUALS

| District | Demands In Favor | Demands Opposed | Requests Information | Supplies Information |
|---|---|---|---|---|
| Coldren Corners | 23% | 11% | 18% | 48% |
| Barwig Park | 0 | 12 | 6 | 82 |
| Nelsonville | 2 | 8 | 19 | 71 |
| Leeville | 32 | 17 | 30 | 21 |
| Kentington | 10 | 17 | 38 | 35 |
| Macktown | 29 | 14 | 14 | 43 |
| Ballard City | 19 | 34 | 21 | 26 |
| Drummond Falls | 25 | 17 | 23 | 35 |
| Hartshorne Hts. | 33 | 5 | 34 | 28 |
| Grahamdale | 6 | 37 | 24 | 33 |
| Stumont | 8 | 3 | 8 | 81 |
| Mean | 17 | 16 | 21 | 46 |

characterized by a high proportion of administrator demands and a low level of performance satisfaction.

Not part of the organizational fabric of support and information, individuals provide the most consistent source of dissent, although they are relatively inactive. Not only do individuals speak with comparative infrequency, but they also interrupt the tranquility of the communications of the more active participants. Tables 5.20 and 5.21 indicate that unaffiliated individuals are more dissent-oriented than are members of organized groups.

## DEMANDS: A FURTHER ANALYSIS

We have seen that all actors articulate at least some demands. However, since participation varies by actor, further analysis is necessary to identify which actors are the primary sources of positive and negative demands.

Identification of negative demand articulators is of particular interest. The

TABLE 5.22

DEMAND ARTICULATION

(In Percentages)

| Actor | Coldren Corners | Barwig Park | Nelsonville | Leeville | Kentington | Macktown | Ballard City | Drummond Falls | Hartshorne Hts. | Grahamdale | Stumont |
|---|---|---|---|---|---|---|---|---|---|---|---|
| Superintendent | 13% | *% | 12% | 8% | 3% | 12% | 10% | 4% | 13% | 11% | 2% |
| Other Admin'r. | 8 | 3 | 7 | 4 | 5 | 20 | 11 | 3 | 8 | 22 | 4 |
| School Board | 67 | 95 | 66 | 70 | 91 | 63 | 70 | 71 | 58 | 34 | 92 |
| Public | 12 | 1 | 14 | 17 | 2 | 4 | 8 | 21 | 20 | 28 | 3 |
| Groups[1] | 44 | 67 | 38 | 33 | 69 | 77 | 73 | 49 | 73 | 59 | 75 |
| Individuals[1] | 56 | 33 | 62 | 67 | 31 | 23 | 27 | 51 | 27 | 41 | 25 |

\* Less than 1%

[1] Percent of public demands

TABLE 5.23

NEGATIVE DEMAND ARTICULATION

(In Percentages)

| Actor | Coldren Corners | Barwig Park | Nelsonville | Leeville | Kentington | Macktown | Ballard City | Drummond Falls | Hartshorne Hts. | Grahamdale | Stumont |
|---|---|---|---|---|---|---|---|---|---|---|---|
| Superintendent | 1% | 0% | 9% | 6% | 6% | 8% | 2% | 2% | 15% | 3% | 0% |
| Other Admin'rs. | 26 | 14 | 9 | 3 | 4 | 15 | 2 | 3 | 6 | 15 | 20 |
| School Board | 36 | 29 | 27 | 67 | 87 | 54 | 72 | 56 | 61 | 19 | 40 |
| Public | 35 | 57 | 49 | 23 | 3 | 23 | 24 | 39 | 18 | 53 | 40 |
| Groups[1] | 32 | 50 | 24 | 37 | 17 | 67 | 71 | 36 | 81 | 55 | 75 |
| Individuals[1] | 68 | 50 | 76 | 63 | 83 | 33 | 29 | 64 | 19 | 45 | 25 |

[1] Percent of public negative demands

overall predominance of information exchange and positive demands indicates that the normal pattern of decision-making does not involve the presentation of competing demands at school board meetings. On the contrary, negative demands are so infrequent that disagreement at school board meetings is clearly episodic conflict. Thus, identification of the sources of negative demands will pinpoint conflict articulation, the focus of the selective view of the previous chapter.

Table 5.22 provides information about the proportion of demands each actor makes. It is clear that the school board assumes the demand-making role. In 10 districts, a majority of demands are made by the board. The single exception is Grahamdale, where the board only makes about ⅓ of the demands. Even in Grahamdale, however, the board makes more demands than any other actor.

The public is the second most frequent demand-maker in five districts; other administrators place second in five, and the superintendent only once. Public demands are normally articulated by groups. They make a majority of public demands in seven districts, and in the others they make at least ⅓.

The pattern of demand articulation meets the specifications of both the polyarchal and bargaining modes in all districts. Laymen dominate the demand

TABLE 5.24

NEGATIVE DEMANDS AS A PROPORTION OF ALL DEMANDS
(In Percentages)

| Actor | Coldren Corners | Barwig Park | Nelsonville | Leeville | Kentington | Macktown | Ballard City | Drummond Falls | Hartshorne Hts. | Grahamdale | Stumont |
|---|---|---|---|---|---|---|---|---|---|---|---|
| Superintendent | 1% | 0% | 14% | 20% | 31% | 3% | 3% | 8% | 23% | 8% | 0% |
| Other Admin'rs. | 32 | 8 | 30 | 21 | 15 | 3 | 3 | 16 | 15 | 22 | 11 |
| School Board | 5 | 1 | 9 | 26 | 16 | 4 | 21 | 15 | 21 | 19 | 1 |
| Public | 27 | 67 | 67 | 37 | 23 | 23 | 60 | 33 | 17 | 63 | 25 |
| Groups | 20 | 50 | 42 | 42 | 1 | 20 | 59 | 24 | 19 | 51 | 25 |
| Individuals | 33 | 100 | 83 | 35 | 63 | 33 | 65 | 41 | 13 | 86 | 25 |

articulation function. Furthermore, groups are quite active in expressing demands from the lay public.

Beyond the quantity of demands, it is possible to examine the quality of demands. Tables 5.23 and 5.24 present information about the relation between positive and negative demands. Just as they dominate the total demand process, laymen also dominate the making of negative demands. However, the role of the board is more subdued. The lay public plays a more active role. The board is still the most frequent negative demand articulator in seven districts. In six of those districts the public is in second place. In three districts, the public makes more negative demands than any other actor. In one district, the board and public share negative demand articulation equally.

Within the public, individuals now assume more of an active role. In five districts, a majority of negative public demands are made by individuals; in five they are made by groups, and in one there is a tie. Thus, the negative demand-making process reveals a more even balance between board and public, and within the public, between individuals and groups.

Finally, we explore the ratio of negative demands to all demands. A stubstantially different picture appears. Because the boards were so active in the total demand-making process, they also appeared as active negative demand-makers.

However, the board's ratio of negative demands to all demands is lower than the public's in ten districts. Further, individual demands are more likely to be negative than are group demands in eight districts.

This analysis of negative demands indicates that conflict is articulated by laymen, and more so by the public than their representatives. While groups are active in positive demand articulation, individuals are more active in negative demand articulation. As we saw earlier, individuals are infrequent participants without an influence group. Thus, their contribution to the communications process is less conditioned by a linkage between groups and the system.[6]

## DEMANDS AND MOST IMPORTANT ISSUES

Regardless of source and nature, what are the most frequent topics of demands and do they correspond to a school district's most important problems? We have seen that the overall agendas of school boards are not particularly concerned with most important problems variously defined. We also know that only a minor portion of board agendas are occupied with demands. Nevertheless, the possibility exists that when topics of greatest concern arise, they generate an abnormally high proportion of demands.

Table 5.25 presents those which attract the highest and lowest proportion of demands in each school district. No single issue is either most or least demand-inducing in more than three districts. Moreover, issues which attract most demands in some districts attract fewest demands in others.

TABLE 5.25

CONFLICT AT SCHOOL BOARD MEETINGS[*]

| District | Greatest | % of Demands | Least | % of Demands |
|----------|----------|--------------|-------|--------------|
| Coldren Corners | Teachers | 31 | Finance | 13 |
| Barwig Park | Students | 37 | District Op. | 7 |
| Nelsonville | Curriculum | 24 | Local Schools | 2 |
| Leeville | Finance | 44 | District Op. | 28 |
| Kentington | Finance | 44 | Teachers | 26 |
| Macktown | Administ'rs | 38 | Finance | 13 |
| Ballard City | Teachers | 41 | Student Svcs. | 27 |
| Drummond Falls | Teachers | 40 | Curriculum | 9 |
| Hartshorne Hts. | Parents | 36 | Curriculum | 15 |
| Grahamdale | School Bd. | 13 | Students | 3 |
| Stumont | Finance | 24 | School Board | 8 |

[*] Topics which attract greater than 3% of statements

TABLE 5.26

CORRESPONDENCE BETWEEN ISSUES OF GREATEST AND LEAST
CONFLICT AND ISSUES FROM PUBLIC SURVEYS,
SCHOOL OFFICIAL SURVEYS, AND NARRATIVES

| District | Corresponds with Issues from Public Survey | | Corresponds with Issues from School Official Survey | | Corresponds with Narrative Issues | |
|---|---|---|---|---|---|---|
| | Greatest | Least | Greatest | Least | Greatest | Least |
| Coldren Corners | No | Yes | No | Yes | No | Yes |
| Barwig Park | Yes | No | No | Yes | Yes | No |
| Nelsonville | Yes | No | No | No | No | Yes |
| Leeville | Yes | No | Yes | Yes | Yes | Yes |
| Kentington | No | Yes | Yes | No | No | Yes |
| Macktown | No | Yes | No | No | No | Yes |
| Ballard City | Yes | No | No | No | Yes | No |
| Drummond Falls | No | Yes | Yes | No | Yes | No |
| Hartshorne Hts. | No | Yes | No | Yes | No | No |
| Grahamdale | No | Yes | No | No | No | Yes |
| Stumont | No | No | Yes | No | No | Yes |

Ironically, not only are the topics which stimulate the greatest proportion of demands infrequently cited as most important issues, topics which stimulate fewest demands are more closely matched to most important issues (table 5.26). In only one district (Leeville), do topics of greatest concern to the public, school officials, and the media (in terms of coverage) generate the greatest number of demands. However, in four districts (Hartshorne Hts., Macktown, Grahamdale, and Coldren Corners), topics which stimulate the most demands are present in no one's list of most important issues. Further, in Coldren Corners the issues of greatest concern receive the lowest proportion of demands.

We conclude that, with the possible exception of Leeville, that portion of the school board agenda which consists of demands does not correspond to the most important issues in the district.

## Policy Proposal

After the agenda has been set and discussion has been completed, some sort of decision is in order. We now turn to the question, "Who makes policy proposals at school board meetings?" Our unit of analysis is the discussion, and we will be focusing on how discussions in which decisions are intended are resolved. This question differs from that of agenda-setting because the person who initiates discussion may or may not make a policy proposal. We define a proposer as the first person who articulates a proposal that is decided upon (favorably or negatively) by the school board.

TABLE 5.27

POLICY PROPOSALS

| District | N | School Board | Supt. | Staff Experts | Line Experts | Public | Gov't. Off'ls. |
|---|---|---|---|---|---|---|---|
| Coldren Corners | 150 | 25% | 69% | 5% | 0% | 1% | 0% |
| Barwig Park | 158 | 90 | 1 | 9 | 0 | 0 | 0 |
| Nelsonville | 124 | 65 | 35 | * | 0 | 0 | 0 |
| Leeville | 319 | 81 | 9 | 3 | 1 | 5 | 1 |
| Kentington | 410 | 97 | 1 | 1 | 0 | * | 0 |
| Macktown | 117 | 44 | 53 | 2 | 1 | 2 | 0 |
| Ballard City | 384 | 36 | 33 | 23 | 6 | 1 | 0 |
| Drummond Falls | 183 | 96 | 3 | 1 | 1 | 1 | 0 |
| Hartshorne Hts. | 93 | 60 | 28 | 2 | 1 | 9 | 0 |
| Grahamdale | 221 | 34 | 57 | 9 | 0 | 0 | 0 |
| Stumont | 203 | 90 | 1 | 7 | 1 | 0 | 0 |
| Mean | | 65 | 26 | 6 | 1 | 2 | * |

* Less than 1%

Our definition of policy proposals is not, it should be clear, merely the making of a formal motion. In many districts, legal motions can only be made by the board. We sought to identify for each proposal the first person who proposed a course of action ultimately accepted or rejected by the board.

The fact that the school board members initiate a majority of policy proposals in seven districts and a plurality in another is not a trivial finding (see table 5.27). In three districts the superintendent makes a majority of policy proposals. Only in one district, Ballard City, do staff experts set a substantial portion of the agenda. However, in two districts, Stumont and Barwig Park, staff experts make more policy proposals than do superintendents, and are the second most frequent source of policy proposals. Line experts, the public, and other government officials are quiescent. Thus, the board and superintendent, in combination, dominate the policy proposal process. In only one district, Coldren Corners, does the superintendent propose policy to the virtual exclusion of the board.

## Voting

Decisions at board meetings are of varying levels of importance. Some are trivial; others involve the adoption of major policy options. We have chosen to focus upon those decisions reached by formal vote as an objective indicator of importance. Policy-making—voting in this case—is what boards are supposed to do.

School board handbooks state—to the point of redundancy—that boards should avoid involvement in administrative matters and confine themselves to policy making:

> It is agreed by authorities in the field of educational administration that the legislation of policies is the most important function of the school board and that the execution of these policies should be left wholly to the professional expert, the superintendent of schools. Boards of education do not have the time to execute policies, nor do they have the technical training needed for such work. In summary, the function of the board of education is not to run the schools but to see that they are run effectively.[3]

Rarely, however, are boards cautioned about the reverse situation—the introduction of the superintendent into policy-making. In fact, they are urged to expect that superintendents will initiate policy recommendations: "It is often said that the board makes policy and the superintendent administers it. This is not the way in which effective boards operate. In actual practice, the superintendent generally initiates policy-making and provides the evidence on which the board makes decisions." [3]

Superintendent recommendations would appear at first glance to violate the notion of separation of administration from policy-making. Remember, however, that boards are told to stay away from administrative matters. They are not told to be wary of a superintendent's intrusion into policy-making. Indeed, executive recommendation is expected and honored. It appears only reasonable that those who set the agenda should also recommend appropriate policy actions. The frequency and importance of executive recommendation stems from a variety of sources.

The most important reason for executive recommendation is to make use of professional expertise. Although superintendents act as executives, their basic resource is expertise rather than more traditional political skills. Deference to expertise is a well-established tradition in American education, a curious phenomenon in view of the tradition of lay control (Zeigler, Tucker, and Wilson, 1977). Respect for the superintendent's expertise is so basic to the board-superintendent exchange that any loss of such respect (as indicated by failure to adopt an executive recommendation, or perhaps by the reluctance of an executive to recommend) or even a hint of a loss of such respect is regarded as a serious crisis. Superintendents regard even a few events which suggest diminished respect and authority as an indication that they should begin seeking a new position. They do not regard such incidents as evidence that they should employ traditional political skills to bargain and compromise. Their posture is that of the expert. When faced with the probability of substantial dissent, experts do not bargain (modify their position) or persuade. These are the tasks of politicians. To engage in them jeopardizes one's status as expert. Quotes from texts in educational administration and from board handbooks proclaim the theme of deference to experts in an *eroica* fashion:

the board must rely for leadership on its chief executive officer, the superintendent. . . . the board may be regarded in much the same light as a board of directors of a business corporation and the superintendent as the president or general manager in immediate charge of operation . . . . Legislation must be guided by what administration knows about schools. . . . a superintendent may be expected to be somewhat in advance of the boards' thinking because of his special interest and preparation. . . . it is perfectly correct for him to participate in policy-making because of his special knowledge and preparation. . . . [recommendation] should be carefully considered and adopted substantially and proposed or sent back for further study or possible change. A board has authority, of course, to formulate policies and pass motions to give policies effect on their own initiative, by-passing the superintendent. This should occur rarely. . . . when it occurs frequently the lack of rapport between the board and superintendent and the misunderstanding of respective spheres calls for a drastic remedy in the form of replacing the superintendent, changing the composition of the board, or both . . . Occasionally, the board will disagree with the superintendent's recommendation and act contrary to it. If this occurs more than occasionally, it indicates lack of understanding between the board and the superintendent. . . . the superintendent must have the wholehearted support of the board. When he/she is no longer deserving of such support, it is time for a change in administration [Greider, *et. al.,* 1961, pp. 113–143].

The essence of these ideas is that the superintendent, as expert, should be opposed only when such opposition is intended to imply a vote of "no confidence." One does not vote merely against the superintendent's policies, one votes against the superintendent. Thus, superintendents propose policy, and these recommendations are followed (table 5.28).

Additionally, as superintendents will be charged with implementation, it is only natural that their opinions about policy execution be taken into account (Zeigler and Tucker, 1978). Concern with policy implementation is extremely important because school boards must necessarily grant wide latitude to the executive. Even more so than members of other lay legislative bodies, they are part-time, amateur, volunteer officials.

Given this widely held belief in the key role of the superintendent: the superintendent—far more than the board—is identified publicly as the "governor" of education. Although superintendents are rarely selected by public election, they are, because of the expectations placed upon them, the symbol of school government.

If making recommendations is expected, what happens when a superintendent does not do so? In three districts (Leeville, Ballard City, and Macktown) the superintendent is more reluctant than normal. In Macktown, the superintendent's reluctance is largely a matter of personal style. He controls the agenda and, in many cases, is content to let the board act without recommendation. In Leeville and Ballard City, the situation is quite the reverse. In neither case does the superintendent control the agenda. In Leeville, the reluctance of the superintendent may be a reaction to the active school board chairman who has an independent base of political influence in municipal government. In Ballard City, the

TABLE 5.28

VOTING DECISIONS

| District | Total Votes | Unanimous Votes | Supt. Pos. Known | Supt. Pos. Adopted |
|---|---|---|---|---|
| Coldren Corners | 134 | 84% | 84% | 95%** |
| Barwig Park | 154 | 97 | 83 | 100 |
| Nelsonville | 98 | 86 | 89 | 100 |
| Leeville | 268 | 67 | 46 | 98* |
| Kentington | 411 | 91 | 68 | 99* |
| Macktown | 110 | 98 | 37 | 100 |
| Ballard City | 270 | 72 | 5 | 100 |
| Drummond Falls | 179 | 96 | 87 | 100 |
| Hartshorne Hts. | 67 | 88 | 75 | 100 |
| Grahamdale | 157 | 99 | 81 | 100 |
| Stumont | 197 | 62 | 68 | 96 |
| Mean | | 85 | 66 | 99 |

*
 Includes one tie vote

**
 Includes one non-binding vote where superintendent's position is consistent with majority vote; but absolute majority is lacking and so motion is not adopted

remarkably reticent behavior of the superintendent can be understood as part of his deteriorating position with the board—he was "giving up."

## Superintendent Defeats

The reluctance of the superintendent to "behave professionally" is a better barometer of tension than is actual defeat. Such defeats are extremely rare. When they occur, they are the object of considerable attention and are offered as proof that the board is not a "rubber stamp." In spite of variance in agenda-setting participation, in mode of presentation, and in the making of policy proposals, the end result is usually the same—a unanimous vote adopting the recommendation of the superintendent. The input may vary; the end result rarely does. Unity—as expressed in unanimous votes and in acceptance of executive recommendation—is clearly the norm.

One might argue that the important votes are the nonunanimous votes. However, when the district with the lowest number of nonunanimous votes (Stumont) still votes unanimously ⅔ of the time, the argument seems strained.

With regard to superintendent recommendation, one might argue, as does Boyd (1976) that superintendents avoid recommendations on "controversial" issues. This is arguable in only 2 of 11 districts. Finally, one might agree that the board dissents from the superintendent's recommendation when important issues are involved. To agree with this argument is to accept the notion that 98 percent of a board's decisions are trivial. There is no escaping the fact that the dominant mode of decision-making is unanimous deference to experts. The tradition of unanimity and deference discussed in chapter 1 is well-established and well-followed.

As table 5.29 shows, in the 11 districts in our study, there were only 13 examples of superintendent defeat (excluding 3 cases in which his position was ultimately adopted). In five of these votes, the position adopted by the board was consistent with the views expressed by those who spoke for the public. In these cases especially, the laymen defeated the experts. Because superintendent defeat is such a rare and important event, we shall explore the cases in detail.

# STUMONT

## CONTRACT WITH LOCAL TELEVISION STATION

The administrative recommendation that the board approve a contract with a local television station to produce a series of reading programs was initially rejected by the board in a 4–3 vote (a subsequent motion to defer decision on the matter passed 5–2). Under the proposed agreement, the district would print and distribute to students program scripts and supplementary materials prepared and produced by the station. A contract was required to legalize the board-approved expenditure. The problem was that the scripts had not yet been prepared or presented by the station to the district for approval. The superintendent's recommendation was a cautious one. He proposed that the board approve the contract, but delay formal signing until the scripts were presented and accepted.

A board member pulled this item from the consent agenda "so [he] could vote no." The discussion among board members and superintendent focused on the question of curriculum control. The superintendent asserted that "the school board has no responsibility for review of curriculum." Two board members strongly objected. They claimed board responsibility for reviewing the content of curriculum.

Another recommendation to approve and sign the contract was presented at the next board meeting as an item in a blanket agenda and was routinely approved without comment. The advisory memo from the associate superintendent for curriculum noted that the scripts had been prepared by the station, distributed to board members and staff, and generally approved by the staff.

TABLE 5. 29

CASES OF BOARD-SUPERINTENDENT OPPOSITION

| Topic of Motion | Vote Yes | No | Supt. Pos. |
|---|---|---|---|
| STUMONT | | | |
| A Approve contract with local TV station | 3 | 4 | Y |
| Authorize air-conditioning feasibility studies | 1 | 6 | Y |
| Do not authorize air-conditioning feasibility studies | 5 | 2 | N |
| A Approve purchase order for band uniforms | 3 | 4 | Y |
| Defer action: reclassify administrative position | 6 | 1 | N |
| Defer action: approve contract with Chamber of Commerce | 7 | 0 | N |
| LEEVILLE | | | |
| * Extend busing to/from school | 4 | 3 | N |
| Adopt new teacher hiring procedures | 3 | 4 | Y |
| * Direct departments to recommend 5% decrease in 1976-77 budgets | 7 | 0 | N |
| COLDREN CORNERS | | | |
| * Grant tuition waiver | 4 | 3 | N |
| * Abolish military education program | 5 | 2 | N |
| * Ban smoking at school board meetings | 7 | 0 | N |
| Reject central menu planning, retain present food food service system | 7 | 0 | N |
| Grant tuition waiver | 4 | 2 | N |
| A Change distance criterion for busing eligibility | 3 | 4 | Y |
| KENTINGTON | | | |
| Amend report on groups using school facilities | 8 | 0 | N |

*-Board position and public position consistent
A-Superintendent's position adopted in a later vote

## AIR-CONDITIONING FEASIBILITY STUDIES AUTHORIZATION

Providing air-conditioning for all the district schools had been under discussion prior to 1974–75. The first feasibility study recommended by the superintendent would have been used for drawing up detailed plans for a bond issue. Spokesmen from the County Council of PTA's, from a school PTA, and from the State Board of Managers attended the meeting and urged the board to authorize the study. The board rejected the proposal by a 6–1 vote, giving "present economic conditions" as the reason. Board opinion was that such expenditures should await improvements in the economy. The rejection of the feasibility study was regarded as a decision against a bond issue referendum.

A second related item—to begin procedures for feasibility studies for air-conditioning two specific high schools was on the agenda because (according to the superintendent's memo) "Several board members have requested that this project be considered." This more limited proposal was defeated 5–2.

## PURCHASE ORDER FOR BAND UNIFORMS

The agenda item was a purchasing order for blazers for the marching band at a high school. The board did not approve the order, by a 4–3 vote, but voted to defer action 5–2.

This item brought to the board's attention the fact that at some schools students in the band were required to pay a nonrefundable fee. Two board members objected to such a policy, and the superintendent suggested that a report on band fees be prepared for the board's consideration at the next meeting. The associate superintendent for operations recommended that this particular purchase order be approved rather than delayed. The board rejected the recommendation.

A report on student fees in secondary schools was presented by the administration at the next board meeting. Board members strongly objected to the wide variation in fee amounts across schools, and argued that the quality of a school's extracurricular program should not depend on the ability of children's parents to "buy excellence." In addition to the inequity across schools, board members were concerned that children might be barred or inhibited from participating in such activities because of their families' inability to pay the fees. They acknowledged, however, that the school district could not bear the entire cost of such programs. The superintendent also expressed concern about students being kept from activities by the fees, but pointed out to the board that the band parent groups would not want the board to standardize fees because they thought it would stifle creativity, individuality, and striving for excellence. The board unanimously accepted a motion instructing the superintendent to draft an "equal opportunity" policy on extracurricular fees that would provide equity throughout the system. Later at the same meeting, the board approved the purchase order for the band blazers in accordance with the superintendent's original recommendation by a 5–2 vote.

## RECLASSIFICATION OF ADMINISTRATIVE POSITION

The superintendent proposed that an unfilled administrative position, Director of Instructional Communications, be defined more broadly and upgraded to Director of Educational Technology. The board did not approve the recommendation, but voted 6–1 to defer decision on it. The only objection to the proposal recorded in the meeting logs was a request for a detailed report on the use of computer-assisted instruction and instructional television, and how these areas would "come together" under one director.

A more specific report was prepared by the associate superintendent for curriculum for the next meeting. The report advocated expanding and making more flexible present instructional television services by setting up a school district broadcasting system. The report was accepted for information in the consent agenda.

### Contract with Chamber of Commerce

The board unanimously voted to defer action on the superintendent's recommendation to contract with the Chamber of Commerce for "career awareness services," to be paid for from a fund earmarked for vocational improvement programs.

The school district had previously cooperated with a junior college in a contract with the Chamber of Commerce for the services of a "professional" who was a liaison between the schools and business community. The junior college had dropped out of the arrangement; the proposal was to continue the agreement with the Chamber of Commerce. The nature of the services to be provided was not made clear in the superintendent's memorandum, and this ambiguity about past and projected benefits caused the reservations expressed by board members. They questioned the administrators about the expenditure of funds. Would such services be an unnecessary duplication of functions performed by district employees? Could more vocational educational benefits be provided by a different use of the earmarked fund? The board voted unanimously to defer action on the proposal.

## LEEVILLE

### Busing Extension

Throughout the school year a group of parents from a neighborhood area had expressed their demand that the school district provide bus transportation for their children. They had argued that the route was too hazardous for the children to walk. The administration had maintained that the conditions did not warrant busing under current district policy.

The superintendent's advisory memorandum for this meeting—reiterating his original recommendation to refuse the request—gave this background summary:

> A petition was filed by the parents requesting busing. Following a hearing on the petition at a school board meeting, the item was referred to Administration. At a later board meeting . . . a report was made in which it was indicated that police who viewed the route did not consider it to be hazardous.
>
> At the same meeting, a spokeswoman for the parents indicated that they would be willing to pay for a bus. Following the discussion, it was moved and voted on a roll call vote of 5–0:

That the School Committee request Administration to set up a meeting with the bus company officials and the petitioners to work out a solution.

Administration communicated with the spokeswoman requesting that a contact be made with a representative of Administration to set possible dates for a meeting. The request was responded to.

The school board decided not to suspend the rules governing provision of transportation to make an exception for this area. To avoid setting a troublesome precedent, the board voted 4–3 to declare the route hazardous, and thereby make it eligible for bus service within existing policy guidelines.

## NEW TEACHER HIRING PROCEDURES

The administration had been requested "to review teacher hiring procedures in light of recent heavy application loads to determine if a new procedure should be established to minimize the amount of administrative time required for recruiting, without negatively affecting the quality of teacher appointments." The superintendent presented a report which recommended modifications in the criteria used for determining which applicants should be interviewed. Board members who opposed adoption of the recommendations wanted administrative time spent on recruitment to be cut more than the 10 percent proposed by the superintendent. The committee rejected the superintendent's proposals in a 4–3 vote, and voted 6–1 to refer the matter back to the administration. The committee wanted a procedure whereby only those applicants who had a "realistic" prospect of being hired would be interviewed, not all who met minimum requirements.

## REDUCTION IN FUTURE BUDGET

This action occurred at a special meeting for review of the budget, which was probably the most heated of the year. A very vocal crowd ("jeering," according to a newspaper account) packed the city council chambers to overflowing. Police were assigned to the meeting for crowd control. The board chairman taunted and insulted other members and the superintendent. At one point, according to the newspaper, he "wandered through the chamber, bringing giggles and smiles as he showed a sign to the crowd [that] read: 'O Lord, help me keep my big mouth shut until I know what I'm talking about.' "

The original $43 million school budget submitted by the administration had been cut by the board to $41 million. At this meeting, the committee certified a final budget of $40.5 million, after voting for cuts in three specific accounts. The board passed a motion directing each administrative department to submit recommendations to reduce the following year's budget by five percent, over the superintendent's opposition.

## COLDREN CORNERS

### TUITION WAIVER

The superintendent had denied a request for a renewal of a tuition waiver; the student and her parents were appealing his decision to the board. Discussion on this item was lengthy. The superintendent's opposition was based on his position that tuition waivers should never be granted. The discussion brought out several facts deemed salient by some board members, including: (1) the petitioner's legal guardianship was assumed by her grandparents (who lived in the district) after the start of the academic year, (2) the petitioner was an honor student, and (3) the petitioner was a member of the gymnastics squad. The board granted the waiver by a 4–3 vote.

## MILITARY EDUCATION PROGRAM

The board had approved continuing the existing military education program at the July 15, 1974 meeting; reconsideration of that decision was by board initiation. The superintendent recommended retention of the program. The board voted 5–2 to rescind approval, after lengthy public discussion.

Several board members appeared initially to be in favor of military education as an option. However, one board member, supported by local peace groups (such as the Women's International League for Peace and Freedom), and various university-affiliated individuals, prepared a lengthy statement arguing that military education was fundamentally different from other educational experiences. In response, National Guard officers read a statement in defense of military training, calling it a vocational educational program. The issue had been given considerable coverage by the media, and the superintendent's support of military education was well publicized.

## SMOKING AT SCHOOL BOARD MEETINGS

At the request of a member of the Student Advisory Council (student representatives to the board), the board chairman asked that the board consider a ban on smoking at board meetings. The board unanimously approved such a ban. The superintendent was in opposition to the motion and spoke in defense of the civil liberties of smokers.

## CENTRAL MENU PLANNING

A committee of food service personnel proposed that the district adopt central menu planning. The superintendent endorsed this proposal because of expected economies from more extensive bulk purchasing. The committee's report noted that the majority of the district's food service personnel were against the proposal. Board members cited this opposition and a concern that centralization would remove opportunities for nutrition education as reasons for rejecting the proposal. It was also noted that a new food service manager had been hired for the next year. The main reason for rejecting the proposal was the lack of hard data to substantiate the claim that savings would be realized. Given doubt about cost effectiveness and personnel opposition, the board voted unanimously to retain the present system.

## TUITION WAIVER

This item was an appeal of a denied tuition waiver. The superintendent cited explicit board policy as the reason for refusing the request for the waiver. The mother of the student presented her case at this meeting; her husband's illness and their lack of awareness that they had moved out of the district were given as reason for the waiver. The board overruled the superintendent, 4–2.

## BUSING ELIGIBILITY

The superintendent had presented his recommendations for changing transportation policy to accommodate budget cuts at a previous meeting. He proposed that the 1-mile limit be retained for the elementary children, but that the 1½-mile boundary be extended to 2 miles for secondary students.

This proposal was the major agenda item at the meeting. Discussion focused on the distribution of hardship, the feasibility of student use of public mass transit, and the added cost to parents. The board rejected the proposed change in a 4–3 vote, and directed the administration to report to the board at the next meeting on alternative ways to provide transportation within the budget estimate. According to the newspaper account, the decision was "applauded enthusiastically" by the audience, which our observer estimated at 35.

Several alternatives were presented at the next meeting. The alternative recommended by the superintendent was the proposal rejected at the previous meeting: he asked for reconsideration. Discussion was again fairly extended, and again several members of the public participated. This time, the superintendent's recommendation was adopted by a 6–1 vote. The observer noted "audience left noisily" at this point.

# KENTINGTON

## REPORT ON GROUP USING SCHOOL FACILITIES

The Kentington Community Association had requested the use of a school in connection with their community development project. The Construction and Maintenance Committee of the board brought a motion to the full board "without recommendation" that the community group be permitted to use the facilities without charge until the end of the year (December 31). One of the board trustees proposed an amendment to strike "free of charge" from the motion. This amended motion received unanimous approval.

One of the board trustees noted that the assistant superintendent had made a plea to carry the community program until the end of December, and asked the assistant superintendent if the amendment (to charge the community group for use of the school) would upset his plans. He replied that the community school would have to be financed in some way. He argued that making the school available without charge would be one means of support. Hence, the administration was opposed to the amendment which was approved.

# SUMMARY OF SUPERINTENDENT DEFEATS

In 11 school districts for a 9-month period, there were 16 examples of superintendent recommendations being rejected. In three cases, the superintendent's recommendation was ultimately adopted. Thus, 13 examples of superintendent defeat remain. Taken as a proportion of total votes in which the superintendent's position is known, the superintendent is defeated less than one percent of the time. While such defeats are occasionally dramatic, they are hardly typical. Further, only two cases are concerned with curriculum or the educational program. Six cases do not deal with district-wide policy, but rather are the redress of individual, or neighborhood, grievances. Thus, we are left with seven examples of the board enacting district-wide policy in opposition to administrative recommendation. Moreover, the issues involved in superintendents' defeats are not important issues identified by news media narratives or our survey research. Only a finance controversy in Leeville is a case of school board failure to adopt a superintendent's recommendation on an issue of major importance.

## Nonunanimous Votes

The extent to which school boards resemble corporate directors more than admittedly political legislatures is also well illustrated in their abhorrence of public displays of disagreement. Expertise must be accorded unanimous support. Breaking ranks is evidence that expertise is subject to question. Various manuals advise: "Individual board members should do everything possible to avoid the formation of factions within the board." "Once a decision is reached, all members of the board should support it." "No other action is more damaging to a board—to its internal relations or its prestige with the public—than for a board member to quarrel publicly with a decision the board has made." "The board should view as a danger signal any frequent occurrence of a split vote along similar lines." "Experience has shown that the continuance of factions and permanent dissenting minorities generally leads to conflicts of personalities and a decline in public confidence in the board and superintendent." [7] Some school board handbooks make a distinction between casting a dissenting vote (one even urges "courage" to those who cannot support the board) and criticizing a board decision in public. Dissenting votes are discouraged; criticizing a decision in public is anathema.

A preoccupation with unanimity is clearly not typical of other legislative bodies. Elected bodies normally contain a "loyal opposition." This opposition is expected to articulate alternative points of view (from majority factions or political parties), and to seek public support for the minority position. Most legislative proceedings are adversary in nature. The atmosphere of a school board meeting is one of harmony. Why? Because nonunanimity either questions the expertise of administrators or questions expertise as an appropriate basis for decision-making. There is an expert-lay tension operating which dictates that public meetings should be displays of consensus. A crack in consensus will provide an opening for the lay public to challenge experts.

As we noted earlier, the norm of unanimity is well heeded. An average of 85 percent of all votes are unanimous. In five districts, over 90 percent of votes are unanimous. As nonunanimous votes do occur, their significance extends beyond their numbers. Nonunanimity is regarded by all participants as a serious breach of proper conduct.

Zeigler, *et al.* (1974, pp. 198–201); and Peterson (1976, pp. 56–78) explain the extent to which intraboard conflicts (as measured by split votes) are indicative of stable or floating factions. While both are evidence of bargaining, the more stable a factional division becomes, the more likely a board is to develop a "loyal opposition." Such a development is visible (that is, public) evidence of a board's behaving more in a traditional legislative style. We need, therefore, to analyze those districts in which such votes occur more than occasionally to learn the extent to which they are reflective of ideological competitions (stable factions) or idiosyncratic disagreements (floating factions).

Three districts fall significantly below the mean rate of unanimity (85%) in board voting: Stumont (62%), Leeville (65%), and Ballard City (71%). The nonunanimous votes in these districts were examined using bloc analysis techniques developed by Schubert (1959). This analysis assesses the cohesion of dissenting blocs.[8] Following Schubert, scores of 0 to .39 are interpreted as low cohesion, .40 to .49 as moderate cohesion, and .50 to 1.0 as high cohesion. Table 5.30 presents blocs which exhibit at least moderate cohesion in dissent.

In Stumont, one bloc of two board members is highly cohesive in dissent. However, this bloc existed in only 12 percent of nonunanimous votes. In Leeville, high cohesion was exhibited by one bloc of two and moderate cohesion was exhibited by two blocs of two and two blocs of three. The most cohesive (and most frequent) bloc existed in only 28 percent of nonunanimous votes. In Ballard City, seven pairs, four trios, and one quartet of board members exhibited high cohesion in dissent. One trio and two quartets exhibited moderate cohesion. The most cohesive (and most frequent) bloc existed in twenty-four percent of nonunanimous votes. Thus, while some highly cohesive blocs exist in dissent, bloc voting does not account for most or an even significant minority of nonunanimous voting.

As table 5.31 indicates, nonunanimous votes are frequently caused by a single dissenter. In no district does a bloc account for a greater proportion of dissent than does solo dissent. Almost all school board members vote against the majority on occasion. In each district the most frequent dissenter is also the greatest solo dissenter, and this dissenter accounts for more than 40 percent of nonunanimous votes. In Stumont the solo dissenter is a former board chairman; in Leeville the solo dissenter is the board chairman.

School board factions, as indicated by dissent from majority opinion, rarely occur. In the three districts with greatest overall dissent some cohesive dissenting blocs can be identified. However, each bloc accounts for only a small proportion of dissent. In no district does a "loyal opposition" exist. Opposition is a function of shifting factions and solo dissent.

## Conclusion

The selective views of chapter 4 suggested that school board meetings were forums of considerable public participation and conflict over major issues facing each school district. The comprehensive views of the present chapter verify that major events are quite different from common events at school board meetings.

Our comprehensive observation of school board meetings in 11 school districts led us to conclude:

School district officials are the dominant actors. Public attendance and participation are low, and are concentrated in a few meetings. Moreover, public

TABLE 5.30

SCHUBERT INDEX OF COHESION IN DISSENT
IN THREE DISTRICTS

| District | School Board Members | Blocs of Two | | Blocs of Three | | Blocs of Four | |
|---|---|---|---|---|---|---|---|
| Leeville | 7 | AC | 64 | ACG | 41 | | |
| | | FD | 46 | FDE | 41 | | |
| | | FE | 40 | | | | |
| Ballard City | 9 | EA | 90 | EAH | 75 | EAHC | 68 |
| | | EH | 71 | EAC | 74 | EAHI | 42 |
| | | EC | 70 | EHC | 64 | EAHF | 40 |
| | | AH | 63 | AHC | 60 | | |
| | | AC | 64 | IFG | 41 | | |
| | | AC | 53 | | | | |
| | | IF | 51 | | | | |
| Stumont | 7 | EC | 63 | | | | |

TABLE 5.31

LONE DISSENT IN THREE DISTRICTS

| Board Member | Leeville | | Ballard City | | Stumont | |
|---|---|---|---|---|---|---|
| | Dissent | Lone Dissent [*] | Dissent | Lone Dissent [*] | Dissent | Lone Dissent |
| A | 48% | 35% | 29% | 9% | 4% | 0% |
| B | 20 | 17 | 3 | 0 | 19 | 57 |
| C | 39 | 9 | 33 | 16 | 25 | 11 |
| D | 21 | 16 | 12 | 33 | 8 | 13 |
| E | 16 | 14 | 24 | 0 | 25 | 21 |
| F | 18 | 6 | 44 | 45 | 45 | 65 |
| G | 28 | 16 | 13 | 10 | 24 | 33 |
| H | -- | -- | 17 | 0 | -- | -- |
| I | -- | -- | 24 | 22 | -- | -- |
| Solo Dissent | | 35 % | | 39% | | 57 % |

[*] Lone Dissent is the ratio

N member is alone in dissent

N Member dissents

attendance and participation at a school board meeting rarely result in a decision at that meeting. Generally speaking, the meetings with greatest public attendance are not meetings of greatest public demand articulation or total demand articulation.

The topics of supposedly crucial importance to school districts do not occupy most of the school board agenda. Routine housekeeping matters are the object of school board discussions. The distribution of discussions among topic areas is remarkably similar across school districts.

The agenda-setting function is dominated by professional administrators.

School board meetings are forums of information exchange and supportive demands. Negative demands are rare.

Administrators regularly make their policy preferences known.

Boards accept administrative recommendations about 99 percent of the time.

Boards vote unanimously 85 percent of the time. Dissent from majority opinion is a rare and virtually random phenomenon.

Public input is normally expressed by educational groups speaking in support of proposed policy.

Dissent, although low, is normally expressed by laymen unaffiliated with formal organizations.

The substance of the typical school board agenda is unlikely to stimulate widespread lay attendance and participation. Issues deemed important by both experts and laymen are underdiscussed. To be sure, school boards must devote part of their public meetings to ratifying experts' proposals on administrative matters. It is entirely reasonable that lay deference to administrative expertise should be the modal pattern of behavior. It seems less reasonable that school board deference to administrative expertise should be the nearly exclusive pattern of behavior.

Low public participation and high board reliance on experts are both functions of the routine nature of the school board agenda. Since the agenda-setting function is dominated by experts, the emphasis on routine can hardly be regarded as a coincidence. In short, the relevant query is not: why do lay board members defer to experts on technical housekeeping matters? The relevant question is: why do lay board members and the lay public allow experts to dominate all phases of the policy-making process?

## Notes

1. See Eugene R. Smoley, *Community Participation in Urban School Government.* (Washington, D.C.: U.S. Office of Education Cooperative Research Project S-029, 1965) in which written records were used to reconstruct events at board meetings.
2. The precise calculation was to sum the absolute differences of the proportions for each topic area and divide by two.
3. To maintain the anonymity of participating districts the state manuals from which the quotations are taken will not be identified.
4. Quotations are from state school board association manuals.
5. Goffman (1959, 1971) has developed the notion of performance as a component of public decision-making.
6. See John W. Thibault and Harold H. Kelly, *The Social Psychology of Groups.* New York: John Wiley & Co., 1961, p. 139.
7. Quotations are from state school board association manuals.

8. Schubert's cohesion index can be thought of roughly as an aggregate proportion of agreement in dissent. The index is actually the mean members' dyadic agreements.

## Appendix: Topic Categories

1. Curriculum includes: general education programs; basic skills; vocational education; bilingual education; sex education; topical education.
2. Student Services includes: athletics; guidance, counseling; special extra programs; programs for special students; transportation; food, health services; safety programs.
3. Students includes: student values; student performance; student misbehavior; student records; enrollment; attendance.
4. Parents includes: parental responsibilities; parent-teacher conferences; parental participation in decision-making; relations with teachers.
5. Teachers includes: teacher values; teacher performance; teacher-staff unions; teacher support staff.
6. Administrators includes: principals; staff administrators; consultants; superintendent; administrative reports; research; administrative professional activities.
7. Local Schools includes: alternative schools; community schools; other innovative schools; methods.
8. School Board includes: school board evaluation; appointment; election of board members; board behavior.
9. Finance includes: appropriations; revenues; bond issue.
10. Discrimination includes: equality; busing; affirmative action.
11. Other Government includes: activities of federal, state, county, and municipal governments; other educational institutions.
12. District Operation includes: maintenance; facilities; materials.

# 6
# Administrative Cabinet Meetings

"In almost every area of school policy . . . those at headquarters . . . were major policy makers." [1] Given such frequently asserted claims, we decided to observe and record the communication patterns of the administrators in their formal meetings by use of the Demand-Response Log. This decision proved fortunate, as observing the influence of administrators in board meetings naturally leads one to examine their behavior in less public settings. In each of our districts, the superintendent held regular meetings—usually once a week—with his administrative cabinet. Although membership varied, it always included senior central office staff, and often included area supervisors.

It was our expectation that administrative cabinet meetings would be arenas of intraexpert communication. Although open to the public by law in two school districts (Stumont and Coldren Corners), we did not expect cabinet meetings to be important forums of lay-expert interaction.

While we cannot compare the behavior of experts and laymen at cabinet meetings, we can explore other questions of interest. When free from the constraints imposed by public scrutiny do experts engage in adocacy proceedings (articulating and considering alternative policies), or do they defer to each other's expertise? [2] With respect to substance, do they complement or anticipate school board meetings? Do they confront issues which they would prefer not to discuss publicly? Is there a division of labor between the substance of board and cabinet meetings? Do administrators address the agenda of greatest interest to laymen in their intraexpert communications?

## The Agenda of Cabinet Meetings

The primary function of public school board meetings is decision-making. As table 6.1 indicates, no such single generalization about administrative cabinet meetings is possible. Three distinct patterns emerge. In four districts (Hartshorne Hts., Barwig Park, Coldren Corners, and Kentington), a majority of discussions are intended to result in decisions. In three districts (Nelsonville, Grahamdale, and Drummond Falls), a majority of discussions do not have decisions as a goal, but a substantial minority do. Finally, administrators in three districts (Stumont, Leeville, and Macktown) rarely intend to reach decisions at cabinet meetings. [3] Thus, in four districts the primary function of cabinet meetings, like board meetings, is decision-making. In the six remaining districts, cabinet meetings provide a forum for expert deliberation and information exchange.

TABLE 6.1

PURPOSE AND RESOLUTION OF DISCUSSIONS AT CABINET MEETINGS

| District | N of Discussions | Decision Intended | Decision Reached When Intended | Decision By Vote |
|----------|------------------|-------------------|--------------------------------|------------------|
| Coldren Corners | 320 | 81% | 99% | 66% |
| Barwig Park | 95 | 95 | 80 | 0 |
| Nelsonville | 247 | 40 | 97 | 2 |
| Leeville | 159 | 5 | 80 | 25 |
| Kentington | 483 | 59 | 89 | * |
| Macktown | 360 | 13 | 82 | 20 |
| Ballard City | -- | -- | -- | -- |
| Drummond Falls | 211 | 43 | 88 | 0 |
| Hartshorne Hts. | 64 | 88 | 66 | 11 |
| Grahamdale | 192 | 37 | 82 | 55 |
| Stumont | 180 | 6 | 92 | 9 |

* Less than 1%

As was the case with school board meetings, cabinet discussions intended to result in decisions achieve decisions in almost every case. Generally, in contrast to board decisions, cabinet decisions are made by consensus. In two districts, Grahamdale and Coldren Corners, voting plays an important role in cabinet meetings. In Grahamdale, slightly more than half of all decisions are reached by vote; however, only 37 percent of discussions are decision-intended. Coldren Corners exhibits a unique pattern. Decisions are intended 87 percent of the time, and ⅔ of such decisions are made by vote. Only in Coldren Corners do school board and cabinet meetings share both a common focus—decision-making—and a common procedure—voting.

Unlike school board meetings, cabinet meetings are subject to the virtually unlimited discretion of the superintendent. No votes, or even decisions, are legally required. Cabinet decision-making style is entirely a reflection of the professional preferences of the superintendent and his administrative staff. Discussions at cabinet meetings are typically informal, and the style of decisions most frequently chosen is consensual—the mode of experts. Voting, a style more appropriate to the resolution of conflicting preferences, is eschewed. Most cabinets seek a common understanding about mutually acceptable solutions to problems.

The distribution of discussion units among topics is presented in table 6.2. As

TABLE 6.2

DISTRIBUTION OF TOPICS DISCUSSED AT CABINET MEETINGS

(Percentage)

| District | Curriculum | Student Services | Students | Parents | Teachers | Administrators | Local Schools | School Board | Finance | Discrimination | Other Government | District Operation |
|---|---|---|---|---|---|---|---|---|---|---|---|---|
| Coldren Corners | 14% | 11% | 10% | 3% | 22% | 9% | 11% | 1% | 3% | 1% | 3% | 14% |
| Barwig Park | 8 | 15 | 4 | 1 | 12 | 17 | 3 | 6 | 8 | 0 | 3 | 22 |
| Nelsonville | 4 | 11 | 13 | 4 | 20 | 13 | 6 | 1 | 2 | 0 | 8 | 20 |
| Leeville | 3 | 11 | 15 | 1 | 9 | 13 | 9 | 3 | 10 | 3 | 3 | 19 |
| Kentington | 6 | 12 | 7 | 2 | 10 | 11 | 10 | 4 | 11 | 1 | 2 | 26 |
| Macktown | 5 | 9 | 13 | 3 | 10 | 6 | 6 | 1 | 6 | 1 | 11 | 29 |
| Ballard City | — | — | — | — | — | — | — | — | — | — | — | — |
| Drummond Falls | 1 | 13 | 4 | 1 | 9 | 13 | 4 | 2 | 20 | 8 | 4 | 20 |
| Hartshorne Hts. | 8 | 9 | 20 | 3 | 16 | 17 | 8 | 2 | 8 | 0 | 5 | 5 |
| Grahamdale | 9 | 5 | 17 | 1 | 10 | 9 | 2 | 2 | 13 | 2 | 9 | 21 |
| Stumont | 2 | 6 | 13 | 3 | 6 | 12 | 6 | 3 | 11 | 1 | 9 | 28 |

159

TABLE 6.3

PROPORTION OF CABINET DISCUSSIONS CONCERNED

WITH IMPORTANT ISSUES

| District | Public Survey | School Official Survey | Narratives |
|---|---|---|---|
| Coldren Corners | 27% | 17% | 28% |
| Barwig Park | 12 | 30 | 43 |
| Nelsonville | 19 | 13 | 17 |
| Leeville | 37 | 32 | 41 |
| Kentington | 23 | 17 | 42 |
| Macktown | 20 | 29 | 16 |
| Ballard City | -- | -- | -- |
| Drummond Falls | 34 | 29 | 29 |
| Hartshorne Hts. | 28 | 28 | 30 |
| Grahamdale | 36 | * | 28 |
| Stumont | 20 | 11 | 50 |
| Mean | 26 | 21 | 32 |

\* No consensus

was the case in school board meetings, district operation is the most frequent modal topic. In 8 of 10 districts, district operation occupies at least $1/5$ of the administrative cabinet agenda. The exceptions are Coldren Corners and Hartshorne Hts., which devote only 14 and 5 percent respectively of their agenda to district operation.

As was the case with school board meeting discussions, the topic of discrimination is seldom broached. In only one district, Drummond Falls, is more than 3 percent of the cabinet agenda concerned with items such as affirmative action, busing, and educational equity. Moreover, when we examine table 6.3, we see that neither issues of great local importance nor issues that dominate the so-called national agenda of school governance are strongly reflected in the agenda of cabinet meetings.

As we noted in chapter 5, the "hot topics" of educational politics are also under-represented at public meetings. Such a finding is not necessarily surprising. After all, public meetings are orchestrated to create an appearance of unity. Administrators may be more comfortable discussing controversial issues among themselves—an idea that has led proponents of the technological decision-making model to argue the existence of "administrative representation." [4] According to this notion, a division of labor in both style and substance exists between board and cabinet meetings. While board meetings must exhibit harmony and avoid controversy, cabinet meetings can deal realistically with important and conflictual issues. The concept of administrative representation holds that experts represent lay concerns and predicts that the most important issues not discussed at school board meetings will be considered at length by administrative cabinets.

Table 6.3 indicates that the discussions at cabinet meetings do not focus disproportionately on issues of greatest importance to laymen, themselves or the local media. While cabinet meetings in some districts devote more of their agendas to issues of greatest public concern than do boards, overall, school boards devote more discussions to these issues. The same conclusion applies to media-identified issues. Cabinet meetings are, however, more devoted to issues deemed important by school officials than are board meetings. Thus, cabinet meeting agendas complement school board meeting agendas only insofar as they emphasize topics of concern to school officials.

Table 6.4 presents the distribution of statements across topics to assess intensity. District operation is the most prominent topic. However, it is the modal topic in only three districts. Finance and teachers are modal cabinet topics in two districts. No other topic is modal in more than one district.

Are most important topics intensively discussed at cabinet meetings? Table 6.5 indicates that they are not. As was the case with discussion units, cabinet statements do not focus disproportionately on important issues. With few exceptions, more statements concerning issues identified by publics, school officials, and local news media as important are articulated at board meetings than at cabinet meetings. There is no escaping the conclusion that administrative cabinet meetings are not primarily concerned with the most important issues facing the respective school districts. Moreover, cabinet agendas do not fulfill representative functions which complement school board agendas. Our data lead us to conclude that administrative representation is more viable as a normative than as an empirical theory.

Cabinet meetings exhibit much less disproportionality between discussion and statement distributions than do board meetings. Table 6.6 indicates that a strong linear relationship exists between topic distributions of discussions and statements in each district. As was the case for school board meetings, all three models of discussion intensity are represented. The equal share model holds for two districts, the higher intensity model for four districts, and the lower intensity model for four districts. [5]

Overdiscussion and underdiscussion of topics at cabinet meetings, as measured by the residual of actual proportion of statements from the prediction of the regression equation, are summarized in table 6.7. In seven districts there is at least one topic for which the intensity of discussion differs by at least five percent from the prediction of its model. As was the case for board meetings, there are no strong patterns of topic overdiscussion or underdiscussion common to all school

TABLE 6.4

DISTRIBUTION OF STATEMENTS AT CABINET MEETINGS, BY TOPIC

| District | N of Statements | Curriculum | Student Services | Students | Parents | Teachers | Administrators | Local Schools | School Board | Finance | Discrimination | Other Government | District Operation |
|---|---|---|---|---|---|---|---|---|---|---|---|---|---|
| Coldren Corners | 4514 | 1% | % | 11% | 6% | 20% | 5% | 9% | 1% | 4% | 1% | 1% | 14% |
| Barwig Park | 506 | 6 | 24 | 5 | 1 | 8 | 15 | 3 | 4 | 12 | 0 | 2 | 22 |
| Nelsonville | 2499 | 5 | 11 | 13 | 1 | 24 | 11 | 10 | 1 | 2 | 0 | 8 | 14 |
| Leeville | 1972 | 1 | 12 | 11 | 1 | 9 | 13 | 9 | 4 | 19 | 2 | 1 | 18 |
| Kentington | 1909 | 6 | 13 | 8 | 2 | 9 | 8 | 11 | 2 | 11 | 1 | 1 | 26 |
| Macktown | 2582 | 4 | 8 | 17 | 2 | 9 | 3 | 10 | * | 7 | 2 | 12 | 25 |
| Ballard City | — | — | — | — | — | — | — | — | — | — | — | — | — |
| Drummond Falls | 1789 | 1 | 12 | 3 | * | 13 | 9 | 6 | 2 | 23 | 8 | 2 | 19 |
| Hartshorne Hts. | 649 | 9 | 8 | 17 | 1 | 16 | 26 | 7 | 5 | 3 | 0 | 6 | 4 |
| Grahamdale | 3307 | 16 | 5 | 14 | * | 6 | 8 | 6 | 1 | 11 | 7 | 12 | 15 |
| Stumont | 2588 | 1 | 6 | 15 | 6 | 7 | 7 | 6 | 3 | 11 | * | 10 | 31 |

* Less than 1%

TABLE 6.5

PROPORTION OF CABINET MEETING STATEMENTS CONCERNED
WITH IMPORTANT ISSUES

| District | Public Survey | School Officials Survey | Narrative |
|---|---|---|---|
| Coldren Corners | 34 % | 18 % | 35% |
| Barwig Park | 17 | 34 | 42 |
| Nelsonville | 20 | 13 | 21 |
| Leeville | 40 | 38 | 48 |
| Kentington | 23 | 17 | 41 |
| Macktown | 26 | 25 | 16 |
| Ballard City | -- | -- | -- |
| Drummond Falls | 27 | 36 | 36 |
| Hartshorne Hts. | 26 | 20 | 25 |
| Grahamdale | 36 | * | 37 |
| Stumont | 22 | 11 | 56 |
| Mean | 27 | 24 | 36 |

* No consensus

TABLE 6.6

REGRESSION OF STATEMENTS AND DISCUSSIONS
**AT CABINET MEETINGS**

| District | Intercept | Slope | $R^2$ |
|---|---|---|---|
| Coldren Corners | 0.22 | .95 | .86 |
| Barwig Park | -0.27 | 1.06 | .83 |
| Nelsonville | 0.49 | .93 | .84 |
| Leeville | -0.19 | 1.01 | .74 |
| Kentington | -0.50 | 1.02 | .97 |
| Macktown | 0.72 | .90 | .90 |
| Ballard City | -- | -- | -- |
| Drummond Falls | -0.41 | 1.05 | .92 |
| Hartshorne Hts. | -0.61 | 1.08 | .80 |
| Grahamdale | 2.98 | .65 | .63 |
| Stumont | -0.67 | 1.09 | .94 |

## TABLE 6.7

## DISPROPORTIONATE INTENSITY OF DISCUSSIONS AT CABINET MEETINGS

### DEVIATION FROM PREDICTED PERCENTAGE

| District | Curriculum | Student Services | Students | Parents | Teachers | Administrators | Local Schools | School Board | Finance | Discrimination | Other Government | District Operation |
|---|---|---|---|---|---|---|---|---|---|---|---|---|
| Coldren Corners | 5.42 | -1.72 | 1.23 | 2.92 | -1.22 | -3.81 | -1.72 | -.17 | .92 | .17 | -2.08 | .42 |
| Barwig Park | -2.23 | 8.32 | 1.02 | .21 | -4.49 | -2.80 | .08 | -2.11 | 3.77 | .27 | .92 | -1.12 |
| Nelsonville | .78 | .25 | -.39 | -3.22 | 4.86 | -1.61 | 4.92 | -.42 | .35 | .49 | .05 | -5.14 |
| Leeville | -3.87 | 1.05 | -4.00 | .18 | .08 | .02 | .08 | 1.15 | 9.06 | -.85 | -1.85 | -1.05 |
| Kentington | .38 | 1.26 | 1.36 | .46 | -.70 | -2.72 | 1.30 | -1.58 | .28 | .48 | .54 | -.01 |
| Macktown | -1.24 | -.85 | 4.53 | -1.43 | -.76 | -3.14 | 3.86 | -1.62 | .86 | .38 | 1.34 | -1.94 |
| Ballard City | — | — | — | — | — | — | — | — | — | — | — | — |
| Drummond Falls | .36 | -1.24 | -.79 | .64 | 3.96 | -4.24 | 2.21 | .31 | 2.41 | .01 | -1.79 | -.59 |
| Hartshorne Hts. | .95 | -1.13 | -4.03 | -1.64 | -.71 | 8.21 | -1.05 | 3.45 | -5.05 | .61 | .80 | 1.20 |
| Grahandale | 7.15 | -1.24 | -.07 | -3.63 | -3.50 | -.85 | 1.71 | -3.29 | .46 | 2.71 | 3.15 | -1.68 |
| Stumont | -.51 | -.87 | 1.50 | 2.40 | 1.13 | -5.41 | .13 | .40 | .32 | .42 | .86 | 1.15 |

districts. No topic is significantly over or underdiscussed in more than two districts.

How similar are the distributions of the discussions and statements over topics in the ten school district cabinet meetings? To investigate this question, we again calculated difference scores for discussion and statement distributions for each of the 45 unique dyads of school districts. (See tables 6.8 and 6.9.) The difference scores range from 0, indicating identical distribution among twelve topic areas, to 100, indicating maximum dissimilarity.

For distributions of discussions, more than ¾ of the cabinet agendas are common across districts as indicated by the overall mean difference score of 23. This aggregate level of agenda similarity is comparable to that found earlier for school board agendas. All ten school districts' mean difference scores cluster around the grand mean. Barwig Park, which exhibited a unique school board agenda, has an administrative cabinet meeting agenda similar to those of the other nine districts. High levels of agenda similarity also are evident when statements are the unit of analysis (table 6.9). The overall mean difference score of 29 indicates that over ⅔ of the cabinet agendas are common across districts. Thus,

TABLE 6.8

DIFFERENCE SCORES FOR DISCUSSIONS

CABINET MEETINGS

|  | Coldren Corners | Barwig Park | Nelsonville | Leeville | Kentington | Macktown | Ballard City | Drummond Falls | Hartshorne Hts. | Grahamdale | Stumont |
|---|---|---|---|---|---|---|---|---|---|---|---|
| Coldren Corners | -- | 31.5 | 19 | 25.5 | 26 | 30 | -- | 39.5 | 26.5 | 33 | 37 |
| Barwig Park | | -- | 26.5 | 21 | 17.5 | 29.5 | -- | 22 | 28 | 26.5 | 29.5 |
| Nelsonville | | | -- | 19.5 | 26 | 19 | -- | 30.5 | 24.5 | 26 | 22 |
| Leeville | | | | -- | 14.5 | 21.5 | -- | 20 | 23 | 18.5 | 18.5 |
| Kentington | | | | | --- | 20 | -- | 22.5 | 31.5 | 24 | 18 |
| Macktown | | | | | | -- | -- | 33.5 | 30.5 | 21 | 13 |
| Ballard City | | | | | | | -- | -- | -- | -- | -- |
| Drummond Falls | | | | | | | | -- | 40 | 27.5 | 27.5 |
| Hartshorne Hts. | | | | | | | | | -- | 28.5 | 32.5 |
| Grahamdale | | | | | | | | | | -- | 18 |
| Stumont | | | | | | | | | | | -- |
| Mean | 27 | 23 | 21 | 18 | 20 | 22 | -- | 26 | 27 | 22 | 22 |

Grand Mean = 23

TABLE 6.9

DIFFERENCE SCORES FOR STATEMENTS

CABINET MEETINGS

|  | Coldren Corners | Barwig Park | Nelsonville | Leeville | Kentington | Macktown | Ballard City | Drummond Falls | Hartshorne Hts. | Grahamdale | Stumont |
|---|---|---|---|---|---|---|---|---|---|---|---|
| Coldren Corners | -- | 44 | 22.5 | 34 | 30 | 33.5 | -- | 41.5 | 33 | 30.5 | 40.5 |
| Barwig Park | | -- | 38.5 | 23 | 20 | 37.5 | -- | 28.5 | 41 | 39.5 | 34.5 |
| Nelsonville | | | -- | 29.5 | 28.5 | 28 | -- | 38 | 27.5 | 33 | 36 |
| Leeville | | | | -- | 18 | 29.5 | -- | 17.5 | 37 | 33.5 | 29.5 |
| Kentington | | | | | -- | 20.5 | -- | 24.5 | 41 | 31.5 | 23.5 |
| Macktown | | | | | | -- | -- | 38 | 38.5 | 26 | 19 |
| Ballard City | | | | | | | -- | -- | -- | -- | -- |
| Drummond Falls | | | | | | | | -- | 47.5 | 35.5 | 36 |
| Hartshorne Hts. | | | | | | | | | -- | 39.5 | 43.5 |
| Grahamdale | | | | | | | | | | -- | 25 |
| Stumont | | | | | | | | | | | -- |
| Mean | 31 | 31 | 28 | 25 | 24 | 27 | -- | 31 | 35 | 29 | 29 |

Grand Mean = 29

cabinet meeting agendas are even more similar across districts than- are school board agendas.

Are the agendas of cabinet meetings more similar to those of school board meetings *within* a given district, or are cabinet agendas more similar *across* districts? Our analyses of the similarity of administrative cabinet meeting agendas to school board meeting agendas within districts, and similarity to administrative cabinet meetings in other districts, are summarized in tables 6.10 and 6.11.

Table 6.10 employs the discussion as the unit of analysis, and presents for each school district: (1) a correlation between cabinet and school board agendas, and (2) the mean correlation between its cabinet agenda and the agendas of the nine other administrative cabinets. These data indicate that, overall, administrative cabinet agendas are more similar to school board agendas in the same district than they are to administrative cabinet agendas in other school districts. In only two districts are administrative cabinet agendas more similar to other cabinets than they are to their respective school boards. The most conspicuous example is Barwig Park. The low correlation between cabinet and school board agendas (.18)

TABLE 6.10

CORRELATION BETWEEN CABINET AND OTHER MEETING

DISCUSSIONS

| District | Cabinet and School Board Correlation | Mean Correlation of Cabinet with Other Cabinets |
|---|---|---|
| Coldren Corners | .54 | .48 |
| Barwig Park | .18 | .65 |
| Nelsonville | .69 | .67 |
| Leeville | .65 | .72 |
| Kentington | .85 | .70 |
| Macktown | .89 | .66 |
| Ballard City | -- | -- |
| Drummond Falls | .83 | .51 |
| Hartshorne Hts. | .45 | .38 |
| Grahamdale | .73 | .65 |
| Stumont | .87 | .67 |
| Mean | .67 | .61 |

TABLE 6.11

CORRELATION BETWEEN CABINET AND

OTHER MEETING STATEMENTS

| District | Cabinet and School Board Correlation | Mean Correlation of Cabinet with Other Cabinets |
|---|---|---|
| Coldren Corners | .14 | .35 |
| Barwig Park | .29 | .48 |
| Nelsonville | .38 | .45 |
| Leeville | .69 | .53 |
| Kentington | .81 | .60 |
| Macktown | .91 | .52 |
| Ballard City | -- | -- |
| Drummond Falls | .84 | .43 |
| Hartshorne Hts. | .23 | .24 |
| Grahamdale | .54 | .34 |
| Stumont | .81 | .51 |
| Mean | .56 | .44 |

is undoubtedly due to the idiosyncratic nature of the Barwig Park school district agenda. For the second case, Leeville, the correlation between cabinet agenda and other cabinet agendas is only slightly higher than that between the administrative cabinet and school board agenda.

In table 6.11 the unit of analysis is statements made at school board and administrative cabinet meetings. This table reveals a somewhat different pattern of correlations. The means are lower, and variance around means is higher. Cabinet agendas are more similar to other cabinets than to school boards in four districts. However, the correlations in these districts are relatively low. To summarize, cabinet agendas reflect the agendas of local school boards more than they reflect a national administrative agenda.

## Agenda-Setting

Table 6.12 presents the distribution of the agenda-setting function at cabinet meetings for our ten school districts. As was the case for school board meetings, the superintendent and his central staff administrators clearly dominate agenda-setting for cabinet meetings. In four districts, the majority of the cabinet agenda is set by the superintendent. In five districts, the majority of the cabinet agenda is set

TABLE 6.12

AGENDA SETTING AT CABINET MEETINGS

Proportion of Discussions

| District | School Board | Supt. | Staff Experts | Line Experts | Public | Gov't. Officials |
|---|---|---|---|---|---|---|
| Coldren Corners | 0% | 41% | 53% | 6% | 1% | 0% |
| Barwig Park | 0 | 43 | 55 | 1 | 1 | 0 |
| Nelsonville | 0 | 20 | 53 | ** | ** | 0 |
| Leeville | 5 | 50 | 42 | 1 | 1 | * |
| Kentington | * | 51 | 46 | 3 | 0 | 0 |
| Macktown | 1 | 36 | 55 | 4 | 4 | * |
| Ballard City | -- | -- | -- | -- | -- | -- |
| Drummond Falls | 4 | 56 | 29 | 10 | 2 | 0 |
| Harthorne Hts. | 0 | 20 | 64 | 0 | 6 | 2 |
| Grahamdale | 0 | 75 | 24 | 1 | 0 | 0 |
| Stumont | 21 | 31 | 46 | 1 | 1 | 0 |
| Mean | 3 | 42 | 47 | 3 | 3 | * |

* Less than 1%

** Excluded because of uncorrectable observer error

by the central administrative staff. In the tenth district, Stumont, a plurality of the agenda is set by the administrative staff. Thus, we see a much greater division of the agenda-setting function among the participants in cabinet meetings than we saw for the participants in school board meetings. School board members defer to administrative experts—mainly the superintendent—in the setting of their agenda. The superintendent, in turn, shares the agenda-setting function with his fellow experts at the cabinet meeting.

It is not surprising that agenda-setting by school board members and members of the public and government officials is limited in administrative cabinet meetings. Indeed, with the exception of Stumont, school board members rarely, if ever, participate in administrative cabinet meetings. Similarly, public participation in agenda-setting is extremely rare. Lack of participation by government officials is uniform across all school districts. It *is* surprising, however, that there is little participation by school employees below the level of central district administrators. It is sometimes alleged that the superintendent's cabinet meeting is a major forum for discussion and resolution of the day-to-day problems experienced in local schools. This may well be the case. However, our data on agenda-setting indicate that when such local matters are discussed in cabinet meetings, it is not at the initiation of the people most directly affected. The agenda-setting function for administrative cabinet meetings is not only dominated by educational professionals to the exclusion of other actors, it is dominated by educational professionals employed at the most central level of school governance. The notion of administrative representation suggests a chain of communications in agenda-setting from constituent to principal, to central administrator, to school board. Our data indicate that only a small proportion of the school board agenda is set directly by line employees and members of the public. Similarly, only a very small proportion of the administrative cabinet meeting agenda is set by line employees and members of the public. In short, we find no evidence in support of the administrative representation model of school governance in the nature of agenda-setting at cabinet meetings.

We have seen that there is an overall division of labor between superintendent and his staff experts in the setting of administrative cabinet agenda. Does this division of labor reflect a pattern of specialization of agenda-setting common to all school districts? There is limited evidence to support this position. In seven school districts, staff experts set the majority of the cabinet agenda for the topics of student services, and students. Similarly, staff experts initiate a majority of discussions on the topic of district operation in five of six districts in which a single actor dominates. Superintendents dominate the topic school board in seven of nine districts in which a single actor sets a majority of the agenda.

A second method of examining division of labor is to ask who sets a majority of the agenda in each district for the most frequently discussed topic. A single actor sets the agenda for this most frequently discussed topic in eight school districts. In six of these eight, staff experts dominate the agenda-setting function. In the remaining two, the superintendent dominates. Two distinct patterns appear. In five districts, a true division of labor emerges, with the superintendent and the administrative staff setting an almost equal share of the topic agenda. In the other five districts, little or no division of labor is apparent over all topics. The dominant actor—superintendent or administrative staff—sets the agenda for all or almost all topics.

TABLE 6.13

PARTICIPATION IN CABINET DISCUSSIONS

Percentage of Discussions

| District | School Board | Supt. | Staff Experts | Line Experts | Public | Gov't. Officials |
|---|---|---|---|---|---|---|
| Coldren Corners | 0 % | 78% | 99% | 26% | *% | 0% |
| Barwig Park | 0 | 32 | 97 | 5 | 1 | 0 |
| Nelsonville | 4 | 73 | 88 | ** | ** | 0 |
| Leeville | 1 | 78 | 87 | 5 | 4 | 1 |
| Kentington | * | 80 | 88 | 17 | 1 | * |
| Macktown | 2 | 66 | 99 | 7 | 14 | 0 |
| Ballard City | -- | -- | -- | -- | -- | -- |
| Drummond Falls | 0 | 94 | 84 | 33 | 1 | 0 |
| Hartshorne Hts. | 4 | 94 | 78 | 18 | 16 | 3 |
| Grahamdale | 5 | 84 | 88 | 24 | 20 | 1 |
| Stumont | 2 | 99 | 97 | 2 | 4 | 1 |
| Mean | 2 | 78 | 91 | 14 | 13 | 1 |

*    Less than 1%

**   Excluded because of uncorrectable observer error

## Participation in Cabinet Meetings

Superintendents and staff experts participate in virtually all discussions (table 6.13). The sole exception is the superintendent's unusually quiescent behavior in Barwig Park. The Barwig Park superintendent was also silent in board meetings. Thus, his unique behavior appears to be a personal preference for listening rather than speaking. The superintendent speaks more in "his" cabinet meeting than he does in board meetings, which are open to the public. The mode of communication at cabinet meetings is one of exchange between experts—especially those employed at the central office level.

In the discussion of line expert participation in agenda-setting, we commented upon the inapplicability of the administrative representation notion. However, with regard to participation in discussions, there is some evidence which supports administrative representation. In five districts, the line administrators (principals and teachers) participate in about 20 percent of the discussions. It appears that on matters of interest to them there is an opportunity to speak. In the remaining districts, however, there is no evidence of line expert participation. Hence, the notion of administrative representation is not supported.

Public participation also exhibits two clear patterns. In three districts, there is

TABLE 6.14

**STATEMENTS AT CABINET MEETINGS**

Percentage of Statements

| District | School Board | Supt. | Staff Experts | Line Experts | Public | Gov't. Officials |
|----------|------|------|------|------|------|------|
| Coldren Corners | 0 % | 21 % | 71 % | 8 % | * % | 0 % |
| Barwig Park | 0 | 29 | 69 | 1 | 0 | 0 |
| Nelsonville | 1 | 23 | 42 | ** | ** | 0 |
| Leeville | * | 31 | 68 | 1 | * | * |
| Kentington | * | 36 | 56 | 7 | * | * |
| Macktown | 2 | 30 | 60 | 5 | 4 | 0 |
| Ballard City | -- | -- | -- | -- | -- | -- |
| Drummond Falls | 0 | 35 | 52 | 13 | 0 | 0 |
| Hartshorne Hts. | 5 | 35 | 47 | 8 | 4 | 1 |
| Grahamdale | 1 | 27 | 53 | 13 | 6 | 1 |
| Stumont | * | 32 | 64 | 2 | 1 | 1 |
| Mean | 1 | 30 | 58 | 6 | 4 | * |

\* Less than 1%

\*\* Excluded because of uncorrectable observer error

some public participation. The level of participation is not equal to that of staff and superintendent. However, given the fact that these meetings are not typically regarded as public, this participation is appreciable. In six districts, however, there is no substantial public participation. In all districts, neither the board nor other government officials can be regarded as sustained actors in cabinet decision-making.

If we analyze the cabinet meetings in terms of statements as opposed to discussions these findings are subject to some modification (table 6.14). There is less variance in the participation of the superintendent and the central office staff. The superintendent in Barwig Park is no longer exceptional. While most superintendents speak on virtually all topics, the Barwig Park superintendent speaks intensively on a few topics. The result is that his share of total statements is comparable to other superintendents.

The cabinet meeting can be understood largely as a communication exchange between the staff and the superintendent. Only 12 percent of the statements made at cabinet meetings are made by line officials, the public school board, and other governmental officials. Experts are talking to experts at the central office level, with substantial under-representation of the other actors who participate at board meetings. Hence, an analysis of statements does not support the idea of administrative representation. Even by the most generous definition, such representation would require the presentation of information by lower level administrators or laymen for consideration at the central office level. This situation does not exist. Therefore, one can conclude that the cabinet meeting is largely a matter of exchange between experts at the central office level.

## The Nature of Communication at Cabinet Meetings

Our conclusions about the professional nature of cabinet meetings are reinforced by an examination of the types of communications at such meetings. With the exception of Kentington, a majority of statements in each district is classified as supplying information (table 6.15). Next most frequent statements are those requesting information, followed by demands in favor, and finally, a negligible trace of demands opposed. In no district do demands opposed account for more than four percent of all statements made.

TABLE 6.15

PERCENT OF VARIOUS TYPES OF STATEMENTS

AT CABINET MEETINGS

| District | Demands In Favor | Demands Opposed | Requests Information | Supplies Information |
|---|---|---|---|---|
| Coldren Corners | 16 % | 3 % | 25 % | 56 % |
| Barwig Park | 2 | * | 21 | 77 |
| Nelsonville | 4 | 1 | 17 | 79 |
| Leeville | 6 | 1 | 24 | 69 |
| Kentington | 47 | 10 | 16 | 27 |
| Macktown | 15 | 2 | 20 | 63 |
| Ballard City | -- | -- | -- | -- |
| Drummond Falls | 22 | 4 | 19 | 55 |
| Hartshorne Hts. | 14 | 3 | 18 | 65 |
| Grahamdale | 5 | 1 | 18 | 75 |
| Stumont | 21 | 2 | 23 | 53 |
| Mean | 15 | 3 | 20 | 62 |

* Less than 1%

TABLE 6.16

REQUEST AND SUPPLY OF INFORMATION AS A PROPORTION
OF ALL STATEMENTS

| District | Superintendent | | Board | | Staff | | Line | |
|---|---|---|---|---|---|---|---|---|
| | Request | Supply | Request | Supply | Request | Supply | Request | Supply |
| Coldren Corners | 30% | 54% | *% | *% | 25% | 52% | 16% | 79% |
| Barwig Park | 24 | 70 | * | * | 20 | 79 | 0 | 100 |
| Nelsonville | 15 | 80 | 20 | 80 | 15 | 80 | ** | ** |
| Leeville | 30 | 42 | 50 | 50 | 17 | 75 | 10 | 90 |
| Kentington | 14 | 22 | 0 | 100 | 18 | 28 | 12 | 33 |
| Macktown | 30 | 48 | 100 | 0 | 16 | 69 | 9 | 81 |
| Ballard City | -- | -- | -- | -- | -- | -- | -- | -- |
| Drummond Falls | 21 | 53 | * | * | 16 | 60 | 11 | 74 |
| Hartshorne Hts. | 19 | 62 | 39 | 42 | 18 | 64 | 8 | 79 |
| Grahamdale | 29 | 68 | 35 | 30 | 17 | 75 | 5 | 90 |
| Stumont | 38 | 43 | 4 | 38 | 17 | 58 | 1 | 64 |

\* No statements

\*\* Excluded because of uncorrectable observer error

It is clear, therefore, that conflict is conspicuously absent at cabinet meetings. Central office experts are exchanging information. If demands are made, they are likely to be in support of proposed policies. Again, deference rather than advocacy is the mode of discussion.

Although information exchange characterizes most of the communication at cabinet meetings, there are two distinct hierarchies in the exchange of information. An examination of table 6.16 indicates that in most districts line officials supply more information than staff officials, who, in turn, supply more information than the superintendent. It is clear that the participation of line officials is *not* one of offering suggestions (which would be coded as demands), but rather one of supplying information to staff and superintendent. This hierarchy is exactly reversed when we examine requesting of information. The superintendent requests more information than staff experts, who, in turn, request more information than line officials. Therefore, two distinct hierarchies exist; one for the requesting of information, and one for the supplying of information. In short, style of communication is a function of rank.

A quite different pattern obtains with regard to the distribution of demands among the various actors at cabinet meetings (table 6.17). No discernible pattern of specialization occurs, with the exception of Grahamdale in which school board members, who articulate a small proportion of total statements, make an unusually high proportion of demands. Thus, there is little deviation from the overall

TABLE 6.17

DEMANDS AS A PROPORTION OF ALL STATEMENTS

| District | Supt. | Board | Staff | Line |
|----------|-------|-------|-------|------|
| Coldren Corners | 16% | * % | 23% | 5% |
| Barwig Park | 6 | * | 1 | 0 |
| Nelsonville | 4 | 0 | 5 | ** |
| Leeville | 5 | 0 | 8 | 0 |
| Kentington | 64 | 0 | 54 | 55 |
| Macktown | 22 | 0 | 14 | 9 |
| Ballard City | -- | -- | -- | -- |
| Drummond Falls | 26 | * | 24 | 15 |
| Hartshorne Hts. | 20 | 17 | 18 | 13 |
| Grahamdale | 3 | 35 | 9 | 5 |
| Stumont | 20 | 17 | 26 | 26 |

* No statements

** Excluded because of uncorrectable observer error

pattern of infrequent demand-making on the part of any actor. Again, the notion of administrative representation is not supported. Line officials, who are presumably in closest contact with patrons are no more likely than anyone else to make demands.

## The Demand Cycle

Not only are demands rare in the aggregate, they are also concentrated with respect to time. In six of the ten districts, a plurality of demands are made during the first third of the year. In two districts, most demands are made during the second third of the year, and in two districts, most demands are made during the final third of the year (table 6.18). The overall pattern, therefore, is modestly in favor of demands in cabinet meetings being articulated at the beginning of the academic year. Cabinet meetings are not mainly forums of decision-making; their nature is more one of collegial exchange of information. The concentration of

TABLE 6.18

TIMING OF DEMANDS AT CABINET MEETINGS

| District | First-Third of Year | Second-Third of Year | Final Third of Year |
|---|---|---|---|
| Coldren Corners | 68% | 19% | 13% |
| Barwig Park | 29 | 14 | 57 |
| Nelsonville | 89 | 9 | 2 |
| Leeville | 90 | 0 | 11 |
| Kentington | 39 | 42 | 19 |
| Macktown | 35 | 23 | 42 |
| Ballard City | -- | -- | -- |
| Drummond Falls | 43 | 36 | 21 |
| Hartshorne Hts. | 52 | 42 | 6 |
| Grahamdale | 82 | 5 | 13 |
| Stumont | 19 | 61 | 20 |
| Mean | 51 | 30 | 19 |

TABLE 6.19

SCHOOL BOARD AND ADMINISTRATIVE CABINET
DEMAND ARTICULATION OVER TIME

| District | Difference Scores |
|---|---|
| Coldren Corners | 37.0 |
| Barwig Park | 61.0 |
| Nelsonville | 75.5 |
| Leeville | 77.5 |
| Kentington | 53.5 |
| Macktown | 40.0 |
| Ballard City | --- |
| Drummond Falls | 41.0 |
| Hartshorne Hts. | 61.5 |
| Grahamdale | 40.5 |
| Stumont | 22.0 |

demands in early meetings suggests that administrative cabinets establish their problem-solving agendas at the beginning of the academic year. Once the agenda has been set, subsequent discussions are largely exchanges of information among experts.

The idea of administrative representation implies that problems and solutions are first articulated in administrative cabinet meetings, and then in school board meetings. Since administrators set the agenda for school board meetings, it is logical to presume that they present problems and alternatives for solution to the school board at the same time. Therefore, the pattern of demand-articulation over time at school board meetings should reflect the pattern of demand articulation over time in cabinet meetings. To test this prediction, we computed longitudinal difference scores between demands articulated at cabinet meetings and demands made at board meetings for each school district. Table 6.19 presents those difference scores. The difference scores has a range of 0 to 100, with 0 indicating minimum difference, and 100 indicating maximum difference. As is readily apparent from the table, school board meetings do not mirror administrative cabinet meetings in the longitudinal pattern of demand articulation. The overall difference scores are quite high. In only two districts, Stumont and Coldren Corners, were the difference scores less than 40. We interpret this to mean that there are indeed two separate cycles of demand articulation; one at cabinet meetings and one at school board meetings. While for most districts, demand articulation occurs in cabinet meetings at the beginning of the academic year; at school board meetings demand articulation is a process that occurs during the entire academic year. Thus, administrative cabinet demands are not translated into school board demands as implied by the idea of administrative representation.

TABLE 6.20

CONFLICT AT CABINET MEETINGS

| District | Greatest | % of Demands | Least | % of Demands |
|---|---|---|---|---|
| Coldren Corners | Teachers | 63 | Finance | 8 |
| Barwig Park | Student Svcs. | 5˙ | Stud. Tchrs., Fin., Dist.Op. | 0 |
| Nelsonville | Stud., O. Govt. | 6 | Admin. Cadre | 1 |
| Leeville | Student Svcs. | 26 | Finance | * |
| Kentington | School Board | 76 | Teachers | 39 |
| Macktown | Admin. Cadre | 31 | Finance | 1 |
| Ballard City | ---- | -- | ---- | -- |
| Drummond Falls | Dist. Oper. | 32 | Local Schools | 18 |
| Hartshorne Hts. | School Board | 39 | Finance | 1 |
| Grahamdale | Finance | 13 | Admin. Cadre | 1 |
| Stumont | Teachers | 38 | Parents | 8 |

* Less than 1%

## Substance of Demands

Not only do boards and cabinet meetings operate on different demand cycles, they show little similarity with regard to the topics which attract the greatest and least number of demands (table 6.20). In only two districts, Macktown and Coldren Corners, do the topics which attract the greatest number of demands at board meetings and cabinet meetings match. In only three districts, Barwig Park, Coldren Corners, and Kentington, do the topics which attract the least number of demands match. In only one district, Coldren Corners, is there a match on both greatest and least demands for both board and cabinet meetings.

Board meetings and cabinet meetings reflect different sets of concerns and different cycles of demand-making. In short, there are two different worlds of school governance; one for the board and one for the cabinet. One aspect of the two governing systems is common to both. It will be recalled that the topics discussed in school board meetings rarely match the concerns of the public, the school officials, or the media. This generalization also extends to cabinet meetings (table 6.21). The issues of concern to the public receive the greatest number of demands in only one of ten districts. Issues cited as important by school officials receive the greatest number of demands in two of ten. This is not to say that cabinets do not discuss these issues. Rather, it is to suggest that the amount of time spent upon them and the absence of demands indicates that the cabinet

TABLE 6.21

CORRESPONDENCE BETWEEN ISSUES OF GREATEST AND LEAST
CONFLICT OF ISSUES FROM PUBLIC SURVEYS,
SCHOOL OFFICIAL SURVEYS AND NARRATIVES

| District | Issues For Public Greatest | Least | Issues for School Officials Greatest | Least | Narrative Issues Greatest | Least |
|---|---|---|---|---|---|---|
| Coldren Corners | No | Yes | No | Yes | No | Yes |
| Barwig Park | No | Yes | No | Yes | No | Yes |
| Nelsonville | Yes | No | Yes | No | No | No |
| Leeville | No | Yes | No | Yes | No | Yes |
| Kentington | No | Yes | No | No | No | Yes |
| Macktown | No | Yes | No | No | No | Yes |
| Ballard City | -- | -- | -- | -- | -- | -- |
| Drummond Falls | No | No | No | No | No | No |
| Hartshorne Hts. | No | No | No | Yes | Yes | Yes |
| Grahamdale | No | No | * | | No | No |
| Stumont | Yes | No | No | No | Yes | No |

* No consensus

meetings are not arenas of decision-making with regard to the major problems of the district. Apparently, cabinet meetings are as insulated from public concerns as are board meetings.

The collegial style of communication obviates the need for an analysis of proposal development and decision-making. Proposal development in cabinet meetings is consensual. Information typically is exchanged until a single policy wins unanimous agreement. With the exception of two school districts, voting is almost unheard of. As a result, the formal articulation of policy proposals which occurs in school board meetings does not occur in administrative cabinet meetings.

## Conclusion

Comprehensive observation of administrative cabinet meetings in ten school districts leads us to conclude:

The purpose of cabinet meetings is to announce, document and discuss policy implementation problems or to articulate the need for policy development.

Participation is limited to the superintendent and his top staff, even in district which permit attendance and participation by other school employees, school board members, and the lay public.

The agenda setting function is divided between superintendent and central staff.

The style of cabinet discussions is collegial; the dominant mode of discussion is exchange of information.

Cabinet decisions are reached by consensus. Conflict articulation and dissenting opinions are rare.

"Crucial issues" are underrepresented on cabinet agendas.

Even though cabinet meetings are nearly exclusively attended by experts, they may be forums of administrative representation of lay concerns and preferences. However, our analyses of the substance of cabinet meeting agendas, the pattern of cabinet agenda-setting, cabinet meeting participation, and interrelations between cabinet meetings and school board meetings found very little evidence supportive of the notion of administrative representation.

## Notes

1. Marilyn Gittell (1967), p. 1.
2. See McGivney and Haught, 1972 for an explanation of this problem.
3. Cabinet meetings are normally held in Ballard City. All but a few such meetings were cancelled during the observation period. As a result, no data on cabinet meetings in Ballard City will be presented.
4. For example, Boyd (1976) and Mann (1976).
5. It is interesting to note that the same model of intensity of discussions applies to both board and cabinet meeting discussions in five districts. The equal share model characterizes meetings in Kentington; the higher intensity model is common to meetings in Drummond Falls; and the lower intensity model applies to meetings in Nelsonville, Grahamdale, and Coldren Corners.

# 7
# Private Communications

This chapter completes our analysis of the network of school district communications and decision-making by examining private interactions between school officials and the lay public. To state the obvious, these exchanges are much less visible and accessible than are communications at school board and administrative cabinet meetings.[1] Furthermore, fewer lay-school official interactions outside the context of formal meetings are expected to result in policy decisions than are interactions at formal meetings. Nevertheless, in view of the character of lay and expert behavior at formal meetings, private communications are of critical importance for achieving responsive governance.

We saw in chapter 3 that laymen and school officials hold divergent attitudes and preferences. In many policy areas school officials who base choices exclusively on their own perceptions cannot act in a manner responsive to their constituents. Since school officials are not adequate surrogates of laymen, some form of communication between the two is requisite for responsiveness. The quantity and quality of lay participation at school board and administrative cabinet meetings are insufficient. School board meetings are orchestrated by experts and are largely insulated from sustained public input. Cabinet meetings are all but completely insulated. Therefore, if school officials are to be guided by lay preferences, those preferences must be expressed in the context of private communications.

As discussed in chapter 2, the Demand-Response Log recorded information provided by school officials on their contacts with laymen. School board members, superintendents, and other central office staff administrators designated by the superintendent to receive communication from the public in his stead were interviewed by our observers on a regular basis.[2] We define the universe of private contacts between school officials and laymen as all interactions which occur outside board and cabinet meetings. Included are telephone calls, letters, office visits, chance encounters, and other meetings attended by school officials. Because of inevitable failures of memory, we cannot claim to have recorded the universe of school official communications with laymen. We are confident that we have captured school official's perceptions of interactions which they remember. Thus, while our interviews captured only a sample of private contacts, the sample is of contacts important enough for school officials to remember.

Two additional points should be made about our concept of private contact. First, the contact is comprised of a series of interrelated statements by both official and constituent. All recorded information relates to the contact as a whole, not to its component statements. Second, each contact is a unique interaction recalled by a school official. To minimize interview time, our data collection instrument allowed school officials to estimate the number of essentially similar contacts. However, the overwhelming proportion of multiple contacts were not cases of many constituents making similar contacts at different times, but were

179

TABLE 7.1

RECIPIENTS OF PRIVATE COMMUNICATIONS

| District | | Superintendent | | | School Board | |
| | N | Pct. | Average N Per Month | N | Pct. | Average N Per Month |
|---|---|---|---|---|---|---|
| Coldren Corners | 154 | 43 % | 20 | 205 | 57 % | 4 |
| Barwig Park | 165 | 62 | 22 | 102 | 38 | 2 |
| Nelsonville | 106 | 38 | 12 | 170 | 62 | 3 |
| Leeville | 75 | 25 | 10 | 229 | 75 | 4 |
| Kentington | 101 | 58 | 14 | 74 | 42 | 1 |
| Macktown | 74 | 42 | 9 | 103 | 58 | 2 |
| Ballard City | -- | -- | -- | -- | -- | -- |
| Drummond Falls | 321 | 66 | 41 | 160 | 34 | 3 |
| Hartshorne Hts. | 123 | 44 | 17 | 154 | 55 | 3 |
| Grahamdale | 556 | 65 | 71 | 293 | 35 | 5 |
| Stumont | 82 | 32 | 12 | 187 | 70 | 4 |
| Mean | | 47 | 23 | | 53 | 3 |

cases of single interactions made in the presence of others. For example, a superintendent who was asked a question at a Kiwanis Club luncheon reported private contacts with 50 individuals. Because weighting individual contacts by the multiple interview component would seriously distort the data, we chose to analyze unique reports of private contacts.

## Sources of Private Contacts

Table 7.1 indicates a relatively even distribution between private contacts received by school board members and superintendents.[3] The school board figures are sums of contacts with seven to nine individuals; the superintendent figures are contacts with one superintendent and sometimes a surrogate. In only one district, Leeville, does a single board member's total approach that of the superintendent. This is not a surprising finding, because the superintendent is more accessible to the public than are school board members. The superintendent is in his office at least 40 working hours per week and has a secretary to take messages. School board members are not professional legislators. They must devote considerable time to their regular employment and do not have offices, office hours or office staff. A constituent can contact his superintendent by telephoning or visiting the district office. To contact a board member requires more knowledge and effort. In four districts, the superintendent receives a majority of reported contacts; in the other six districts, he receives between 25 and 45 percent.[4]

In each district except Drummond Falls, one school board member receives a disproportionate share of private contacts. The most frequently contacted board member receives two to three times the number of contacts he or she would receive if contacts were evenly distributed. In no case is the most frequent school board target of lay communication the chairman of the school board.

Generally speaking, superintendents and school board members are not inundated with unique private contacts. The average school board member recalls three unique private contacts per month; the average superintendent recalls 23 unique private contacts per month. School officials in Grahamdale report unusually high numbers of private contacts, as does the Drummond Falls superintendent. School board members in Kentington report an average of one lay communication per month.

Table 7.2 presents the sources of private communications with school board members. Lay contactors were identified by the affiliation they claimed during the exchange. Those who mentioned no group affiliation were coded as parent or nonparent. Group affiliations are categorized as governmental, educational or noneducational. Educational groups include PTA's, Citizen Advisory Councils,

TABLE 7.2

SOURCE OF PRIVATE COMMUNICATIONS WITH SCHOOL BOARD

| District | School Officials | Groups | Individuals |
|---|---|---|---|
| Coldren Corners | 3% | 10% | 87% |
| Barwig Park | 1 | 9 | 90 |
| Nelsonville | 6 | 2 | 92 |
| Leeville | 1 | 7 | 92 |
| Kentington | 3 | 19 | 79 |
| Macktown | 7 | 17 | 77 |
| Ballard City | -- | -- | -- |
| Drummond Falls | 10 | 22 | 68 |
| Hartshorne Hts. | 10 | 19 | 71 |
| Grahamdale | 4 | 18 | 78 |
| Stumont | 5 | 27 | 68 |
| Mean | 5 | 15 | 80 |

teachers' unions, administrators' associations, other educational institutions in the area, and so on. Noneducational groups include unions, political parties, civil rights groups, fraternal organizations, business and civic groups, charitable organizations, and so on.[5]

The overwhelming majority of private contacts directed at school board members originate with unaffiliated individuals. This generalization holds for all 10 school districts. The source of private communications with board members contrasts sharply with the source of their lay communications at public meetings. Whereas most private contacts come from individuals in 10 of 10 districts, most lay statements at board meetings are made by group members in 9 of 11 districts. Furthermore, educational groups account for most group statements at board meetings.

In seven districts, the modal source of private contact is individuals who do not identify themselves as parents or group members. Parents are the modal source of private contact in the other three districts. Over all districts, unaffiliated individuals account for 85 percent of school board members' private contacts. In seven districts most group contacts are with members of educational groups. In three districts government officials account for a negligible amount of private contacts in each district. To sum, while most lay-board communications in public settings originate with formally organized educational groups, most lay-board communications in nonpublic settings originate with unattached individuals.

Table 7.3 presents the sources of private communications with superin-

TABLE 7.3

SOURCE OF PRIVATE COMMUNICATIONS
WITH SUPERINTENDENT

| District | Groups | | | Individuals | |
|---|---|---|---|---|---|
| | Educ. | Educ. | Non-Gov't. | Parents | Non-Parents |
| Coldren Corners | 10% | 8% | 4% | 30% | 48% |
| Barwig Park | 2 | 4 | 1 | 14 | 79 |
| Nelsonville | 30 | 20 | 7 | 21 | 22 |
| Leeville | 4 | 1 | 3 | 62 | 32 |
| Kentington | 25 | 17 | 7 | 25 | 27 |
| Macktown | 22 | 13 | 0 | 17 | 48 |
| Ballard City | -- | -- | -- | -- | -- |
| Drummond Falls | 24 | 20 | 8 | 9 | 38 |
| Hartshorne Hts. | 9 | 0 | 1 | 70 | 21 |
| Grahamdale | 9 | 7 | 2 | 64 | 18 |
| Stumont | 9 | 1 | 5 | 60 | 24 |
| Mean | 14 | 9 | 4 | 37 | 36 |

tendents. As was the case for board members, unaffiliated individuals are the most frequent initiators of private contacts. In only two districts are a majority of superintendent private contacts with group members. Superintendents receive a higher proportion of contacts from parents than do board members. As was the case for board members, superintendents receive most group contacts from members of educational groups. One modest specialization in private contacts among school officials can be seen. Superintendents are more likely to receive contacts from government officials than are school board members.

## Purpose of Private Contacts

Our investigation of the purpose of private contacts corresponds directly with our analysis of the nature of communication at the school board and cabinet meetings. In addition to classifying the purpose of private contacts as demands in favor, demands opposed, request for information, or supplying information, we include a fifth category, exchange information. This additional category is necessary for private contacts, because we attempt to characterize the preponderant nature of the communication as a whole. A private communication consists of many statements, some of which may be demands, some of which may be informational statements. The category exchange of information reflects the fact that many private communications could not be placed into a single informational category.

Table 7.4 summarizes purpose of private contacts received by school board members. In every district, the majority are demands. Over all districts, an average of 72 percent of private communications are to articulate demands. In contrast, only about 22 percent of the statements made by members of the public at school board meetings are demands. As was the case with source of communication, purpose of communication reveals a strong contrast between public and private behavior. Demand articulation is private behavior; informational exchanges are public behavior.

In public meetings, the ratio of lay positive to negative demands is 7 to 1. In private communications, the ratio is about 1.3 to 1, indicating virtual equality. Indeed, in three districts there are more negative than positive demands. There is a major contrast between lay public and private behavior. Most lay public communication is informational. Most lay private communication is positive and negative demands to the board. Private communications involve more conflict than do public communications. There are more demands being made and there is more of a balance between positive and negative.

It is important to remember that the average school board member is only receiving about three contacts per month. Thus, the *quantity* of conflict and demand articulation in private communications is low even as the *quality* is high. An average board member will hear two demands in private communication per month, hardly a ground swell of constituent opinion. Boards meet publicly every two weeks and receive a smaller portion of demands than they do in private. However, each case of private and public demand articulation may consist of a number of statements. Thus, from the perspective of board members, their constituents may appear quite demanding.

Table 7.5 provides information about the purpose of private contacts received

TABLE 7.4

PURPOSE OF PRIVATE COMMUNICATIONS

WITH SCHOOL BOARD

| District | Demand In Favor | Demand Opposed | Request Information | Supply Information | Exchange Information |
|----------|------|------|------|------|------|
| Coldren Corners | 35% | 38% | 18% | 7% | 1% |
| Barwig Park | 43 | 22 | 24 | 12 | 0 |
| Nelsonville | 30 | 31 | 22 | 6 | 11 |
| Leeville | 44 | 38 | 14 | 5 | 0 |
| Kentington | 47 | 28 | 25 | 0 | 0 |
| Macktown | 39 | 29 | 19 | 7 | 6 |
| Ballard City | -- | -- | -- | -- | -- |
| Drummond Falls | 59 | 23 | 11 | 6 | 1 |
| Hartshorne Hts. | 43 | 25 | 24 | 8 | 0 |
| Grahamdale | 39 | 34 | 13 | 17 | 1 |
| Stumont | 28 | 38 | 15 | 19 | 0 |
| Mean | 41 | 31 | 19 | 9 | 2 |

TABLE 7.5

**PURPOSE OF PRIVATE COMMUNICATIONS WITH SUPERINTENDENT**

| District | Demand In Favor | Demand Opposed | Request Information | Supply Information | Exchange Information |
|----------|------|------|------|------|------|
| Coldren Corners | 34% | 35% | 26% | 2% | 2% |
| Barwig Park | 23 | 16 | 51 | 9 | 1 |
| Nelsonville | 27 | 10 | 27 | 18 | 18 |
| Leeville | 27 | 68 | 3 | 3 | 0 |
| Kentington | 27 | 53 | 18 | 2 | 0 |
| Macktown | 37 | 4 | 34 | 18 | 8 |
| Ballard City | -- | -- | -- | -- | -- |
| Drummond Falls | 40 | 13 | 24 | 21 | 2 |
| Hartshorne Hts. | 10 | 29 | 41 | 20 | 0 |
| Grahamdale | 36 | 12 | 34 | 18 | 1 |
| Stumont | 0 | 7 | 39 | 54 | 0 |
| Mean | 26 | 25 | 31 | 17 | 3 |

by superintendents. Demand statements are again higher than they are in public lay communications. However, superintendents report fewer demand contacts than do school board members. In only four districts do superintendents report the majority of their private contacts as demands. In all districts a majority of private communications to the board are demands. Thus, the difference between communication to expert officials and lay officials is substantial. Fewer demands are being placed upon the superintendent privately than upon the board privately.

We suggest three explanations for the fact that superintendents report more informational exchanges, and less demand exchanges, than do board members. First, superintendents, not board members, are publicly identified experts. Hence, it is reasonable for a person seeking information to contact the school official who has a virtual monopoly on information by virtue of his expertise. Board members—elected laymen—are part-time public officials who are not expected to know as much as superintendents. Second, just as superintendents load the public agenda with trivia, they may deflect a private demand into a private request for information. An expert may reply to a demand as if it were a request for information. For example, instead of ascertaining the preferences of a constituent, the superintendent may reply with information about his own preferred course of action. Finally, superintendents may misperceive. Professional ideologies define demands as inappropriate. Hence, they are re-coded when received into less threatening exchanges.

## Agreement and Disagreement in Private Communications

If school officials are like other public officials, most private communications should be with supporters rather than opponents. Constituents prefer to communicate with sympathetic public officials. Hence, most constituent communication tends to be encouraging. Two legislators from the same constituency who take opposing points of view on a particular issue are therefore probably speaking the truth when they claim that an overwhelming majority of their constituent communications supports the position they have taken. As V.O. Key writes: "Those who write letters to the White House tend to write in support or approbation rather than in criticism. . . . The tendency to write letters of approval doubtless gives Presidents, Senators, Congressmen and other officials a distorted notion of the nature of public response to their actions and positions" (Key, 1961, p. 418).

Board members' private communications prove to be typical. In every district board members report that most private contactors express agreement with their position (table 7.6). On the average, half the communications are in agreement, compared to only 16 percent in opposition. The absence of disagreement contrasts with the finding that there is a balance between positive and negative demands. Most private communication is reinforcing, rather than critical. Thus, the notion of conflict is modified: laymen may express discontent in general, but they rarely articulate disagreement with an individual board member.

Table 7.7 reports the same information for the superintendent. In contrast to the board, the superintendent's private communication is less reinforcing. Communication expressing agreement is the modal response in only three districts. However, the superintendent does not report more critical private communication than does the board. Rather, he is unable to ascertain the position of the source of

TABLE 7.6

**SCHOOL BOARD AGREEMENT WITH CONSTITUENT**

| District | Agree | Neutral | Disagree | Don't Know |
|---|---|---|---|---|
| Coldren Corners | 51% | 16% | 14% | 19% |
| Barwig Park | 50 | 15 | 17 | 19 |
| Nelsonville | 51 | 27 | 12 | 10 |
| Leeville | 55 | 8 | 15 | 22 |
| Kentington | 64 | 12 | 11 | 13 |
| Macktown | 46 | 13 | 9 | 31 |
| Ballard City | -- | -- | -- | -- |
| Drummond Falls | 46 | 8 | 18 | 28 |
| Hartshorne Hts. | 63 | 6 | 18 | 13 |
| Grahamdale | 38 | 18 | 20 | 24 |
| Stumont | 40 | 36 | 25 | 0 |
| Mean | 50 | 16 | 16 | 18 |

TABLE 7.7

**SUPERINTENDENT AGREEMENT WITH CONSTITUENT**

| District | Agree | Neutral | Disagree | Don't Know |
|---|---|---|---|---|
| Coldren Corners | 29% | 17% | 32% | 23% |
| Barwig Park | 19 | 4 | 19 | 57 |
| Nelsonville | 36 | 4 | 10 | 50 |
| Leeville | 72 | 8 | 19 | 4 |
| Kentington | 46 | 13 | 37 | 5 |
| Macktown | 57 | 11 | 20 | 12 |
| Ballard City | -- | -- | -- | -- |
| Drummond Falls | 26 | 11 | 18 | 45 |
| Hartshorne Hts. | 28 | 10 | 15 | 46 |
| Grahamdale | 22 | 16 | 10 | 52 |
| Stumont | 5 | 1 | 0 | 94 |
| Mean | 34 | 9 | 18 | 39 |

the communication. Hence, "don't know" is the modal response in six districts. A conspicuous exception is Coldren Corners, where the superintendent reports a modal pattern of disagreement. The exceptional nature of the perception of Coldren Corner's superintendent can be appreciated if we recall that in no district did a board member recall a modal pattern of negative private communications; hence, the Coldren Corners superintendent is the single example of a school official reporting a predominance of negative input.

It is not surprising that board members do not hear much criticism. Insofar as constituents seek interaction with officials with whom they agree, they have quite a range of choice. The norm of unanimity requires consensus in voting, and in discussion after voting. Prior to voting, however, board members may be less constrained. Thus, a constituent may have a choice of at least seven individuals with whom to communicate. He may be able to find a sympathetic listener. It is surprising that the superintendent does not receive more negative communications than the school board. If the constituent wishes to communicate with the superintendent, there is only one, irrespective of whether or not the source and recipient are in agreement.

It is possible to consider simultaneously the source and nature of private communication by focusing upon the modal *type* of communication of the most frequent *source* of communication. Tables 7.8 and 7.9 list the most frequent source and modal nature of communications as reported by board members and

TABLE 7.8

MODAL PURPOSE OF MOST FREQUENT SOURCE
OF PRIVATE COMMUNICATIONS WITH SCHOOL BOARD

| District | Source | % of Private Communications | Modal Purpose | % of Private Communications |
|---|---|---|---|---|
| Coldren Corners | Individuals | 75 | DO | 39 |
| Barwig Park | Individuals | 71 | DF | 44 |
| Nelsonville | Individuals | 70 | DO | 34 |
| Leeville | Individuals | 71 | DF | 42 |
| Kentington | Individuals | 51 | DF | 47 |
| Macktown | Individuals | 51 | DF | 39 |
| Ballard City | -- | -- | -- | -- |
| Drummond Falls | Individuals | 52 | DF | 62 |
| Hartshorne Hts. | Individuals | 35 | DO-RI (tie) | 28 |
| Grahamdale | Individuals | 34 | DF-DO (tie) | 32 |
| Stumont | Parents | 41 | DO | 49 |

DF = Decision in Favor
DO = Decision Opposed
RI = Request Information
SI = Supply Information

TABLE 7.9

MODAL PURPOSE OF MOST FREQUENT SOURCE
OF PRIVATE COMMUNICATIONS WITH SUPERINTENDENT

| District | Source | % of Private Communications | Modal Purpose | % of Communications |
|---|---|---|---|---|
| Coldren Corners | Individuals | 46 | DO | 37 |
| Barwig Park | Individuals | 79 | RI | 52 |
| Nelsonville | Ed. Group | 24 | SI | 28 |
| Leeville | Parents | 60 | DO | 73 |
| Kentington | Individuals | 27 | DO | 57 |
| Macktown | Individuals | 46 | DF | 33 |
| Ballard City | -- | -- | -- | -- |
| Drummond Falls | Individuals | 36 | DF | 39 |
| Hartshorne Hts. | Parents | 65 | DO-SI (tie) | 37 |
| Grahamdale | Parents | 62 | RI | 33 |
| Stumont | Parents | 57 | SI | 70 |

DF = Decision in Favor
DO = Decision Opposed
RI = Request Information
SI = Supply Information

superintendents. With regard to the board, the pattern is quite consistent. In all districts except one, the modal source is unaffiliated individuals who are not parents, and the predominant mode of communication is the making of demands.

The modal pattern of most frequent source of communication to the superintendent reveals that the superintendent receives a somewhat more varied distribution. He receives more communications from parents than does the board. Additionally, the superintendent receives more requests for information than does the board. There is an even distribution between informational exchange and making of demands. When the superintendent does hear demands, they are likely to be negative. There are two different patterns, one for the board and another for the superintendent. The superintendent's pattern—considering only the most active communications—is more varied both in source and nature of communication.

Finally, we provide an overview of the modal pattern of private communication for all sources in all districts (table 7.10). This table presents the modal pattern of each actor for each district. There is a reasonably consistent pattern of behavior for each. Government officials, educational groups, and noneducational groups are likely to make positive demands. Parents are equally divided between positive and negative demands. Unaffiliated individuals are likely to make negative demands. Those groups which are most attached to the school system—government officials, educational groups, and noneducational groups—are making positive demands. Only individuals provide a consistent source of dissent. Un-

TABLE 7.10

MODAL PURPOSE OF PRIVATE
COMMUNICATIONS BY SOURCE

| District | Gov't. Officials | Educ. Goups | Non-Ed. Groups | Parents | Individuals |
|----------|---------|-------|--------|---------|-------------|
| Coldren Corners | DF | RI | DF | DO | DO |
| Barwig Park | RI | DF-RI | DF | DF | RI |
| Nelsonville | DF | RI-SI | RI | DF | DO |
| Leeville | DO | DF-DO | DF | DO | DO |
| Kentington | DF | DF | DO | DO | DO |
| Macktown | -- | DF | RI | DF | DF |
| Ballard City | -- | -- | -- | -- | -- |
| Drummond Falls | SI | DF | DF | DF | DF |
| Hartshorne Hts. | DF | DF | DF | DO | RI |
| Grahamdale | RI | DF | RI | DF | DF |
| Stumont | RI | DF-RI | DO | DO | SI |
| Mode | DF | DF | DF | DF-DO | DO |

DF = Decision in Favor
DO = Decision Opposed
RI = Request Information
SI = Supply Information

affiliated individuals were also most likely to make negative demands in public. Whatever the forum—public or private—laymen unaffiliated with formal organizations are the most frequent and consistent source of dissent.

## Scope of Request

Since we have observed different participants in private and public communication, we might expect that the goals of participants also differ in private and public exchanges. It is possible to describe the substance of a communication according to its scope. A communication may propose a policy which affects the entire district or may be limited to the resolution of an individual problem. Scope of request refers to the range of people who would be affected by a lay proposal.

The narrowest scope requests actions affecting only isolated individuals. For example, a parent requests that a child be transferred to another teacher within a school. The next level is requests which involve more than one individual but less than an entire school. The scope can be broadened to include communications that deal with a single school and those that deal with a unit larger than a single school, but less than an entire district (for example, all high schools, all grammar schools, or all the schools on the west side of town). Even more expansive are requests which require decisions affecting the entire school district. Finally, some communications raise issues larger than the school district that can be resolved only at the state or national level, such as appeals to change school finance regulations. For this latter category, school officials lack legal authority to make policy changes, but may nevertheless be responsive to constituent demands by expressing concern to officials at other governmental levels.

This classification scheme represents a policy orientation continuum. At the individual level there are few direct district policy implications. The person seeking the redress of an individual grievance is simply asking that his or her case be considered and resolved. For example, a parent may request that his or her child be transferred to another school. The request can be handled without involving more than a single individual. Suppose, however, the parent asks for a reconsideration of district policy on student transfers. This latter request has clear district policy implications.

Whereas all requests arguably may have district policy implications, the wider the scope of request the greater the probability that policy considerations will have to be attended. The broader the scope of request, the greater the probability that more than one set of behaviors will have to be modified.

Tables 7.11 and 7.12 array scopes of request by district for private and public communications by the lay public. District-wide requests are the plurality category for private contacts in 6 of 10 districts. However, in only 3 districts are a majority of private contacts of district or greater scope. Thus, school officials hear private communications across the entire range of the policy orientation continuum. Policies which affect the entire school district are a prominent, but only partial, component of this pattern.

Demands articulated by laymen at public meetings are far more concentrated in scope (table 7.12). About 60 percent of such demands require a district-wide response. In 10 of 11 districts, district-wide demands comprise a plurality; in 9 districts they are a majority. School-neighborhood demands are next most prominent, comprising about ¼ of all demands. In only 1 district do such demands exceed those that are district-wide in scope. Narrower scopes are less represented. For example, individual requests, which are well represented in private communications, are nonexistent in 5 districts, and comprise only about 3 percent of the aggregate.

A clear distinction in scope between public and private demands can therefore be made. Individual level requests are made more often in private. District-wide policy requests are made more often in public.

Board members' private communications are quite similar in scope to what they hear at public meetings (table 7.13). Private communications concerning district-wide requests are a plurality in 8 of 10 districts, and a majority in 6. About half the contacts received in private and public by the school board have to do with district-wide policy, another third are concerned with policy at less than the district level, and approximately 15 to 20 percent involve individual service requests.

Private lay contracts with superintendents are quite different from lay requests at school board meetings. Superintendents receive a higher proportion of individual service requests in private (table 7.14). The aggregate distributions do not reflect the complexity of individual school districts. In two districts, Stumont

TABLE 7.11

DISTRIBUTION OF PRIVATE COMMUNICATIONS

BY SCOPE OF REQUESTS: ALL SCHOOL DISTRICT OFFICIALS

| | Individual | < School | School/Nbrhd. | < District | District | > District |
|---|---|---|---|---|---|---|
| Coldren Corners | 10% | 2% | 16% | 8% | 57% | 4% |
| Barwig Park | 29 | 5 | 9 | 7 | 47 | 2 |
| Nelsonville | 14 | 4 | 23 | 9 | 43 | 5 |
| Leeville | 35 | 7 | 12 | 2 | 41 | 1 |
| Kentington | 17 | 2 | 10 | 3 | 64 | 2 |
| Macktown | 24 | 10 | 39 | 5 | 22 | 1 |
| Ballard City | | | | | | |
| Drummond Falls | 14 | 1 | 11 | 7 | 46 | 17 |
| Hartshorne Hts. | 34 | 4 | 20 | 11 | 30 | 1 |
| Grahamdale | 26 | 4 | 30 | 8 | 23 | 8 |
| Stumont | 35 | 6 | 16 | 11 | 30 | 0 |
| Mean | 29 | 4 | 19 | 7 | 45 | 4 |

TABLE 7.12

DISTRIBUTION OF PUBLIC DEMANDS AT SCHOOL BOARD MEETINGS

BY SCOPE OF REQUEST

| | Individual | < School | School/Nbrhd. | < District | District | > District |
|---|---|---|---|---|---|---|
| Coldren Corners | 7% | 0% | 14% | 7% | 64% | 7% |
| Barwig Park | 0 | 0 | 33 | 0 | 67 | 0 |
| Nelsonville | 0 | 0 | 62 | 0 | 38 | 0 |
| Leeville | 6 | 6 | 13 | 13 | 55 | 6 |
| Kentington | 0 | 0 | 23 | 0 | 77 | 0 |
| Macktown | 13 | 0 | 38 | 0 | 50 | 0 |
| Ballard City | 4 | 4 | 24 | 4 | 53 | 9 |
| Drummond Falls | 1 | 0 | 24 | 11 | 63 | 1 |
| Hartshorne Hts. | 0 | 3 | 16 | 16 | 63 | 3 |
| Grahamdale | 6 | 0 | 35 | 12 | 47 | 0 |
| Stumont | 0 | 0 | 13 | 0 | 87 | 0 |
| Mean | 3 | 1 | 27 | 6 | 60 | 2 |

TABLE 7.13

DISTRIBUTION OF PRIVATE COMMUNICATIONS WITH SCHOOL BOARD

BY SCOPE OF REQUEST

|  | Individual | < School | School/Nbrhd. | < District | District | > District |
|---|---|---|---|---|---|---|
| Coldren Corners | 7% | 1% | 12% | 8% | 68% | 2% |
| Barwig Park | 19 | 8 | 8 | 8 | 55 | 2 |
| Nelsonville | 12 | 3 | 21 | 8 | 51 | 2 |
| Leeville | 24 | 9 | 14 | 2 | 50 | 1 |
| Kentington | 13 | 0 | 7 | 4 | 75 | 0 |
| Macktown | 29 | 11 | 33 | 4 | 21 | 1 |
| Ballard City |  |  |  |  |  |  |
| Drummond Falls | 11 | 3 | 10 | 10 | 61 | 5 |
| Hartshorne Hts. | 16 | 6 | 24 | 12 | 41 | 1 |
| Grahamdale | 17 | 2 | 37 | 8 | 25 | 10 |
| Stumont | 22 | 6 | 18 | 13 | 41 | 1 |
| Mean | 17 | 5 | 18 | 9 | 49 | 2 |

TABLE 7.14

DISTRIBUTION OF PRIVATE COMMUNICATIONS WITH SUPERINTENDENT

BY SCOPE OF REQUEST

|  | Individual | < School | School/Nbrhd. | < District | District | > District |
|---|---|---|---|---|---|---|
| Coldren Corners | 14% | 3% | 20% | 9% | 44% | 7% |
| Barwig Park | 12 | 0 | 21 | 0 | 64 | 3 |
| Nelsonville | 18 | 4 | 26 | 10 | 32 | 9 |
| Leeville | 72 | 3 | 7 | 1 | 17 | 0 |
| Kentington | 21 | 3 | 8 | 3 | 59 | 3 |
| Macktown | 29 | 11 | 33 | 4 | 21 | 1 |
| Ballard City |  |  |  |  |  |  |
| Drummond Falls | 16 | 1 | 12 | 6 | 39 | 23 |
| Hartshorne Hts. | 0 | 0 | 23 | 39 | 31 | 8 |
| Grahamdale | 23 | 7 | 15 | 10 | 33 | 14 |
| Stumont | 81 | 6 | 6 | 6 | 0 | 0 |
| Mean | 29 | 4 | 17 | 9 | 34 | 7 |

and Leeville, superintendents receive an extraordinarily high proportion of individual requests. In Barwig Park and Kentington, a majority of private communications with the superintendent is of district scope. However, even with such wide variance, the superintendent is still receiving fewer district-wide requests and more individual requests than is the board. Whereas for school boards district-wide requests were the modal scope in all but two districts, in only six districts are district-wide requests the modal scope for superintendents. There is a division of labor between superintendents and school board members concerning the scope of lay requests heard in private. The superintendent deals more with requests beneath the district level than does the board; the board deals more with the requests at the district level.

We also inquired as to the type of action requested by the initiator of private contact. Laymen either requested actions to be taken by the board, to be taken by the superintendent, to be taken by other administrators, requested other action, or sought information. For board members (table 7.15), it is almost invariably the case that a private communication involves a request for actions by the school board itself. This generalization holds regardless of scope of action requested. It is logical to contact school board members to request school board action. However, the logic breaks down when nondistrict policies are at stake. Specifically,

TABLE 7.15

MODAL ACTION REQUESTED OF SCHOOL BOARD

BY SCOPE OF REQUEST

|  | Individual | < School | School/Nbrhd. | < District | District | > District |
|---|---|---|---|---|---|---|
| Coldren Corners | AB | AB | AB | AB | AB | AB |
| Barwig Park | AB | AB | AB | AB | AB | AB |
| Nelsonville | AB | AA | AB | AB | AB | AB |
| Leeville | AB | AB | AB | AB | AB | -- |
| Kentington | I | -- | AB | AB | AB | -- |
| Macktown | AB | AB | AB | AB | AB | AB |
| Ballard City | -- | -- | -- | -- | -- | -- |
| Drummond Falls | AB | AB AA I | AB | AB | AB | AB |
| Hartshorne Hts. | AB | AB | AB | AB | AB | AB |
| Grahamdale | AB | AB | AB | AB | AB | AB |
| Stumont | AB | AB | AB | AB | AB | AB |

AB = Action by Board
AS = Action by Superintendent
AA = Action by Administration
OA = Other Action
I  = Information

TABLE 7.16

MODAL ACTION REQUESTED OF SUPERINTENDENT

BY SCOPE OF REQUEST

| | Individual | < School | School/Nbrhd. | < District | District | > District |
|---|---|---|---|---|---|---|
| Coldren Corners | AS | AA / I | AS | AS | AS | AS |
| Barwig Park | I | AA | AS / I | I | I | I |
| Nelsonville | AS | AS | AS | AB AS AA | I | AS |
| Leeville | AS | AS | AS | AS | AS | AS |
| Kentington | AS | AS | AB AS | AS | AB | I |
| Macktown | AS | AS | AS | AS | AS | AS |
| Ballard City | -- | -- | -- | -- | -- | -- |
| Drummond Falls | AS | AB | AS | AA | AS | AS |
| Hartshorne Hts. | AA | -- | AA | I | I | -- |
| Grahamdale | AA | AA | AA | AA | I | I |
| Stumont | AA | AA | AA | AA | AA | I |

AA = Action by Board
AS = Action by Superintendent
AA = Action by Administration
OA = Other Action
I  = Information

school boards rarely take formal action on requests affecting isolated individuals. Lay requests for school boards to act on individual-scope requests may indicate ignorance of the powers and responsibilities of school boards.[6]

Private communications received by the superintendent (table 7.16) request a variety of actions. Superintendents are most frequently contacted to request that they or other administrators take some action. They are less frequently requested to facilitate board action or to supply information. In all districts and for all scopes, action by superintendent or other administrator is the modal request.

The difference in private requests addressed to superintendents and school board members generally reflect their different levels of power and expertise. Laymen contact lay school board members concerning requests for school board action on district-wide matters. Laymen contact superintendents to ask them to take action personally, to refer a problem to another administrator or to the board, or to supply information on matters across the policy continuum. Expert school officials are contacted in private more often to make a greater range of requests than are lay school officials. Members of the lay public rarely ask school board members to influence superintendents. On the other hand, they quite frequently ask superintendents to influence school board members.

## TABLE 7.17

## TOPIC OF PRIVATE COMMUNICATIONS WITH SCHOOL BOARD

| District | Curriculum | Student Services | Students | Parents | Teachers | Administrators | Local Schools | School Board | Finance | Discrimination | Other Government | District Operation |
|---|---|---|---|---|---|---|---|---|---|---|---|---|
| Coldren Corners | 19% | 13% | 7% | 0% | 6% | 6% | 8% | 12% | 20% | 1% | 0% | 8% |
| Barwig Park | 10 | 16 | 20 | 1 | 10 | 6 | 2 | 8 | 3 | 2 | 1 | 20 |
| Nelsonville | 10 | 13 | 11 | 1 | 10 | 3 | 12 | 2 | 5 | 4 | 1 | 28 |
| Leeville | 9 | 17 | 12 | 4 | 6 | 5 | 10 | 3 | 22 | 3 | 0 | 9 |
| Kentington | 8 | 11 | 11 | 7 | 12 | 3 | 12 | 9 | 1 | 5 | 0 | 20 |
| Macktown | 10 | 14 | 29 | 6 | 14 | 1 | 3 | 7 | 2 | 1 | 1 | 14 |
| Ballard City | — | — | — | — | — | — | — | — | — | — | — | — |
| Drummond Falls | 11 | 11 | 8 | 4 | 10 | 2 | 7 | 4 | 28 | 8 | 1 | 9 |
| Hartshorne Hts. | 12 | 17 | 25 | 2 | 5 | 1 | 9 | 3 | 6 | 1 | 1 | 19 |
| Grahamdale | 15 | 6 | 20 | 1 | 10 | 2 | 16 | 5 | 1 | 4 | 2 | 15 |
| Stumont | 7 | 15 | 23 | 6 | 14 | 5 | 3 | 10 | 4 | 2 | 1 | 10 |
| Mean | 11 | 13 | 17 | | 10 | 3 | 8 | 6 | 9 | 3 | 1 | 15 |

195

## Subject of Private Contacts

In our discussion of school board and cabinet meetings, we noted that there was a disproportionate focus on the topic of district operation. As one might anticipate, the private contacts to the board are not so concentrated around district operation as was true of the discussions and statements at public board meetings (table 7.17). In only three cases is district operation the modal category, and in one of those three it is tied with students. There is more of a dispersion of topics characterizing the traffic in private communications as contrasted with public communications. Students attract a substantially higher share of private communication than is reflected in the discussions at school board meetings.

How similar are the public and private agendas? The correlation between the topics discussed publicly at school board meetings and the topics of private communications to school board members in table 7.18 reveals a wide range over school districts. The mean correlation is .48, the range is from .01 to .91. There are two distinct categories of districts: those in which there is little or no correlation between the public and private agendas, and those in which there is a high correlation.

TABLE 7.18

CORRELATIONS BETWEEN SCHOOL BOARD PRIVATE COMMUNICATIONS
TOPICS AND SCHOOL BOARD MEETING DISCUSSION TOPICS

| District | r |
|---|---|
| Coldren Corners | .01 |
| Barwig Park | .74 |
| Nelsonville | .91 |
| Leeville | .33 |
| Kentington | .68 |
| Macktown | .39 |
| Ballard City | -- |
| Drummond Falls | .64 |
| Hartshorne Hts. | .67 |
| Grahamdale | .37 |
| Stumont | .27 |
| Mean | .48 |

TABLE 7.19

PROPORTION OF PRIVATE COMMUNICATIONS WITH SCHOOL BOARD

CONCERNED WITH IMPORTANT ISSUES

| District | Public | School Officials | Narratives |
|----------|--------|------------------|------------|
| Coldren Corners | 46% | 28% | 58% |
| Barwig Park | 23 | 23 | 46 |
| Nelsonville | 26 | 11 | 25 |
| Leeville | 49 | 40 | 44 |
| Kentington | 31 | 9 | 40 |
| Macktown | 32 | 14 | 16 |
| Ballard City | -- | -- | -- |
| Drummond Falls | 47 | 38 | 38 |
| Hartshorne Hts. | 38 | 31 | 35 |
| Grahamdale | 45 | * | 39 |
| Stumont | 39 | 4 | 57 |
| Mean | 38 | 22 | 40 |

* No consensus

The subject of private communication is closer to unarticulated lay concerns than is lay communication at board meetings (table 7.19). This greater correspondence is, of course, a function of the fact that at school board meetings administrators set most of the agenda, whereas in private contacts a lay initiator defines the subject. There is very little difference between the proportion of private and public communications which reflects major issues identified by school officials and news media. However, private communications reflect unarticulated lay concerns substantially better than public communications do.

What is the substance of the private contacts received by the superintendent? As was the case with the school board, the superintendent hears far fewer private communications on the topic of district operation than he hears at board and cabinet meetings (table 7.20). District operation is the modal topic of private communications with the superintendent in only one district. Students is the most

TABLE 7.20

TOPICS OF PRIVATE COMMUNICATIONS WITH SUPERINTENDENT

| District | Curriculum | Student Services | Students | Parents | Teachers | Administrators | Local Schools | School Board | Finance | Discrimination | Other Government | District Operation |
|---|---|---|---|---|---|---|---|---|---|---|---|---|
| % | 12% | 17% | 14% | 2% | 6% | 8% | 9% | 3% | 16% | 1% | 2% | 9% |
| Coldren Corners | 10 | 12 | 25 | 1 | 4 | 7 | 4 | 1 | 2 | 7 | 3 | 21 |
| Barwig Park | 6 | 12 | 8 | 8 | 15 | 6 | 8 | 1 | 2 | 2 | 13 | 18 |
| Nelsonville | 9 | 27 | 23 | 3 | 9 | 7 | 7 | 0 | 12 | 0 | 0 | 4 |
| Leeville | 11 | 6 | 16 | 6 | 17 | 2 | 13 | 4 | 10 | 2 | 1 | 13 |
| Kentington | 14 | 5 | 32 | 3 | 7 | 8 | 9 | 0 | 3 | 7 | 1 | 11 |
| Macktown | — | — | — | — | — | — | — | — | — | — | — | — |
| Ballard City | — | — | — | — | — | — | — | — | — | — | — | — |
| Drummond Falls | 8 | 10 | 6 | 4 | 8 | 11 | 5 | 1 | 16 | 4 | 12 | 14 |
| Hartshorne Hts. | 17 | 16 | 35 | 1 | 10 | 1 | 2 | 0 | 6 | 6 | 1 | 6 |
| Grahamdale | 15 | 13 | 26 | 7 | 9 | 3 | 8 | 2 | 2 | 2 | 2 | 12 |
| Stumont | 10 | 26 | 28 | 11 | 6 | 5 | 0 | 0 | 4 | 4 | 1 | 5 |
| Mean | 11 | 14 | 21 | 5 | 9 | 6 | 7 | 1 | 7 | 4 | 4 | 11 |

frequent topic of private communications in four school districts, and student services is the modal topic in three districts. These substantive areas reflect the narrow scope of private communication to superintendents.

As was the case for private communications with school board members and the agenda of school board meetings, there is a range of correspondence between superintendents' private communication and their cabinet meeting agendas (table 7.21). In four districts the correlations between cabinet meeting topics and topics of superintendent private contacts are greater than .50; in six districts they are lower. Three of the four higher correlation districts—Nelsonville, Drummond Falls, and Hartshorne Hts.—also had high correlations between school board private contacts and meeting agendas.

Just as was the case with the school board, when laymen communicate with the superintendent in private, the topics reflect their major concerns as identified by survey research (table 7.22). Superintendents' private communications are more representative of lay public concerns than are the cabinet meeting agendas. Superintendents' private contacts are much more representative of the concerns of laymen than they are of school officials and local news media.

## Public Preferences and Three Modes of Communication

How well do the three forums of lay-school official communication reflect the concerns and preferences of the public? We have seen that private communications more accurately represent lay opinion than do either cabinet or board meet-

TABLE 7.21

CORRELATIONS BETWEEN SUPERINTENDENT PRIVATE
COMMUNICATIONS TOPICS AND CABINET DISCUSSION TOPICS

| District | r |
|---|---|
| Coldren Corners | .37 |
| Barwig Park | .39 |
| Nelsonville | .84 |
| Leeville | .51 |
| Kentington | .46 |
| Macktown | .33 |
| Ballard City | -- |
| Drummond Falls | .78 |
| Hartshorne Hts. | .58 |
| Grahamdale | .48 |
| Stumont | .04 |
| Mean | .53 |

TABLE 7.22

PROPORTION OF PRIVATE COMMUNICATIONS WITH SUPERINTENDENT
CONCERNED WITH IMPORTANT ISSUES

| District | Public | Administration | Narratives |
|---|---|---|---|
| Coldren Corners | 42% | 25% | 45% |
| Barwig Park | 27 | 23 | 45 |
| Nelsonville | 16 | 8 | 13 |
| Leeville | 53 | 25 | 16 |
| Kentington | 44 | 21 | 41 |
| Macktown | 42 | 11 | 10 |
| Ballard City | -- | -- | -- |
| Drummond Falls | 30 | 24 | 24 |
| Hartshorne Hts. | 58 | 41 | 47 |
| Grahamdale | 50 | * | 43 |
| Stumont | 38 | 4 | 39 |
| Mean | 40 | 20 | 32 |

* No consensus

ings. Public concerns are best expressed in private contacts, next best in school board meetings, and least in administrative cabinet meetings. It seems as though the less control experts exercise over the agenda of discussion, the greater the congruence between the agenda of lay-official interaction, and the agenda preferred by laymen.

## Conclusion

Although school officials are hardly inundated with private communications from the lay public, the character of private communications is an important complement to school official-lay interactions at public meetings. Private contacts with laymen provide school officials with a greater quantity of (1) input from individuals unaffiliated with interest groups, (2) communications made to articulate demands, (3) requests which are less than district-wide in scope, and (4) topics of major concern to the public than do school board or administrative cabinet meetings. There are important differences in the quantity and quality of private communications received by superintendents and school board members. The superintendent is likely to have as many private contacts with members of the lay public as the entire school board. His private communications will cover a broader range of requests for action and scope of request; board members' private communications will be more reinforcing in tone.

The linkages between the substance of private contacts and school board and administrative cabinet meetings are uneven across school districts. Yet the linkages between unarticulated lay concerns and the substance of private communications are generally high. Clearly, interactions which do not occur at school district meetings are an important element in the communications system which links school officials and their constituents.

## Notes

1. Although we use the generic title "private communications," many exchanges take place in the presence of other people. Private communications include, for example, interactions which occur at service club meetings, athletic contests, PTA functions, and so forth.
2. Generally, twice each month.
3. Superintendent contacts are reported as the sum of contacts with superintendents and their designated staff administrators.
4. School officials in Ballard City cancelled so many interviews that we cannot present reliable data for that district.
5. This coding scheme follows that developed in Zeigler, *et al.*, 1974.
6. This confirms the findings of research by the National School Boards Association. See NSBA (1975-1), p. 21.

# 8

# Responsiveness

In chapter 1 the concept of responsiveness as the key to American democracy was introduced. The purpose of the present chapter is to explore the responsiveness of school district officials to their constituents. As discussed in chapter 1, we define responsiveness as a relationship between constituent preferences and government activity.

A central problem for the empirical measurement of responsiveness is created by the difficulty of identifying constituent preferences. As we have documented here and others have shown elsewhere, direct citizen communication of demands and preferences to government officials is rare. Moreover, those who do communicate are not broadly representative of the larger public. The upshot is that articulated constituent preferences may differ greatly from unarticulated constituent preferences.

The dilemma that low quantity and quality of public preference articulation poses for evaluating responsiveness is well known. Although the dilemma has not been completely resolved, two approaches have evolved. What we have designated as the representational school focuses exclusively on articulated constituent preferences: responsiveness exists to the extent that government does what its citizens say they want to be done. There can be no responsiveness in school districts without lay demand articulation. Accordingly, the proper empirical base for measuring representational responsiveness is all cases in which constituents articulate policy preferences to school district officials. What we have designated as the congruence school focuses on both articulated and unarticulated preferences: responsiveness exists to the extent that government does what its citizens want it to do. The proper empirical base for measuring congruence responsiveness is all cases in which constituents hold policy preferences.

In this chapter we will develop measures of both congruence and representational responsiveness. The former will link data on attitudes and preferences from survey research and data on behavior of school officials in meetings and private communications. The latter will link data on articulated preferences and ensuing action by school officials from the Demand-Response Logs. Two definitions of congruence responsiveness will be offered: agenda responsiveness and symbolic responsiveness. Three definitions of representational responsiveness will be offered: service responsiveness, policy responsiveness, and influence responsiveness. Interrelations of indices within and across definitions will be examined. Finally, the levels and patterns of responsiveness of local school districts to their constituents will be briefly explored.

## Agenda Responsiveness

Our first congruence definition of responsiveness focuses on how well representatives articulate the policy concerns of their constituents. This concept of responsiveness posits a meaningful connection between constituent policy preferences and representatives' policy conduct. This is what Miller and Stokes (1963) call congruence, and what Verba and Nie (1972) call concurrence. Whatever the term, the operational definition is the same. If representative and constituency agree on a particular policy position, no matter how the agreement has come about, then the representative is responsive.

Our index of agenda responsiveness links constituent preferences as to what should be on the school district's policy agenda and the policy agenda addressed by school district officials. Constituent preference is operationalized in terms of answers to the survey question: at the present time, what do you consider the most important problems facing the public schools in your community that school officials try to take care of? School district behavior is operationalized in terms of topics of discussions at various meetings during the academic year. Four different operational measures of school district agenda-setting are presented. The first measure defines the agenda in terms of discussions at school board meetings. A second measure defines the agenda in terms of discussions at school board meetings in which there is public participation. Thus, the second operational definition is actually a subgroup of the first definition. A third measure focuses on discussions at administrative cabinet meetings as the agenda. A fourth measure aggregates *all* discussions at meetings during the academic year as the agenda. These agendas are matched with the preferences of public, elite, and school official survey respondents.

Putting the three survey groups in combination with the four agenda definitions yields 12 different indices of agenda responsiveness for each school district. The operational definition of the index of agenda responsiveness is as follows: Concurrence scores were calculated for each constituent survey respondent, and then aggregated by district, employing the methodology described by Verba and Nie (1972, pp. 302–304; pp. 412–414). Agenda concurrence scores are summarized in tables 8.1, 8.2, and 8.3. Consideration of agenda responsiveness scores will be structured by two overriding questions. First, which forum most accurately reflects the concerns of each constituency? Second, which group's concerns are most accurately reflected by each of the four forums of discussion and decision-making?

Which forum of school district discussion and decision-making most accurately reflects the concerns of the public? (table 8.1.) In four districts, the administrative cabinet meeting agendas are most responsive to the policy concerns of the general public. However, in the other seven districts, the school board meeting agendas are more responsive to the concerns of members of the public. One cannot generalize over all districts that either school board meetings or administrative cabinet meetings are more responsive to lay concerns.

It is somewhat surprising that the school board meeting is not more uniformly most responsive over all the districts. One might expect the school board meeting, as a forum of both discussion and decision-making, to have the broader agenda. Additionally, since it is the forum of discussion most accessible to the members of the public, one would expect a higher level of board meeting responsiveness.

TABLE 8.1

AGENDA RESPONSIVENESS--PUBLIC PREFERENCES

| District | Public Participation at School Board Meetings | School Board Meetings | Administrative Cabinet Meeting | All Meetings |
|---|---|---|---|---|
| Coldren Corners | 53 | 59 | 82 | 87 |
| Barwig Park | 39 | 64 | 56 | 69 |
| Nelsonville | 39 | 60 | 76 | 77 |
| Leeville | 61 | 77 | 78 | 83 |
| Kentington | 40 | 86 | 81 | 95 |
| Macktown | 41 | 68 | 57 | 73 |
| Ballard City | 44 | 79 | 56 | 79 |
| Drummond Falls | 73 | 78 | 75 | 82 |
| Hartshorne Hts. | 69 | 73 | 67 | 74 |
| Grahamdale | 45 | 68 | 70 | 87 |
| Stumont | 38 | 48 | 46 | 50 |
| Mean | 49 | 69 | 68 | 78 |

Empirically, it is the case that there is virtually no public participation at administrative cabinet meetings. Nevertheless, in four school districts, administrative cabinet meeting agendas are more responsive to the major concerns of the public than are school board meeting agendas. In two districts the difference between board and cabinet agenda responsiveness is virtually negligible. In two other districts cabinet agendas are substantially more responsive to lay concerns than are school board agendas.

The aggregate agenda responsiveness scores for each school district are quite high. Stumont is the sole exception, with a responsiveness score of 50 for all meetings. The interpretation is that, in the aggregate, only half of the issues of greatest concern to the constituents are being discussed at meetings of school officials during the academic year. The other school districts have much higher aggregate scores. All districts have scores of at least 50, and 10 have scores indicating that they consider more than ⅔ of the agenda concerns of laymen. Most of the scores are in the 70's and the 80's.

One should bear in mind that public preferences express a range of policy concerns that is virtually unconstrained, and largely uninformed by substantive knowledge of the history of school district concerns and issues. Even rudimentary knowledge of the legal constraints and scope of policy discretion allowed school officials is lacking. For example, a high proportion of respondents to our community survey indicated that school district officials should take steps to insure that fundamental religious doctrines are taught in the public schools. This, of course, is beyond the legal scope and capacity of any school official. In each district, a rather substantial minority of responses from the public named policy actions which is beyond either the scope or authority of the school district. With this in mind, scores in the 70's and 80's are rather substantial.

In all school districts, each type of meeting adds something to the aggregate level of responsiveness. While there is a great overlap of discussion topics at board and cabinet meetings, both school board meetings and administrative cabinet meetings make an independent contribution to the aggregate level of responsiveness. The single exception is Ballard City, where cabinet meeting discussions completely overlap school board meeting discussions with respect to agenda responsiveness. That is, the school board meeting agenda responsiveness score of 79 is also the agenda responsiveness score for *all* meetings, while administrative cabinet meetings yield the responsiveness score of 56. Administrative cabinet meetings yield no additional increments of responsiveness to that already generated at school board meetings for Ballard City.

We can further divide the agenda responsiveness scores of school board meetings into discussions in which there is public participation, and discussions in which there is no public participation. The column on table 8.1 labeled 'Public Participation at School Board Meetings' gives the agenda responsiveness score for each school district for those discussions in which there was some public participation. For each district more than half of the total responsiveness score for school board meetings overlaps with discussions in which there is public participation. To be sure, in every district discussions in which there is no public participation add substantially to the overall level of agenda responsiveness. Nevertheless, it is interesting to note that the greater proportion of agenda responsiveness occurs when there is some public participation. One should not infer that it is the public which is initiating these discussions. It is more likely that these agenda items were introduced by school board members or experts. Nevertheless, the operant finding is that the public participates directly in the majority of the discussions which yield agenda responsiveness at school board meetings.

Table 8.2 presents data on the responsiveness of school district agendas to preferences of community elites. As was the case for public preferences, elite preferences are most accurately reflected by cabinet meeting agendas in some school districts, and by school board meeting agendas in other districts. In four districts the administrative cabinet meeting is the forum whose agenda is most responsive to the preferences of community elites. In five districts the school board meeting agenda is most responsive to the preferences of the elites. In one district there is a tie between the level of responsiveness of cabinet and school board meetings.

Agenda responsiveness of all meetings to elite preferences is higher than responsiveness to public preferences. The low district for responsiveness to public preferences is Stumont, with a score of 50. The low district with respect to elite preferences is also Stumont, but the score is 63. Most of the other school districts' scores were in the range of 70's and 80's for public preferences; most of the school district scores are in the range of 80's and 90's with respect to elite preferences. Obviously, the agendas of meetings in school districts are quite responsive to the major policy concerns of community elites. As one shifts attention from public to elite concerns, not only does the overall level of agenda responsiveness increase, but the minimum level of agenda responsiveness also increases.

The division of responsiveness to elites at school board meetings between discussions with and without public participation also diverges from the pattern from public preferences. For public preferences in each school district, more than half of the overall school board responsiveness score was linked with public

TABLE 8.2

AGENDA RESPONSIVENESS--ELITE PREFERENCES

| District | Public Participation at School Board Meetings | School Board Meetings | Administrative Cabinet Meetings | All Meetings |
|----------|-----------------------------------------------|-----------------------|---------------------------------|--------------|
| Coldren Corners | 40 | 47 | 82 | 85 |
| Barwig Park | 33 | 76 | 59 | 80 |
| Nelsonville | 22 | 47 | 71 | 75 |
| Leeville | 86 | 95 | 95 | 95 |
| Kentington | 7 | 90 | 68 | 97 |
| Macktown | 55 | 77 | 88 | 92 |
| Ballard City | -- | -- | -- | -- |
| Drummond Falls | 79 | 86 | 83 | 90 |
| Hartshorne Hts. | 95 | 95 | 90 | 95 |
| Grahamdale | 37 | 55 | 82 | 89 |
| Stumont | 46 | 63 | 60 | 63 |
| Mean | 50 | 73 | 78 | 86 |

TABLE 8.3

AGENDA RESPONSIVENESS--SCHOOL OFFICIALS' PREFERENCES

| District | Public Participation at School Board Meetings | School Board Meetings | Administrative Cabinet Meeting | All Meetings |
|----------|-----------------------------------------------|-----------------------|--------------------------------|--------------|
| Coldren Corners | 58 | 69 | 82 | 92 |
| Barwig Park | 51 | 92 | 66 | 92 |
| Nelsonville | 22 | 59 | 86 | 87 |
| Leeville | 71 | 83 | 81 | 83 |
| Kentington | 20 | 96 | 88 | 98 |
| Macktown | 42 | 74 | 77 | 86 |
| Ballard City | -- | -- | -- | -- |
| Drummond Falls | 52 | 67 | 60 | 78 |
| Hartshorne Hts. | 78 | 87 | 78 | 87 |
| Grahamdale | 32 | 68 | 85 | 88 |
| Stumont | 47 | 60 | 60 | 60 |
| Mean | 47 | 76 | 76 | 85 |

participation in discussions. This is the case for only 7 of the 10 school districts with respect to elite preferences. In three districts less than half of the overall agenda responsiveness score for elite preferences is a function of discussions at school board meetings in which there is public participation. We should reiterate at this point that there is overlap in our elite survey sample and those who participate at school board meetings. Our elite sample was drawn, in part, from those people who were recognized as ongoing participants in school affairs. Thus, those who were frequent participants in school board meetings were likely to receive a survey questionnaire which became part of our elite file. Thus, it is fascinating to note that overall, there is even *less* overlap between elite preferences and what might be called elite participation at school board meetings than occurred for public preferences.

Table 8.3 summarizes agenda responsiveness to the preferences of school officials. When we ask which of the forums most accurately reflects the concerns of school officials, we again find a division between the two types of meetings. Neither administrative cabinet meetings nor school board meetings are most representative of the preferences of school officials over all school districts. For four school districts, the administrative cabinet meeting is the more responsive forum. In five districts, school board meetings yield a higher responsiveness score vis-à-vis school officials' preferences. In one district, Stumont, there is a tie between cabinet meeting and school board meeting responsiveness scores. Thus, as has been the case for elite preferences and public preferences, neither the school board meeting nor the administrative cabinet meeting is the universally superior form of school official behavior.

Aggregate agenda responsiveness to school officials' preferences is quite similar to the pattern discussed for responsiveness to elite preferences. As has been the case for elite and public preferences, Stumont shows the lowest responsiveness score. However, the score for school official preferences is 60, which is quite comparable to the 63 score for elite preferences. Similarly, most of the scores for the other school districts are in the range of 80's and 90's, and the overall mean of 84 is virtually the same as that for responsiveness to elite preferences. Thus, the agendas of meetings in school districts are quite responsive to the preferences of school board members and administrators.

In 6 of 10 school districts, both school board meetings and cabinet meetings make an independent contribution to the overall level of responsiveness. In 4, administrative cabinet meetings do *not* make an independent contribution to the overall responsiveness score independent of school board meetings. In 1, the responsiveness scores of school board meetings and administrative cabinet meetings are identical, indicating perfect overlap.

When we divide responsiveness scores of school board meetings into discussions with and without public participation, we find that in three districts most discussions which are responsive to the preferences of school officials do not stimulate public participation. In three districts fewer than half of the responsive discussions at school board meetings contain public participation. It is interesting to note that two of those three are districts in which there was a similar pattern of low public participation with respect to discussions responsive to elite preferences.

When we reconsider the question, Which forum is most responsive to the preferences of our various survey populations? we find no consistent pattern. In five districts, the school board meeting is the forum which is the most responsive to the preferences of each of our survey populations. In three districts, the administrative cabinet meeting is the forum most responsive to the preferences of each of our three survey populations. In two districts, there is shifting among the three survey populations. Thus, a division of labor with respect to responsiveness is plausible. For five districts, school board meetings are the major forum of responsiveness; for three districts, administrative cabinet meetings are the major forum of responsiveness.

Which group's concerns are most reflected in the responsiveness scores of the various forums of decision-making? For all meetings, elite preferences are most closely matched in six districts. In four districts the preferences of school officials are most closely matched. In *no* district are public preferences most closely matched. For cabinet meetings, matching of elite and school official preferences is balanced. In four districts, elite preferences are most closely matched by the agendas of cabinet meetings. In four districts, the preferences of school officials are most closely matched by the agendas of cabinet meetings. In two, there is a tie between matching elite preferences and school official preferences at cabinet meetings. School board meetings most closely match the preferences of community elites in five districts. The preferences of school officials are most closely matched by school board meetings in three districts. The public's preferences are most closely matched in school board meetings in one, and in one district, there is a tie between the matching of public preferences and school officials' preferences. Considering only the discussions at school board meetings in which there is public participation; the public is the most closely matched in three districts, elite preferences are most closely matched in four districts, and school officials' preferences are most closely matched in three districts.

When we inquire: which group's concerns are most reflected over *all* types of meetings? we find that in five districts the concerns of community elites are most frequently matched at school district meetings, and in three districts, the concerns of school officials are most frequently matched in school district meetings. In the other districts no single actor's agenda is most frequently addressed. In no district are the concerns of the public most frequently matched in all or most forums of discussion and decision-making.

## Symbolic Responsiveness

A second congruence definition of responsiveness is symbolic responsiveness. Symbolic responsiveness focuses on the behavior of school officials and perceptions of constituents. School officials engage in symbolic responsiveness when they manipulate political symbols in order to generate and maintain support. Eulau and Karps note that

> The need for giving symbolic reassurance is being demonstrated by the "reach out" efforts of the new President of the United States—walking down Pennsylvania Avenue after his inauguration, fireside chats, telephonic call-athons, visits to stricken economic areas, being "Jimmy" Carter, etc. The purpose of all of these symbolic acts is to project an image that the President is truly the people's representative and ready to be responsive to them [1977, pp. 246–247].

Symbolic responsiveness can also be measured in terms of constituent perceptions. For constituents, what matters in symbolic responsiveness is that the constituents feel represented, quite regardless of whether the representative is responsive in his policy stance or the service or public goods he provides for his constituency.

Table 8.4 presents information on symbolic behaviors by the 11 school boards. The focus is on the opportunities boards present to the public for participating in the school board legislative session. School board meetings are nominally open to the public, and all school boards solicit public attendance and participation in discussions. However, the opportunity for public attendance is, in large measure, a function of how frequently meetings are held and when the public can voice their concerns. The range of meeting frequency is from one to four per month, with most boards holding two meetings per month. Seven boards hold all meetings in the evenings, three hold some meetings in the afternoon, and one holds all meetings in the afternoon. It is obviously more convenient for the average person to attend evening meetings. Holding meetings in the mornings or afternoons is a subtle, but effective, method of reducing public participation. Finally, it is possible to examine when, during the meetings, constituents may make comments on items not on the formal agenda. Five school boards reserve time at the beginning of each meeting to hear general comments, three make constituents wait until the formal agenda has been completed, and three have no regular arrangement for general comments.

Although these indicators of symbolic responsiveness behavior by school boards are qualitative, it is clear that school boards vary widely in convenience of

TABLE 8.4

SYMBOLIC RESPONSIVENESS

OPPORTUNITY FOR PUBLIC PARTICIPATION

| District | Regular School Board Meetings Per Month | Time | Items From Constituents |
|---|---|---|---|
| Coldren Corners | 2 | Evenings | End of meeting |
| Barwig Park | 2 | Evenings | Beginning of meeting |
| Nelsonville | 2 | Evenings | Beginning of meeting |
| Leeville | 2 | Evenings | No regular agenda item |
| Kentington | 1 | Evenings | Beginning of meeting |
| Macktown | 2 | One morning or afternoon, one evening | Beginning of meeting |
| Ballard City | 2 | Afternoons | Beginning of meeting |
| Drummond Falls | 4 | Three afternoon, one evening | End of meeting |
| Hartshorne Hts. | 2 | one morning, one evening | No regular agenda item |
| Grahamdale | 2 | Evenings | End of meeting |
| Stumont | 1 | Evenings | No regular agenda item |

TABLE 8.5

SYMBOLIC RESPONSIVENESS

CONSTITUENT PERCEPTION OF SCHOOL OFFICIALS

| District | Satisfied With School Board | Satisfied With Superintendent | District Efficacy Score |
|---|---|---|---|
| Coldren Corners | 48 | 39 | 48 |
| Barwig Park | 53 | 61 | 53 |
| Nelsonville | 55 | 62 | 51 |
| Leeville | 39 | 48 | 39 |
| Kentington | 51 | 57 | 54 |
| Macktown | 56 | 66 | 49 |
| Ballard City | 36 | 45 | 41 |
| Drummond Falls | 36 | 39 | 45 |
| Hartshorne Hts. | 43 | 45 | 48 |
| Grahamdale | 54 | 46 | 46 |
| Stumont | 45 | 51 | 44 |
| Mean | 47 | 46 | 47 |

lay participation. We can say that, in terms of frequency of meetings, the school board in Drummond Falls gives the public greatest opportunity for participation by meeting. In terms of *when* during the day the school board meeting is held, the Drummond Falls district is seen to be much less responsive. Three meetings per month are held during the afternoon. Moreover, there is a distinct tendency for the evening meetings to resemble public hearings and for legislative sessions to be confined almost entirely to the afternoon sessions. The Ballard City school board is similarly unresponsive in the sense that both its monthly school board meetings are held in the afternoon. In Hartshorne Hts. and in Macktown, the two school board meetings are held at different times. One school board meeting per month is held during the evening, and the other school board meeting is held during the morning or afternoon. In the other seven school districts, all school board meetings are held in the evening.

Table 8.5 summarizes three indices of symbolic responsiveness that focus on public attitudes. The first is a score based on the survey responses to a question soliciting overall satisfaction with school board performance. The second is a score concerning satisfaction with the superintendent, and the third is the average efficacy score presented in chapter 3. These scores are an attempt to capture the intensity of satisfaction with school board, superintendent, and overall intensity of efficacy in each of the 11 school districts. The mean satisfaction score for school boards is 47; the range is from a low of 36 to a high of 56. The mean satisfaction score for superintendents is 46, with a range from 39 to 66. The mean for school district efficacy is a score of 47, with a range from 39 to 54.

Clearly, constituents do not give their school boards or superintendents particularly high satisfaction ratings. However, it is important to note that these scores are generally in line with satisfaction ratings for the President, Congress, and other political figures. The mean satisfaction scores for school boards and superintendents are generally quite close within each school district. It is also interesting that in 9 of 11 school districts, the superintendent's satisfaction score is higher than the school district's satisfaction score. Generally speaking, constituents are slightly more satisfied with their superintendent than they are with their school board.

The rhetoric of symbolic responsiveness is employed by all school officials virtually all the time; they all express a desire to hear and respond to public preferences. Efficacy scores gauge the extent to which laymen are persuaded by promises (and to a lesser extent, by performance) that school officials will respond favorably to constituent demands.

The 11 school districts exhibit only moderate levels of lay efficacy. The mean scores of the three perceptual indices of symbolic responsiveness are nearly identical. Variation across indices within districts is minor. It seems that the public views school boards and superintendents as being about as symbolically responsive as other legislative bodies and executive officials. They are perceived as only moderately responsive.

## Service Responsiveness

Service responsiveness is our first measure of representational responsiveness. As Eulau and Karps state,

> Service responsiveness concerns the non-legislative services that a representative actually performs for individuals or groups in his district. Service responsiveness, then, refers to the advantages and benefits which the representative is able to obtain for particular constituents [1977, p. 243].

Service responsiveness concerns demands made by constituents that are limited in scope, and responses of school officials.

The concept of service responsiveness is most clearly relevant to the state and federal levels of governments. Those units are so large and complicated that constituents often ask legislators and others to intervene for them with large and distant bureaucracies. Since school districts are units of local government, distance is no impediment to direct constituent input. The average citizen can easily communicate with teachers, principals, and school district administrators. Size, however, may be an impediment to direct citizen contact with school officials. Many school districts are such large and complex organizations that laymen may still contact school board members and superintendents to intervene with or to direct them to appropriate school district officials.

As was documented in chapter 7, school district residents do contact school board members and administrators to ask favors. Our measures of service responsiveness focus on the disposition of requests for action made by the public in private communications with school board members and superintendents. Not all demands articulated by laymen in private are service requests. Service respon-

TABLE 8.6

SERVICE RESPONSIVENESS: ACTION

| District | School Board Action Taken | School Board Not Refused | Superintendents Action Taken | Superintendents Not Refused | All School Officials Action Taken | All School Officials Not Refused |
|---|---|---|---|---|---|---|
| Coldren Corners | 14 | 100 | 28 | 84 | 23 | 91 |
| Barwig Park | 20 | 93 | 45 | 73 | 38 | 78 |
| Nelsonville | 33 | 100 | 60 | 77 | 44 | 90 |
| Leeville | 71 | 97 | 66 | 93 | 69 | 96 |
| Kentington | 50 | 94 | 27 | 95 | 34 | 94 |
| Macktown | 49 | 97 | 40 | 100 | 45 | 98 |
| Ballard City | -- | -- | -- | -- | -- | -- |
| Drummond Falls | 22 | 92 | 11 | 98 | 12 | 97 |
| Hartshorne Hts. | 59 | 98 | 64 | 85 | 62 | 91 |
| Grahamdale | 44 | 93 | 43 | 97 | 43 | 96 |
| Stumont | 42 | 83 | 93 | 99 | 64 | 90 |
| Mean | 40 | 95 | 48 | 90 | 43 | 92 |

siveness is a concept relevant to requests which entail less than entire school districts. For example, a parent who asks that his or her child be transferred from one school to another is making a service request. A parent who proposes a district-wide procedure for transferring students between schools is making a policy request. Our indices of service responsiveness are based on private communications which include requests for action whose consequences are less than district in scope.

Table 8.6 presents two indices of service responsiveness for school board members, superintendents, and all school officials. The first service index is the proportion of times school officials comply with the request for action made by the petitioning constituent. The second service index is the proportion of requests for action which are not refused by school officials. Not all service requests are either refused or granted. Requests could also be pending or be referred to more appropriate officials.

Passive responsiveness scores are much higher than the active responsiveness scores for all actors in all school districts. The mean passive scores are 92 for all school officials, 90 for administrators, and 95 for school board members. The mean active service responsiveness scores are 43 for all school officials, 48 for administrators, and 40 for school board members. There is much greater variation across districts in active service responsiveness scores than in passive service responsiveness scores.

It is interesting to note that, of the five districts in which the superintendent is more responsive according to the *active* measure of service responsiveness, the school board is more responsive according to the *passive* measure of service responsiveness. This indicates that the superintendent is more active in both granting and denying service requests. Superintendents and other top administrators have greater authority to grant or deny service requests from a constituent than do board members. The overall high level of passive school board member responsiveness, coupled with low levels of active school board responsiveness, suggests that service requests made to school board members are typically passed along to other officials.

How should one interpret the levels of service responsiveness? Obviously, school officials in all districts are extremely responsive in a passive sense. Service requests are rarely refused. Even the most refusing actors refuse only one in four requests. Active responsiveness to service requests is another matter. We interpret the mean scores of less than 50 percent as low. Unlike interactions at public meetings, private communications between school officials and the lay public can be lengthy exchanges. The school official has an opportunity to indicate when an action requested is beyond his or her ability or authority to take. The constituent then has an opportunity to make a more appropriate request for action which the official can fulfill. For example, after a board member explains that he or she cannot order a principal to have a playground swing repaired, the constituent can ask the board member to refer the request to an appropriate administrator. Similarly, after a superintendent explains that his options on finance are constrained by state law, the constituent can ask that officials of state government be informed of local need.

Only three school boards and four superintendents report active service responsiveness at the level of 50 percent. This is not to say that a majority of service requests in most districts are not ultimately granted. Our data often do not include the final disposition of requests. Nevertheless, it is clear that in most districts most service requests do not receive a timely positive response.

Another set of service responsiveness indices can be based on constituent satisfaction. Table 8.7 presents active and passive measures of service responsiveness satisfaction. Data are school officials' perceptions of lay satisfaction with private contacts dealing with requests less than district in scope. While a school official may not be able or disposed to fulfill a constituent's request for action, the constituent may nevertheless be satisfied because the school official was courteous, gave good reasons why action could not be taken at the time, suggested a more appropriate target for the request, etc. Thus, we would expect that virtually all cases of action taken as requested would also be cases of satisfaction, and that some cases of action not taken would also be cases of perceived constituent satisfaction.

As table 8.7 indicates, satisfaction scores are higher than action scores for service responsiveness. Passive satisfaction scores are higher than are active satisfaction scores. School board members perceive that they achieve greater satisfaction in service requests than do superintendents. Board active scores are higher than superintendent active scores in eight districts. Board passive scores are higher in seven districts. In only one district does the superintendent report greater active and passive constituent satisfaction than do school board members.

In the passive sense, all districts are quite responsive in satisfying constituents who make service requests. Active satisfaction is also quite high. All districts achieve combined active scores above 60. Only one disaggregated score is lower than 50. School officials clearly perceive that they do a good job

TABLE 8.7

SERVICE RESPONSIVENESS: SATISFACTION

| District | School Board Satisfied | Not Dis- satisfied | Superintendent Satisfied | Not Dis- satisfied | All School Officials Satisfied | Not Dis- satisfied |
|---|---|---|---|---|---|---|
| Coldren Corners | 82 | 82 | 64 | 76 | 70 | 78 |
| Barwig Park | 76 | 83 | 55 | 64 | 71 | 79 |
| Nelsonville | 54 | 93 | 83 | 88 | 68 | 90 |
| Leeville | 76 | 77 | 74 | 81 | 75 | 79 |
| Kentington | 82 | 82 | 77 | 86 | 79 | 85 |
| Macktown | 91 | 96 | 43 | 93 | 73 | 95 |
| Ballard City | -- | -- | -- | -- | -- | -- |
| Drummond Falls | 76 | 76 | 66 | 73 | 69 | 74 |
| Hartshorne Hts. | 62 | 67 | 50 | 50 | 62 | 67 |
| Grahamdale | 74 | 75 | 65 | 65 | 72 | 73 |
| Stumont | 69 | 77 | 85 | 85 | 71 | 78 |
| Mean | 74 | 81 | 66 | 69 | 71 | 80 |

of satisfying constituents who make private contacts—even when requested action is not taken. This index of responsiveness based on school officials' perceptions of constituents' feelings indicates that school officials are responsive to those who articulate private requests in private settings.

## Policy Responsiveness

At the opposite end of the scope of impact continuum from service requests are policy proposals. Proposals are deemed policy in scope if they would apply throughout the district. Policy requests may be articulated either in private communications or in public meetings. Action on most policy scope issues is ultimately taken by the school board in a regular legislative session. In this section indices of policy responsiveness will be developed from both objective and subjective data in the Demand-Response Logs. Policy responsiveness in public meetings and private contacts will be evaluated.

## POLICY RESPONSIVENESS AT PUBLIC MEETINGS

Objective measures of policy responsiveness at public meetings focus on the extent to which school boards defer to lay preferences articulated at school board meetings. Constituent behavior is operationalized as demands made at school board meetings—statements in support of or opposition to specific policy pro-

TABLE 8.8

OPPORTUNITY FOR SCHOOL BOARD POLICY RESPONSIVENESS

| District | % Discussions With Public Demands | % Discussions With Public Demand And Decision | % Discussions With Public Plurality Position And Decision |
|---|---|---|---|
| Coldren Corners | 13 | 8 | 7 |
| Barwig Park | 1 | 0 | 0 |
| Nelsonville | 5 | 0 | 0 |
| Leeville | 33 | 24 | 24 |
| Kentington | 1 | 0 | 0 |
| Macktown | 6 | 2 | 2 |
| Ballard City | 8 | 1 | 1 |
| Drummond Falls | 15 | 1 | 1 |
| Hartshorne Hts. | 24 | 11 | 11 |
| Grahamdale | 4 | 2 | 2 |
| Stumont | 4 | 2 | 1 |
| Mean | 10 | 5 | 4 |

TABLE 8.9

SCHOOL BOARD POLICY RESPONSIVENESS

| District | % Decisions Which Match Public Plurality Preference | % Voting Decisions Which Match Public Preference & Division of Opinion |
|---|---|---|
| Coldren Corners | 45 | 30 |
| Barwig Park | * | * |
| Nelsonville | * | * |
| Leeville | 51 | 40 |
| Kentington | * | * |
| Macktown | 100 | 100 |
| Ballard City | 100 | 50 |
| Drummond Falls | 33 | 0 |
| Hartshorne Hts. | 68 | 42 |
| Grahamdale | 75 | 75 |
| Stumont | 67 | 33 |
| Mean | 67 | 46 |

*Data unavailable

posals. School board behavior is operationalized in terms of decisions reached. The policy responsiveness score is the proportion of school board decisions which match the plurality preference position of constituent statements.

Three elements must be present in a school board discussion unit for it to provide an opportunity for policy responsiveness. First, public demands must be articulated. Second, a school board decision relating to public demands must be made. Third, a public plurality preference must be ascertainable. Public demand articulation at school board meetings was rare and tended to cluster in a few meetings. Table 8.8 documents how rarely the conditions necessary to gauge policy responsiveness at school board meetings occurred in each district. In three districts the conditions never existed even though hundreds of discussions and decisions were recorded! In another five districts fewer than two percent of discussions qualify. Only Leeville, Hartshorne Hts., and Coldren Corners present more than minimal opportunities to evaluate policy responsiveness. Even in these three districts the numbers of cases are small: 81 in Leeville, 19 in Hartshorne Hts., and 20 in Coldren Corners.

Since the index of policy responsiveness at school board meetings is based on so few cases, evaluation of district scores in table 8.9 must, of necessity, be tentative. Of the eight districts for which scores can be computed, five are responsive in at least two of every three opportunities. On this responsiveness continuum, Macktown and Ballard City cluster at the top, followed by Grahamdale, Hartshorne Hts., and Stumont. Leeville, Coldren Corners, and Drummond Falls are in the unresponsive range of this potentially unstable continuum.

The normative and empirical emphasis on unanimous school board approval of policy measures make a second index of policy responsiveness at school board meetings desirable. An obvious problem of unanimous decision-making is that, when division of public opinion exists, some preferences must be unrepresented. A school board which consistently makes decisions unanimously even though constituent opinion is narrowly divided, is in some sense unresponsive, even though all decisions may be in accordance with the preferences of a majority of constituents. This larger concept of responsiveness requires both acceptance of majority lay preferences and representation of minority lay preferences.

A distributional index of policy responsiveness at school board meetings is also presented in table 8.9. Operationalization of constituent behavior is the same as for the first policy responsiveness index. School board behavior is operationalized as voting decisions. Matching occurs when (1) all lay comments are in support of the proposal under discussion and the school board vote is unanimously in favor, (2) all lay comments are in opposition and the vote is unanimously to reject, or (3) lay comments are divided and the board adopts the lay plurality preferences by a divided vote.

The lower scores of this distributional index are a consequence of unanimous school board voting despite divided lay preferences. Only two districts' distributional responsiveness scores are as high as their scores on the less restrictive index. Only Macktown and Grahamdale achieve scores of higher than 50. While school board decisions may generally match constituent preferences in some school districts, school board acknowledgment of minority preferences is low. In the larger, distributional sense, school boards are not very responsive in their decision-making behavior.

A subjective index of school board policy responsiveness at meetings can be based on Demand-Response Log data collected from individuals who articulated policy preferences at meetings. Table 8.10 presents proportions of lay participants at school board meetings who reported that they were satisfied and not dissatisfied with school officials' responses to their presentations. All cases of lay demand articulation are included in this index, regardless of whether a decision was made. Thus, the subjective indices of school board meeting policy responsiveness include discussions which did not qualify for inclusion in the objective indices.

Subjective satisfaction scores are generally lower than objective scores of matching lay preferences. This is largely due to the different data bases of the two indices and the fact that laymen are usually not satisfied when school boards defer action on their requests. Only three school boards satisfied more than half of our sample of articulate laymen. Six boards do not dissatisfy half or more of our sample of articulate laymen.

## POLICY RESPONSIVENESS IN PRIVATE CONTACTS

Our objective measure of policy responsiveness in private contacts focuses on the extent to which constituent requests for action are fulfilled. Our subjective measure focuses on constituent satisfaction resulting from the private contact as perceived by the reporting official. These indices directly parallel those developed

TABLE 8.10

PUBLIC SATISFACTION WITH RESPONSE AT SCHOOL BOARD MEETINGS

| District | N | % Satisfied | % Not Dissatisfied |
|---|---|---|---|
| Coldren Corners | 171 | 64 | 70 |
| Barwig Park | 27 | 7 | 41 |
| Nelsonville | -- | -- | -- |
| Leeville | 65 | 3 | 29 |
| Kentington | 9 | 33 | 89 |
| Macktown | 9 | 44 | 89 |
| Ballard City | -- | -- | -- |
| Drummond Falls | 27 | 56 | 67 |
| Hartshorne Hts. | 44 | 57 | 80 |
| Grahamdale | 18 | 33 | 50 |
| Stumont | 8 | 25 | 38 |
| Mean | 42 | 36 | 61 |

TABLE 8.11

POLICY RESPONSIVENESS FOR PRIVATE CONTACTS: ACTION

| District | School Board | | Administrators | | All School Officials | |
|---|---|---|---|---|---|---|
| | Action Taken | Not Refused | Action Taken | Not Refused | Action Taken | Not Refused |
| Coldren Corners | 10 | 96 | 43 | 79 | 25 | 88 |
| Barwig Park | 32 | 86 | 59 | 84 | 48 | 85 |
| Nelsonville | 26 | 96 | 67 | 87 | 33 | 94 |
| Leeville | 48 | 77 | 27 | 91 | 46 | 79 |
| Kentington | 30 | 94 | 58 | 93 | 34 | 94 |
| Macktown | 42 | 100 | 47 | 80 | 44 | 89 |
| Ballard City | -- | -- | -- | -- | -- | -- |
| Drummond Falls | 40 | 91 | 49 | 93 | 46 | 91 |
| Hartshorne Hts. | 43 | 86 | 58 | 83 | 46 | 85 |
| Grahamdale | 36 | 97 | 74 | 97 | 60 | 97 |
| Stumont | 25 | 84 | 100 | 100 | 31 | 85 |
| Mean | 33 | 91 | 58 | 89 | 41 | 89 |

earlier for service responsiveness. The difference between service and policy responsiveness is scope of action requested. Service requests include only less than district-wide scopes; policy requests include district and greater level scopes.

Table 8.11 indicates that active responsiveness scores are very low, and passive responsiveness scores are quite high. In 9 of 10 districts, superintendent active scores are higher than school board active scores. This reflects the reality that individual school board members are less capable of granting private policy demands at the time they are made than are superintendents. Superintendents frequently have the power to take policy action on their own. Individual school board members almost never have that authority.

Superintendents are fairly responsive to policy requests made in private in a more absolute sense. Six of 10 superintendents report an active responsiveness rate of greater than 50 percent. Laymen are better advised to make their policy requests in private to executive school authorities. Because of scarcity of data on active policy responsiveness at school board meetings, comparisons between rates of policy responsiveness in public and private must be extremely tentative. However, if one considers the probability of receiving *any* official response as well as the probability of receiving a favorable response it is our judgment that active policy responsiveness results more from private lay contacts than from public lay presentations.

TABLE 8.12

POLICY RESPONSIVENESS FOR PRIVATE CONTACTS:  SATISFACTION

| District | School Board | | Superintendent | | All School Officials | |
|---|---|---|---|---|---|---|
| | Satisfied | Not Dis-satisfied | Satisfied | Not Dis-satisfied | Satisfied | Not Dis-satisfied |
| Coldren Corners | 65 | 77 | 80 | 84 | 72 | 81 |
| Barwig Park | 77 | 79 | 65 | 71 | 73 | 77 |
| Nelsonville | 43 | 92 | 94 | 94 | 56 | 93 |
| Leeville | 61 | 62 | 82 | 82 | 63 | 64 |
| Kentington | 72 | 86 | 80 | 85 | 76 | 86 |
| Macktown | 83 | 100 | 57 | 57 | 69 | 77 |
| Ballard City | -- | -- | -- | -- | -- | -- |
| Drummond Falls | 67 | 67 | 71 | 83 | 70 | 78 |
| Hartshorne Hts. | 50 | 59 | 0 | 0 | 49 | 57 |
| Grahamdale | 86 | 90 | 96 | 96 | 89 | 92 |
| Stumont | 67 | 75 | -- | -- | 67 | 75 |
| Mean | 67 | 79 | 69 | 72 | 68 | 78 |

Table 8.12 presents indices of perceived lay satisfaction resulting from policy-oriented private contacts. As was the case for service responsiveness, school officials perceive constituent satisfaction even when they do not take policy action. Both active and passive measures of satisfaction are quite high. Schools clearly think themselves to be extremely responsive in the sense that they satisfy constituents who articulate policy demands to them in private.

## Influence Responsiveness

Our final measure of representational responsiveness is responsiveness as public influence on school officials' attitudes and behavior. The operational focus is on the extent to which constituents and school officials perceive that the latter are influenced by the former. While service and policy responsiveness can be measured objectively, influence is a purely subjective assessment.

An influence concept of representational responsiveness is a useful complement to our other definitions for two reasons. First, most policy decisions are not presented as choices between "policy X or *not* policy X." As they are used in all political processes, compromises and amendments are employed by the school boards and administrators. While a citizen who voices opposition to a proposal may see his policy preferences voted down at a school board meeting, he may nevertheless achieve *some* desirable modification as a result of his participation. For example, a group of parents may fail to prevent the adoption of a sex education curriculum, but by their protest may influence the board to initiate the program on a limited trial basis. The black and white distinction between match and nonmatch of policy action and constituent preference made by some service and policy measures does not accurately reflect the grayness of a policy process. A second reason for including an influence concept of responsiveness follows from the fact that a vast majority of decisions are recurring, routine matters which will be subject to review and revision in the near future. Thus, while a school board may fail to enact a constituent proposal today, school board members may be influenced to reconsider and pass the proposal later. A school board may be unable to start an extracurricular soccer program, when asked to do so by a student and some parents, due to lack of funds. Although the board refuses the requested action today, they may be influenced to make soccer the highest priority item for the following fiscal year. In many cases, an objective observation of constituent requests and school official action may present a picture of nonresponsiveness. Yet, according to the subjective perceptions of constituents and school officials, the officials *were* responsive to the extent that they were influenced by constituents.

To assess influence responsiveness, we (1) asked citizens who made policy requests at school board meetings whether they thought their presentation influenced school officials, (2) asked school officials if they were influenced by those presentations, and (3) asked school officials if they were influenced by constituents who initiated private contacts. Thus, from public meetings we have subjective data, from the perspective of both the constituents and school officials. Our data from meetings are limited to school board meetings due to low level of public participation in administrative cabinet meetings. We also have subjective data on the influence of constituents in their private contacts with school officials. These data, of course, express the perspectives of the school officials only.

What levels of influence responsiveness should we expect from school board members, school administrators, and all school officials? Public participation in school board meetings is extremely rare. On the average, constituents speak in only one of five discussions at school board meetings. Since public participation is so rare, we might expect that on those few occasions when the public does participate, such participation would be heeded and deemed influential by school board members and school administrators. Similarly, the average school board member receives on the average of three unique private contacts from constituents per month, and the average superintendent receives about one per working day. By any standards, the frequency of contact between constituents and school officials is low. Thus, using the same reasoning, we might hypothesize that since private contacts are so rare, on those few occasions when members of the public do speak, they will exert influence over school board members and administrators.

Table 8.13 summarizes influence of lay participants at school board meetings. School board members and administrators report that they are generally not influenced by constituents who speak at school board meetings. The mean influence score for school board members is 28, the mean influence score for superintendents is 25, and the mean influence score for all school officials is 28. The mean influence scores mask the fact that superintendents perceive greater lay influence than board members do in three school districts. Not surprisingly, constituents

TABLE 8.13

PUBLIC INFLUENCE AT SCHOOL BOARD MEETINGS

| District | School Board Perspective | Administrators' Perspective | All School Official Perspective | Public's Perspective |
|---|---|---|---|---|
| Coldren Corners | 23 | 31 | 23 | 56 |
| Barwig Park | 20 | 0 | 20 | 27 |
| Nelsonville | 50 | 25 | 45 | * |
| Leeville | 49 | 36 | 51 | 55 |
| Kentington | 16 | 57 | 21 | 57 |
| Macktown | 12 | 0 | 10 | 33 |
| Ballard City | -- | -- | -- | -- |
| Drummond Falls | 43 | 39 | 42 | 42 |
| Hartshorne Hts. | 33 | 36 | 34 | 70 |
| Grahamdale | 16 | 10 | 15 | 43 |
| Stumont | 18 | 15 | 16 | 25 |
| Mean | 28 | 25 | 28 | 45 |

* Insufficient data


TABLE 8.14

PUBLIC INFLUENCE IN PRIVATE CONTACTS

| District | School Board | Super-intendent | All School Officials |
|---|---|---|---|
| Coldren Corners | 52 | 13 | 36 |
| Barwig Park | 64 | 4 | 37 |
| Nelsonville | 57 | 63 | 60 |
| Leeville | 51 | 68 | 56 |
| Kentington | 53 | 61 | 58 |
| Macktown | 59 | 60 | 58 |
| Ballard City | — | — | — |
| Drummond Falls | 49 | 33 | 40 |
| Hartshorne Hts. | 28 | 15 | 24 |
| Grahamdale | 32 | 25 | 28 |
| Stumont | 30 | 75 | 31 |
| Mean | 48 | 42 | 43 |

perceive a greater level of influence than do school officials. The mean constituent perception score is 45. In only one case is the constituent perception score not higher than the corresponding school board, superintendent, or total school official perception score. These aggregate figures reflect the common situation where the person who attends and speaks out at school board meetings sees himself as an active, informed, influential citizen; while school officials see him as a chronic meeting attender. (In seven school districts one or a few individuals do make a disproportionate amount of public demands.) [1]

There is substantial variance among school districts concerning the level of influence reported by school officials and members of the public. It is interesting to note that there is only one school board perspective score, one administrator perspective score, and one total school official score over 50. However, it is a different district in every case. In seven districts, board members report greater influence scores than do administrators. Apparently, it is easier for laymen to influence members of the school board than it is for them to influence superintendents.

According to school officials, laymen participating in public meetings generally fail to influence school board members and superintendents. However, from the perspective of the constituents who are the participants, lay participation is influential.

Public influence is greater in private contacts than in public meetings (table 8.14). The mean private influence score reported by school board members is 48. The mean score reported by administrators is 42. The mean score reported by all school officials is 43. The mean level of public influence from private contacts is higher than the mean level of public influence resulting from appearances at school board meetings, and the scores for all school officials are higher for all but two districts. Thus, it is a fair generalization that members of the public exert greater influence over school officials when they discuss their concerns in private than when they discuss their concerns at a public school board meeting.

It is important to bear in mind that we are dealing with slightly different units of analysis when we consider private interactions and public interactions. In the public interaction, the constituent makes a formal statement to the school board. In terms of discussion and statement units, the participation is limited to a single discussion period and usually a very small number of statements. The private contact is an extended interaction between an individual constituent and an individual school official. Virtually all private contacts contain both elements of information exchange and requests for action. Presentations at school board meetings to request action are more uniform in the nature of statements—most are policy demands. In a private contact a school official may be influenced by either demand or informational statements. Private communications present greater opportunities for lay influence because school officials may be influenced by the demand articulation or the information exchange component of the interaction.

We saw that at school board meetings, it was easier for constituents to exert influence over school board members than administrators. In private contacts, the same pattern holds for the mean scores for all districts. However, on a district-by-district basis, a mixed pattern emerges. School board members report higher levels of influence than administrators do in five school districts. In the other four school districts, administrators report greater levels of lay influence in private contacts than do school board members. Thus, while the public seems to exert a consistently higher level of influence with school board members than with administrators as a result of participation in school board meetings, the influence they exert in private contacts is much more mixed.

The range of influence among superintendents is appreciably greater than it is among school boards. Five districts' superintendent influence scores are 60 and above; the other five districts' scores are 33 and below. Two administrative styles are apparent. The first is a style in which lay input rarely influences professional judgment. The second is a style in which professional perceptions are frequently modified by lay input.

Are levels of influence resulting from public presentations and private communications related? Do school officials who report that lay demand articulation at school board meetings is influential also report that lay private communications are influential? These questions can be answered by correlation analysis. The results indicate that influence levels resulting from public and private lay communications are largely independent. The correlation coefficient for school board scores is .10, for superintendent scores is .16, and for all school officials scores is .27. There is no consistent pattern of influence responsiveness. In one district, neither board nor superintendent is subject to influence through public or private contact. In one the board alone is not subject to influence; in another the superintendent alone is not subject to influence. In seven districts both are subject to influence—some in private only and some in private and public. In short, the constituent who wishes to influence school district officials is best advised to make both private and public contact with board members and superintendents. However, there is certainly no guarantee that either mode of contact with any school official will result in influence. Overall, influence results in a minority of school official-constituent interactions. Nevertheless, in spite of the fact that some school officials are virtually impermeable to public influence, the best opportunities for success are in private communication. In no district is public communication alone the most likely means of influence.

## Differential Responsiveness in Private Communication

Which requests for action are most likely to be met with a timely positive response from school district officials? Because so few cases of lay requests for action made at public meetings result in prompt favorable disposition, analysis must focus on private communications data. This section inquires about the characteristics of requests for action that are more successful than average in each school district: which sources, tones, scopes, and topics are most likely to achieve favorable response from school district officials.

Source of request is not a helpful predictor of superintendent responsiveness. However, the nature of communication is a good predictor. Although private communications usually contain both demand and informational components, an overall tone of demand articulation or information exchange characterizes almost all interactions. Communications perceived as informational are more likely to generate a positive response from superintendents than are those more demanding in tone.

Policy requests to superintendents are more successful than service requests. Additionally, the chances of positive response are enhanced if the request is conveyed to the superintendent so that he can agree with the premises of the requester. Finally, requests involving the topics of parents and parental participation in educational affairs are more likely to be well received. In summary, a private request made of a superintendent is more likely to be successful if it is policy in scope, informational in tone, concerning ideas with which the superintendent agrees, or concerning the role of parents.

While superintendents tend to be more responsive to policy requests, school board members tend to be more responsive to service requests. School board members tend to be more responsive to parents than to other sources of private communication, but they do not seem to vary their response by topic of private communication. As do superintendents, board members react more positively to communications which are informational in tone. Board members are also more sympathetic to lay communicators with whom they are in agreement. Clearly, for both superintendents and school board members, the process by which a demand is communicated is of equal or greater importance than the content of the demand.

The layman who desires a timely positive response from school district officials to a request for action would be well advised to consider how the request might be most effectively communicated. The probability of success will be enhanced if the petitioner acknowledges the expert-lay relationship by articulating his demand in the context of a larger exchange of information. Requests should be phrased so that the school official can agree with the layman's point of view. Policy requests should be directed to superintendents, service requests to board members. Parents should contact board members, but those who wish to discuss parents should contact superintendents. As do other public officials, school district officials react to both the substance and the style of citizen communications.

## Responsiveness in Perspective

Are school district officials responsive to their constituents? The answer to this question will vary sharply according to the kind of responsiveness being measured. We have discussed two major conceptions of responsiveness, congruence and representational. Within this framework, five theoretical definitions of responsiveness have been presented, and multiple operational definitions of each have been explored. On no measure have all school districts been found either extremely responsive or unresponsive. No individual district has been deemed responsive by all measures; no district has been deemed unresponsive by all measures.

If all operational indicators of responsiveness are treated equally, and each school district is assigned an aggregate responsiveness level, three levels of responsiveness emerge. Ballard City is the least responsive district. Barwig Park and Stumont achieve responsiveness on fewer than half of the indicators. The remaining eight districts achieve responsiveness on more than half.

Although gross aggregate rankings designate districts which are more and less responsive, it is nevertheless the case that each school district is in some senses responsive and in other senses unresponsive. Table 8.15 arrays school districts in nominal rank order on 19 operational indicators of responsiveness which measure on a district-wide basis. Each district achieves some extremely high rankings; each also achieves some extremely low rankings.

## TABLE 8.15:

## RANKINGS OF DISTRICTS ON RESPONSIVENESS INDICES

| | Ag. S.B. | Ag. Cab. | Ag. All | Symbolic | Service--Action | Service--Not Refused | Service--Sat. | Service--Not Dissat. | Policy, S.B. Dec. | Policy, Distribution | Sat.-S.B. Dec. | Not Dissat. S.B. Dec. | Pol. Action Taken | Pol. Resp. Priv. Cont. Not Refused | Pol. Resp. Priv. Cont. Satisfied | Pol. Resp. Priv. Cont. Not Dissatisfied | Influence-S.B. Meet. Sch. Offic. Perspect. | Influence-S.B. Meet. Public Perspect. | Influence-Priv. Contacts |
|---|---|---|---|---|---|---|---|---|---|---|---|---|---|---|---|---|---|---|---|
| Coldren Corners | 10 | 1 | 2.5 | 5.5 | 9 | 6.5 | 7 | 6.5 | 7 | 7 | 1 | 4 | 10 | 6 | 4 | 4 | 5 | 3 | 7 |
| Barvig Park | 8 | 9.5 | 10 | 2 | 7 | 10 | 5.5 | 4.5 | — | — | 8 | 7 | 2 | 8 | 3 | 6.5 | 7 | 8 | 6 |
| Nelsonville | 9 | 4 | 7 | 3 | 5 | 8.5 | 9 | 2 | — | — | — | — | 8 | 2.5 | 9 | 1 | 2 | — | 1 |
| Leeville | 4 | 3 | 4 | 11 | 1 | 3.5 | 2 | 4.5 | 6 | 4 | 9 | 9 | 4 | 10 | 8 | 9 | 1 | 4 | 4 |
| Kentington | 1 | 2 | 1 | 1 | 8 | 5 | 1 | 3 | — | — | 5.5 | 1.5 | 7 | 2.5 | 2 | 3 | 6 | 2 | 2.5 |
| Macktown | 6.5 | 8 | 9 | 4 | 4 | 1 | 3 | 1 | 1.5 | 1 | 4 | 1.5 | 6 | 5 | 6 | 6.5 | 10 | 7 | 2.5 |
| Ballard City | 2 | 9.5 | 6 | 10 | — | — | — | — | 1.5 | 3 | — | — | — | — | — | — | — | — | — |
| Drummond Falls | 3 | 5 | 5 | 8 | 10 | 2 | 8 | 8 | 8 | 8 | 3 | 5 | 4 | 4 | 5 | 5 | 3 | 6 | 5 |
| Hartshorne Hts. | 5 | 7 | 8 | 5.5 | 3 | 6.5 | 10 | 10 | 4 | 5 | 2 | 3 | 4 | 8 | 10 | 10 | 4 | 1 | 10 |
| Grahamdale | 6.5 | 6 | 2.5 | 7 | 6 | 3.5 | 4 | 9 | 3 | 2 | 5.5 | 6 | 1 | 1 | 1 | 2 | 9 | 5 | 9 |
| Stumont | 11 | 11 | 11 | 9 | 2 | 8.5 | 5.5 | 6.5 | 5 | 6 | 7 | 8 | 9 | 8 | 7 | 8 | 8 | 9 | 8 |

School districts exhibit inconsistent patterns of responsiveness on different theoretical and operational measures. This is consistent with Eulau and Karps' (1977) contention that different components of responsiveness may be independent of each other. No theoretical linkages among our five components of responsiveness have been specified. For example, school officials who achieve high agenda responsiveness may achieve low service responsiveness. Similarly, influence and policy responsiveness may be unrelated. It is theoretically possible for school district officials to be responsive on any component of responsiveness and either responsive or unresponsive on any other component. One example is Stumont, a district which is relatively unresponsive in the aggregate. It is deemed unresponsive in the agenda, symbolic, and influence senses. Yet, it is deemed responsive on half of the policy responsiveness indicators and all of the service responsiveness indicators.

The intercorrelations of responsiveness indices across districts produce a similarly inconsistent pattern (table 8.16). Only 12 of 171 possible pairs of indicators are significantly positively correlated at the .05 level of confidence. Moreover, only 6 of 40 coefficients for pairs of operational measures from the same component of responsiveness are significantly positively correlated. Thus, we conclude that operational measures of responsiveness are for the most part mutually independent, both within and across components of responsiveness.

Responsiveness is a complex concept. Our analysis of multiple, theoretical, and operational notions of responsiveness in 11 school districts yields the following conclusions:

School district agendas are quite responsive to public concerns and even more responsive to elite public and school official concerns.

Generally speaking, all forums of school district discussion and decision-making contribute to agenda responsiveness.

In the symbolic sense, school districts seem only moderately responsive.

Service responsiveness is uneven across districts, but is generally not high. Passive service responsiveness and perceived satisfaction, however, are quite high.

Opportunities for policy responsiveness in public forums are rare because of infrequent lay demand articulation and infrequent resolution of issues at the time lay demands are made.

Lay satisfaction with the results of demand articulation at school board meetings varies greatly across districts.

School officials are more responsive to policy requests made in private than to policy requests made in public.

School officials are generally not influenced by constituents who speak at school board meetings.

Constituent influence is greater in private contacts than in public meetings.

There is a considerable range of responsiveness on each operational measure.

School districts' levels of responsiveness vary from index to index.

Each school district is responsive by some definitions and unresponsive by other definitions.

The five theoretical components of responsiveness are mutually independent—both theoretically and empirically.

Operational measures within components of responsiveness are generally independent.

TABLE 8.16:

INTERCORRELATIONS OF RESPONSIVENESS INDICES

| | 1 | 2 | 3 | 4 | 5 | 6 | 7 | 8 | 9 | 10 | 11 | 12 | 13 | 14 | 15 | 16 | 17 | 18 |
|---|---|---|---|---|---|---|---|---|---|---|---|---|---|---|---|---|---|---|
| 1. Agenda S.B. Meetings | -- | | | | | | | | | | | | | | | | | |
| 2. Agenda Cab. Meetings | .42 | -- | | | | | | | | | | | | | | | | |
| 3. Agenda All Meetings | .70* | .84* | -- | | | | | | | | | | | | | | | |
| 4. Symbolic Respon. | -.06 | .15 | .14 | -- | | | | | | | | | | | | | | |
| 5. Svc.-Action Taken | -.21 | -.40 | -.47 | -.41 | -- | | | | | | | | | | | | | |
| 6. Svc. Action Not Refus. | .41 | .36 | .40 | -.47 | -.03 | -- | | | | | | | | | | | | |
| 7. Svc. Satisfied | .33 | .17 | .35 | .05 | -.08 | .23 | -- | | | | | | | | | | | |
| 8. Svc. Not Dissat. | -.08 | -.05 | .01 | .36 | -.07 | .12 | .48 | -- | | | | | | | | | | |
| 9. Pol. S.B. Meet.,Dec. | .39 | -.32 | .19 | .11 | .19 | .45 | .07 | .48 | -- | | | | | | | | | |
| 10. Pol. S.B. Meet.,Dist. | -.04 | -.34 | .01 | .29 | .32 | .36 | .32 | .59 | .80* | -- | | | | | | | | |
| 11. Pol. S.B. Meet.-Sat. | .02 | .29 | .23 | .16 | -.51 | .36 | -.50 | -.18 | .04 | -.18 | -- | | | | | | | |
| 12. Pol. S.B. Meet.Not Dis | .40 | .27 | .39 | .58* | .41 | .34 | .31 | .52 | .28 | | .72* | -- | | | | | | |
| 13. Pol. Priv.-Act. Taken | .36 | -.14 | .12 | -.20 | .12 | .14 | -.06 | -.34 | .47 | .37 | -.28 | -.22 | -- | | | | | |
| 14. Pol. Priv.-Act.Not Ref | .12 | .28 | .43 | .49 | -.54 | .25 | .12 | .20 | .28 | .26 | .40 | .48 | .09 | -- | | | | |
| 15. Pol. Priv.-Satis. | .08 | .03 | .33 | .09 | -.43 | .12 | .60* | .02 | .10 | .27 | -.16 | -.11 | .31 | .48 | -- | | | |
| 16. Pol. Priv.-Not Dissat | -.15 | .21 | .31 | .43 | -.51 | .03 | .36 | .44 | .07 | .23 | .05 | .11 | -.11 | .84* | .59* | -- | | |
| 17. Influence S.B. Meet. Sch. Off. Perspect. | .31 | .53 | .22 | -.39 | .09 | .12 | -.25 | -.18 | -.47 | -.64 | -.09 | -.28 | -.02 | -.28 | -.57 | -.27 | -- | |
| 18. Influence S.B. Meet. Public Perspective | .56 | .75* | .62* | -.04 | .06 | .30 | -.21 | -.40 | .03 | -.22 | .40 | .39 | -.08 | -.03 | -.40 | -.36 | .50 | -- |
| 19. Influence Resp. Priv. | .33 | .33 | .31 | .17 | -.04 | .27 | .57* | .84* | .28 | .30 | -.29 | .23 | -.26 | .09 | -.10 | .28 | .27 | -.02 |

* Significant at .05

Responsiveness in local school districts is obviously a multifaceted and complex phenomenon. Yet, at a more abstract level, a consistent pattern can be identified. Indicators of responsiveness which reflect the point of view of school officials are consistently higher than indicators which reflect the point of view of their constituents and indicators which are based on third party observation.

School district officials clearly believe that they can and do satisfy constituents who interact with them in public and in private, even though they generally do not respond favorably to constituent requests and generally are not influenced by constituent communications. This belief is consistent with the professional orientation of experts toward lay participation in decision-making: the obligation of the expert is only to hear, acknowledge, and consider lay concerns. The high levels of agenda responsiveness, passive action measures of service and policy responsiveness, and satisfaction measures of service and policy responsiveness indicate that school district officials fulfill these limited obligations quite well. The expert is not obligated to accede to, or even be influenced by preferences articulated by laymen. Once laymen have played a limited role in outlining the agenda, decisions should be made by professionals based on their expertise. The deferential behavior of lay school board members toward school district administrators and the low levels of active action service responsiveness, active action policy responsiveness, and influence responsiveness indicate that these norms prevail in school district governance. The mixed record of school district responsiveness reported here is consistent with the patterns in which experts prefer to respond to laymen.

The preference for lay deference is a natural consequence of any policy process which contains elements of the expert-laymen dialogue. Whether they are elected or appointed, local decision-makers are more likely than the public to regard their performance of governmental tasks as satisfactory. Additionally, decision-makers believe they are more responsive to the public than does the public itself. Further, these leaders believe, in higher proportions than does the public, that governmental services are best delivered by "putting the right men in control of government and letting them run things with the help of the best experts they can find" (Subcommittee on Intergovernmental Relations of the Committee on Government Operations, United States Senate, 1973, pp. 146–147). Among major reasons for holding this opinion, local officials indicate that they are more "knowledgeable" about governmental problems than is the public.

Thus, our findings about patterns of responsiveness seem typical of policy-making in which a major perceived resource is knowledge, the domain of the expert.

## Notes

1. In seven school districts one or a few individuals do make a disproportionate amount of public demands.

# 9
# Preference, Communication, and Response

The roles of experts and laymen in contemporary educational governance in the United States are highly paradoxical. Many institutional, attitudinal, and behavioral norms surrounding local school districts reflect the popular notion that governments should do what people want them to do—should be responsive to their constituents. Other institutions, attitudes, and behaviors in public school districts reflect a strongly professional orientation: lay preferences are insufficient and largely inappropriate bases for educational policy-making. We must acknowledge that school districts are complex organizations which contain examples of the entire spectrum of political relationships and processes. Nevertheless, it is clearly the case that the preponderant form of decision-making in the school districts we have studied is that of the hierarchical or technological model. Experts dominate laymen.

School districts offer unparalleled opportunities for indirect and direct citizen oversight and participation in policy-making. Legal authority flows from the public to its lay legislative body, the school board. Over 90 percent of school board members are chosen by election, the balance are appointed either by elected officials or by commissions named by elected officials. As is the case in nearly all units of local government in the United States, citizens may influence school district policy through the polls.

Important decisions are made at meetings which are held in the local community and are open to the public. Public participation is solicited; many school boards hold regular public hearings to receive communications from their constituents. Most school boards have standing and ad hoc committees, some of whose members are selected from the general public. Key financial decisions are often made directly by the citizenry through referenda. In most school districts a citizen can reach school board members and top administrators—including superintendents—by telephone. More so than in other governments, the channels of citizen access to policy-makers in school districts are numerous, convenient, and open.

Yet, in spite of all the potential for lay control of education, the reality of local school district governance suggests a different picture. The quantity and quality of citizen participation are low, perhaps lower than in any other unit of American government. Only a small minority takes advantage of the opportunity to vote in school district elections, to attend public meetings, to speak at public meetings, or to communicate in private with school district officials. The superintendent and other professional administrators consistently dominate the lay school board and public, regardless of arena or topic of decision-making, largely because the latter abstain from participation. Moreover, when laymen do participate, they are not often successful or influential.

## Preference

One might be tempted to interpret low quantity and quality of public participation as indicative of a high level of satisfaction with the process and content of educational governance. One might argue that laymen, while not entirely happy with everything at all times, have sufficient faith in educational professionals to defer to them in nearly all routine matters. Unfortunately, that argument cannot account for the significant public dissatisfaction and low efficacy reported in this and other studies.

Experts and laymen agree on the major problems facing their school districts: student discipline and finance. Lay concern with the major problems they perceive is emphasized in participatory behavior. A disproportionate amount of their private contacts with school officials and comments at public meetings address the topics of greatest concern to them. Concern with these major problems is not reflected in the amount or intensity of discussion by school officials in their formal meetings. Thus, it is possible to document that school officials and their constituents share recognition of major issues and that constituents' behavior parallels their preferences. Establishing a linkage between perceived major problems and the policy-making behavior of school district officials is more problematic.

School official-public agreement on identification of major problems other than student discipline and finance is much lower. This is largely a function of public ignorance or apathy: most public respondents to our survey could only name one or two important problems facing their school district; others named problems such as nationwide inflation and state taxation laws which are beyond the control of local school districts. The low response rates and some of the content of responses to our community surveys suggest that public attitudes and preferences concerning educational governance may be poorly informed and superficial. It is axiomatic that school officials cannot respond to the overwhelming majority of their constituents who do not articulate, and perhaps do not have, preferences. It also appears to be the case that school officials may not be capable of acting on many of the preferences of the minority who do hold them because of the nature of those preferences. School district responsiveness to unrealistic preferences is impossible.

Important differences were found in the most general attitudes and preferences held by school officials and the public. School officials are consistently more liberal, more satisfied, and more supportive of the district than are their constituents. These attitudes and preferences are clearly related to position and participation in school affairs. The occasionally active public took positions between the inactive public and school officials. From these data we cannot determine whether this pattern is a product of chance, of school officials reflecting the opinions of the active public, or of the active public reflecting the opinions of school officials. We can determine that the attitudes and preferences of those who are most active and those who are least active in school district policy-making differ significantly.

Given these differences, one cannot reasonably expect that a high level of congruence responsiveness would result from school officials acting solely on their own initiative. Indeed, given the nature of public opinion and—more importantly—lack of public opinion, one might conclude that the notion of congruence responsiveness is not useful for assessing the governing of local school districts. The quantity and quality of unarticulated preferences which we were able to identify provide only the broadest outlines for educational policy-making.

## Communication

It is crucial to an understanding of expert-lay communications in public school districts to distinguish between routine and episodic behavior. A selective view focusing only on crisis episodes would suggest ongoing public participation resulting in turmoil. Yet, our systematic analysis of school board meetings selected because of their importance indicates that public participation and conflict are quite rare. Significant public attendance and preference articulation at school board meetings are episodic phenomena concentrated in one or two days of the year. More often than not, public participation follows rather than precedes important decisions. Public input at school board meetings does not result in immediate favorable decisions. The meetings which do contain the most articulated demands and decisions are unusually productive routine school board sessions with little or no public participation. To be sure, public participation and turmoil in school districts do occur. However, the fact that such episodes occur very rarely adds to their significance.

A comprehensive view of school board meetings documents that the vast majority of communications and decisions involve only the lay school board and district level professional administrators. Topics of presumed national importance are rarely discussed. The most important problems identified by the public and school officials occupy less than 20 percent of the agenda. The agenda of public school board meetings is set by the professional educational establishment and is routine in nature.

School board meetings are not arenas of conflict articulation. School board meeting discussions follow a pattern of professional administrators supplying information to school board members that normally includes a policy recommendation by the superintendent. School board members articulate demands in favor of administrative recommendations. Dissent is infrequent and typically originates with an individual who is not part of the educational establishment. School board decision-making is normally by unanimous vote. Dissenting votes are rare and without consistent pattern. Defeat of administrative recommendations is extremely rare and is almost always limited to relatively unimportant matters. In short, the lay school board defers to educational professionals, most often without direct participation by members of the lay public.

Administrative cabinet meetings are forums of communication exchange limited almost exclusively to district level administrators. The substance of these meetings is routine—cabinet meetings do not concentrate on or discuss intensively topics identified as of greatest importance by laymen or experts. The amount of participation of line administrators varies from district to district. The nature of local administrators' participation, however, is quite uniform: they provide information. Clearly, information flows up and decisions flow down the administrative hierarchy of local school districts.

Private communications between school district officials and their constituents are an important supplement to exchanges in public meetings. Private communications more accurately reflect the agenda of lay concerns than do the statements of experts or laymen at formal meetings. Nonpublic communications are school officials' most important source of action-oriented lay requests, requests which are private in scope, and requests articulated by individuals who are not speaking for organized interests. As is the case for lay participation at public meetings, lay expression of preferences in private is infrequent, irregular, concentrated, and more often than not follows rather than precedes major decisions. Lay preferences articulated to school officials might serve as a useful commentary on popular perceptions of some episodic issues. They are of insufficient quantity and quality to guide school district officials in the establishment of most routine and episodic policies.

## Response

The research project reported here attempted to record all communications between school district officials and their constituents in 11 school districts for an academic year. Given the timing, scope, nature, source, and substantive content of public-school official communications, the model of representational responsiveness is irrelevant to the overwhelming majority of school district decisions. The articulation of preferences by constituents requisite to representational responsiveness is rare. The holding of clear, specific policy preferences requisite to congruence responsiveness is also rare. Hence, if all decisions are considered, school districts must be judged unresponsive to their constituents mainly because of the latter's failure to hold and express preferences.

The quest for responsiveness in the routine matters which occupy so much of a modern school district's agenda is bound to be disappointing. Responsiveness may be more fruitfully sought in those less frequent episodes in which members of the lay public hold or articulate policy preferences. The record of responsiveness in this more narrow focus of inquiry is mixed. Indicators of responsiveness which measure school officials' acknowledgment of public concerns and preferences are fairly high. Indicators of responsiveness which measure school officials taking specific action in accordance with constituent wishes are fairly low. The patterns of responsiveness over individual indicators and districts are complex, yet they are consistent with school officials' explicit and implicit norms of professionalism. It seems to be the case that the relevance of constituent preference to school district decision-making is tied most closely not to factors associated with those preferences, but to the perceptions of school district officials.

We conclude that a notion of professional educational administrators beleaguered by lay constituents is not an accurate representation of the aggregate of school governance. The picture which emerges suggests that direct participation by constituents within the school district and actors without the school district is infrequent. Little evidence supports a notion of administrative representation. The overall picture is one of public and school board deference to educational experts.

## A Broader Perspective

How can the apparent contradiction between the findings of this study and the assertion by schoolmen themselves and observers sympathetic to them that they have lost control of the governing of schools be resolved? We suggest that several resolutions are tenable.

1) School districts are not free of conflict, and some school districts do experience a considerable quantity of conflict. However, the conflict mode of educational governance is the exception, not the rule, in American public school districts. When conflict episodes are measured in terms of all decisions, and districts with high conflict are viewed in terms of all districts, the technological decision-making model is seen as predominant.

2) The case study approach has biases which overstate the amount of lay participation and community conflict. Case studies of conflict are selective views which are not intended to describe all incidents, most incidents, or even typical incidents. They are extremely limited in their generalizability. Similarly, the news media find cases of conflict in educational governance newsworthy because it is the unique which is newsworthy. All forms of conflict in educational governance are newsworthy.

3) School officials misperceive the frequency of challenges to the technological decision-making model. The self-reported perceptions of school officials might tend to overstate conflict. When school officials are asked to recall "most important" issues or decisions, conflict will be overstated because that which generates conflict is, by definition, important. Additionally, because school districts are not philosophically or institutionally prepared to accept conflict as a normal aspect of governance, school officials find conflict particularly troublesome and therefore memorable.

The power of local educational professionals may be threatened in the long run by educational professionals in state and federal governments. Their options may be circumscribed by state and federal courts, state and federal economic problems, and other political and nonpolitical forces originating outside the local school district which are beyond their control. We have found little, if any, evidence that the power of local educational professionals is significantly threatened by school boards or by the lay public within the local school district.

The research reported here is exploratory and, in the main, descriptive. An immense amount of information was collected and analyzed in a limited number of school districts. The generalizability of the findings here for 11 school districts to the over 15,000 districts in the United States can only be a subject of speculation. Yet, in spite of the limited basis for broader inference, the commonalities of expert and lay behavior across the 11 districts are striking. Although our sample districts differ significantly in size, wealth, clientele, location, formal structures, and other attributes, the roles played by the various actors in local school district governance seem to be essentially the same.

Theoretically and empirically, the concept of responsiveness to the most broadly defined constituency remains troublesome. A number of independent indicators of responsiveness were advanced and explored. No single leading, aggregate, or integrated definition of responsiveness could be identified. Moreover, the factors requisite to an evaluation of responsiveness which involve the lay public could be identified only infrequently. Although data were collected

Table 9.1
SIGNIFICANT CORRELATES OF RESPONSIVENESS

I. Agenda Responsiveness
   A. School Board Meetings
      1. Positive
         a. % school board agenda set by laymen
         b. % private contacts demands
      2. Negative
         a. % cabinet statements not by superintendent
   B. Cabinet Meetings
      1. Positive
         a. % school board discussions on public priority copies
         b. % school board statements by public
         c. % cabinet discussions on public priority topics
         d. Private contacts per district enrollment
         e. % private contacts demands
         f. % private contacts policy scope
      2. Negative
         a. % minority enrollment
         b. % school board demands by laymen
         c. % school board public statements by groups
         d. % school board public demands by groups
   C. All Meetings
      1. Positive
         a. School board statements on public priority topics

Table 9.1 continued

b. % private contacts demands
c. % private contacts policy scope
2. Negative
a. Enrollment
b. % school board statements by public
II. Symbolic Responsiveness—Efficacy Score ·
1. Positive
a. Issue congruence score
b. Public support score
c. School board % superintendent position known
2. Negative
a. School board % nonunanimous votes
b. School board % discussions with public demands
policy scope
c. Cabinet % decision not intended
d. Cabinet statements on public priority topics
e. % private contacts on public priority topics
III. Service Responsiveness
A. Action Taken
1. Positive
a. School board % nonunanimous votes
b. Private contacts with board
2. Negative
a. Per pupil expenditure
b. School board statements on public priority topics
c. % private contacts policy scope

Table 9.1 continued

B. Action Not Refused
   1. Positive
      a. Cabinet decision not intended
      b. Cabinet statements on public priority topics
      c. School board decision reached when intended
C. Constituent Satisfied
   1. Positive
      a. School board agenda set by public
      b. Cabinet supply information not by superintendent
      c. Private contacts demands
   2. Negative
      a. % school board discussions with public participation
      b. % school board statements by public
D. Constituent Not Dissatisfied
   1. Positive
      a. Public support score
      b. % school board decisions by vote
   2. Negative
      a. School board % discussions with public demands
         policy slope
      b. % private contacts on public priority issues
IV. Policy Responsiveness
   A. School Board Meeting Decisions—Content
      1. Positive
         a. % school board public statements by groups
         b. % school board public supply information by groups

Table 9.1 continued

2. Negative

   a. Program expenditure congruence score

   b. % school board proposals by laymen

   c. School board % superintendent position known

   d. % private contacts policy scope

B. School Board Meeting Decision—Distributional

  1. Positive

   a. % school board public statements by groups

   b. % school board public supply information by groups

   c. % school board supply information by experts

  2. Negative

   a. Expenditure per pupil

   b. % school board statements demands

   c. % private contacts policy scope

C. School Board Presentation—Constituent Satisfied

  2. Negative

   a. % school board decision intended

   b. % school board discussion on public priority issues

   c. % school board demands by laymen

D. School Board Presentation—Constituent Not Dissatisfied

  1. Positive

   a. % school board public supply information by groups

   b. % cabinet statements demands

  2. Negative

   a. School board meetings per month

Table 9.1 continued

E. Private Contacts Action Taken
   2. Negative
      a. Performance satisfaction congruence score
      b. % cabinet agenda not set by superintendent
F. Private Contacts Action Not Refused
   2. Negative
      a. % school board decision intended
      b. % school board statements demands
      c. % school board demands by laymen
      d. % school board proposals by public
      e. % school board nonunanimous votes
      f. % private contacts to school board
G. Private Contacts Constituent Satisfied
   2. Negative
      a. % school board discussions with public participation
      b. % school board statements by public
      c. % school board proposals by public
      d. % cabinet agenda not set by superintendent
      e. % private contacts to school board
H. Private Contacts Constituent Not Dissatisfied
   2. Negative
      a. % school board decision intended
      b. % school board discussions with public participation
      c. % school board statements demands
      d. % school board demands by laymen

Table 9.1 continued

    e. % school board proposals by public
    f. % school board discussions with public demands
        policy scope
V. Influence Responsiveness
  A. School Board Presentation--School Official Perspective
    1. Positive
      a. % minority enrollment
      b. School board meeting attendance
      c. % school board discussions public participation
      d. % school board statements by public
      e. % school board discussions with public demands
         policy scope
    2. Negative
      a. % school board public statements by groups
      b. % school board public supply information by groups
      c. % school board public demands by groups
  B. School Board Presentation--Constituent Perspective
    1. Positive
      a. % school board discussion with public participation
      b. % school board statements by public
      c. % school board proposals by public
      d. % school board discussions with public demands
         policy scope
      e. Competing school board demands
      f. % private contacts on public priority issues

Table 9.1 continued


C. Private Contacts
    1. Positive
        a. % school board decisions by vote
        b. % school board agenda set by laymen
    2. Negative
        a. Enrollment

over an entire academic year, few longitudinal analyses could be supported. What factors are associated with school district responsiveness? What governance institutions and political behaviors promote and inhibit responsiveness? Consideration of these questions must be even more cautious and tentative than the analyses presented earlier. In addition to all the other limitations of this study, consideration of factors associated with responsiveness is constrained by what was observed in our 11 school districts. Insufficient cases of responsiveness were identified to investigate processes occurring over time within individual districts. Only a less desirable correlation of data across 11 school districts is possible. Such a cross-sectional analysis is, of course, insufficient for making inferences about longitudinal changes. At best, ideas for future research may be suggested.

Table 9.1 identifies the significant correlates between the nineteen indicators of responsiveness of chapter 8 and the structural, attitudinal, and behavioral variables presented throughout the earlier chapters. All 19 indices of responsiveness have multiple significant correlates; 15 have both positive and negative significant correlates. Of 79 significant correlates, 68 are behavioral indicators, 5 are attitudinal measures, and 6 are structural variables. Of the behavioral variables, 54 concern behavior at school board meetings, 8 concern private communications, and 6 concern cabinet meetings.

This suggests that, while some school board meeting activities may appear to be performances orchestrated to insure harmony, what occurs at those meetings may be related to responsiveness. Structural and attitudinal variables, which are less malleable, are less frequent correlates of responsiveness. Behaviors which are subject to change—especially the behaviors of laymen—are the most frequent correlates of responsiveness.

Unfortunately, lay participation is not always positively related to responsiveness. Some aspects of lay participation do seem to be consistently positive correlates. For example, the proportion of private communications from constituents that articulate demands is positively linked with three agenda responsiveness and one service responsiveness indicators. However, other elements of lay participation are negatively related to responsiveness. For example, the proportion of demands articulated by the lay public at school board meetings is negatively correlated with indices of influence, policy, and service responsiveness.

A simple interpretation of conditions associated with responsiveness is further complicated by the fact that most independent variables are positively correlated with some responsiveness indicators and negatively correlated with others. For example, public participation in school board meetings is linked positively with influence responsiveness, but negatively with policy and service responsiveness. Statements at board meetings by group members may increase policy responsiveness yet decrease agenda and influence responsiveness. Similarly, private communications to discuss policy may stimulate agenda responsiveness and stifle policy and service responsiveness. Thus, it appears that lay participation may have various impacts on the various dimensions of responsiveness.

This is not to suggest that incremental increases in lay participation will yield increases in school district responsiveness. The information available to school district officials concerning lay constituent preferences is profoundly insufficient in quantity, quality, and diversity to support either a congruence or representational model of responsiveness. Fundamental changes in the structure of public opinion may be necessary for school district responsiveness to be a realistic or desirable goal. Yet, even should such change be forthcoming, school officials would still have to face the dilemma that deference to lay preferences often demands sacrificing professional values. As long as public school districts are expected to meet simultaneously the inconsistent demands of professional judgment and lay preference, they must inevitably fall short of one or the other goal.

# BIBLIOGRAPHY

ALESHIRE, ROBERT A. "Power to the People: An Assessment of the Community Action and Model Cities Experiences," *Public Administration Review,* 32(September 1972), 428–443.

ANDES, JOHN O., JOHNS, ROE L. and KIMBROUGH, RALPH B. *Changes in Organizational Structures of Large School Systems With Special Reference to Problems of Teacher Militancy and Organizational Conflict.* University of Florida, 1971 (Litho.).

AREEN, JUDITH and JENCKS, CHRISTOPHER. "Education Vouchers: A Proposal for Diversity and Choice," *Teachers College Record,* 72:3(February 1971), 327–336.

ARONS, STEPHEN. "Equity, Option and Vouchers," *Teachers College Record,* 72(February 1971), 337–364.

BINDERMAN, MURRAY B. "The Failure of Freedom of Choice: Decision-Making in a Southern Black Community," *Social Forces,* 50(June 1972), 487–498.

BOYD, WILLIAM. "The Public, The Professionals, and Educational Policy-Making: Who Governs?" *Teachers College Record,* (May 1976), 539–577.

BROWN, JULIUS S. "Risk Propensity in Decision Making: A Comparison of Business and Public School Administrators," *Administrative Science Quarterly,* 15(December 1970), 473–481.

BUREAU OF SCHOOL SERVICE AND RESEARCH. "A Summary of Major Findings Concerning Citizen Opinions Toward the Voucher Plan," in MECKLENBERGER and HOSTROP (Eds.), *Education Vouchers: From Theory to Alum Rock.* Homewood, Ill.: ETC Publications, 1972.

BURNS, TOM. "The Direction of Activity and Communication in a Departmental Executive Group: A Quantitative Study in a British Engineering Factory with a Self-Recording Technique," *Human Relations.* 7(February 1954), 73–87.

CALLAHAN, RAYMOND E., and BUTTON, H. WARREN. *The Superintendent of Schools: An Historical Analysis.* St. Louis, Mo.: Washington University Press, 1966.

CAMPBELL, ALAN K. "Who Governs the Schools?" *Saturday Review,* 64(December 21, 1968), 50–52.

CAMPBELL, RAOLD F., BRIDGES, EDWIN M. and NYSTRAND, RAPHAEL O. *Introduction to Educational Administration.* Boston: Allyn and Bacon, Inc., 1977.

CARLSON, RICHARD O. *School Superintendents: Careers and Performance.* Columbus, Ohio: Charles E. Merrill, 1972.

*Confidence and Concern: Citizens View American Government. A Survey of Public Attitudes* by the Subcommittee on Intergovernmental Relations of the Committee on Government Operations, United States Senate, 93d Cong., 1st sess., 1973.

DYKES, ARCHIE. *School Board and Superintendent: Their Effective Working Relationships.* Danville, Ill.: Interstate Printers and Publishers, 1965.

EASTON, DAVIS. "An Approach to the Analysis of Political Systems," *World Politics,* 9(April, 1957), 383–400.

EULAU, HEINZ, and KARPS, PAUL D. "The Puzzle of Representation: Specifying Components of Responsiveness," *Legislative Studies Quarterly,* 2(August 1977).

EULAU, HEINZ, and PREWITT, KENNETH. *Labyrinths of Democracy.* Indianapolis: Bobbs-Merrill, Inc., 1973.

FANTINI, MARIO D. *The Reform of Urban Schools.* Schools for the 70's Series. Washington, D.C.: National Education Association, 1971a.

FANTINI, MARIO D. "Participation, Decentralization, Community Control, and Quality Education," *The Record,* 71(September 1971)b, 93–107.

FRIEDMAN, MILTON. *Capitalism and Freedom.* Chicago: University of Chicago Press, 1962.

GALLUP OPINION INDEX, 135, (October 1976).

GINSBERG, ELI. "The Economics of the Voucher System," *Teachers College Record,* 72(February 1971), 373–382.

GITTELL, MARILYN. *Educating an Urban Population.* Beverly Hills, Calif.: Sage Press, 1967.

GITTELL, MARILYN and HOLLANDER, T. EDWARD. *Six Urban School Districts: A Comparative Study of Institutional Response*. New York: Praeger Publishers, 1968.

GITTELL, MARILYN, BERUBE, MAURICE R., GOTTFRIED, FRANCES, GUTTEN-TAG, MARCIA, and SPIER, ADELE. *Local Control in Education: Three Demonstration School Districts in New York City*. New York: Praeger Publishers, 1972.

GOFFMAN, ERVING, *The Presentation of Self in Everyday Life*. Garden City, N.Y.: Doubleday & Co., 1959.

GOFFMAN, ERVING, *Relations in Public*. New York: Harper & Row, 1971.

GREIDER, CALVIN, PIERCE, TRUMAN, and ROSENSTENGEL, WILLIAM EVERETT. *Public School Administration*. 2nd edition. New York: Ronald Press, 1961.

GROSS, NEAL. *Who Runs Our Schools?* New York: John Wiley & Sons, 1958.

GROSS, NEAL, MASON, WARD H., and McEACHERN, ALEXANDER W. *Explorations in Role Analysis: Studies of the School Superintendency Role*. New York: John Wiley & Sons, 1958. 2nd edition, 1964.

GUTHRIE, JAMES W., *et al.* "The Erosion of Lay Control," in National Commission for Citizens in Education, *Public Testimony on Public Schools*. Berkeley: McCutchan Publishing Co., 1975, 92–101.

HALLMAN, HOWARD W. "Federally Financed Citizen Participation," *Public Administration Review*, 32(September, 1972), 421–427.

HESS, ROBERT D., and KIRST, MICHAEL. "Political Orientation and Behavior Patterns: Linkages Between Teachers and Children," *Education and Urban Society*, 3(August 1971), 453–477.

HINES, C. "A Study of School Board Administrative Relationships: The Development of the Eugene, Oregon, Superintendency, 1891–1944," *American School Board Journal*, 1951, 122(2), 19–21; 122(3), 28–29; 122(4), 17–19.

IANNACCONE, LAURENCE. *Politics in Education*. New York: The Center for Applied Research in Education, Inc., 1967.

JAMES, H. THOMAS. "School Board Conflict Is Inevitable," *American School Board Journal*, 154(March 1967), 5–9.

JAMES, H. THOMAS, *et al. Determinants of Educational Expenditures in Large Cities of the United States*. Stanford, Calif.: School of Education, Stanford University, 1963.

JENCKS, CHRISTOPHER, *et al. Inequality: A Reassessment of the Effect of Family and Schooling in America*. New York: Basic Books, 1972.

JENKINS, MICHAEL A. "Decentralizing High School Administration in Detroit: An Evaluation of Alternative Strategies of Political Control," *Economic Geography,,* 48(January 1972), 95–106.

JENNINGS, M. KENT, and ZEIGLER, L. HARMON. "The Politics of Teacher-Administrator Relations," *Education and Social Science*, Vol. 1, Great Britain: Pergamon Press, 1969, 73–82.

JENNINGS, M. KENT, and ZEIGLER, L. HARMON. "Response Styles and Politics: The Case of the School Boards," *Midwest Journal of Political Science*, 15(May 1971), 290–321.

JENNINGS, M. KENT, and ZEIGLER, L. HARMON. "Interest Representation in School Governance," *Urban Affairs Annual Review*, Vol. 6, 1972a, 201–230.

JENNINGS, M. KENT, and ZEIGLER, L. HARMON. "Avenues to the School Board and Political Competition." Paper read at the American Educational Research Association Annual Meeting, 1972b.

KERR, NORMAN D. "The School Board as an Agency of Legitimation," *Sociology of Education*, 38(Fall, 1964), 45–55.

KEY, V. O., Jr. *Public Opinion and American Democracy*. New York: Alfred A. Knopf, 1971.

KIMBROUGH, RALPH B. *Political Power and Educational Decision-Making*. Chicago: Rand-McNally, 1964.

KNEZEVICH, STEPHEN J. *Administration of Public Education*. New York: Harper & Row, 1969.

KOERNER, JAMES D. *Who Controls American Education? A Guide for Laymen*. Boston: Beacon, 1968.

KOVENOCK, DAVID. "Influence in the U.S. House of Representatives: A Statistical Analysis of Communications," (Unpublished manuscript, 1967).

LANOUE, GEORGE R. "Vouchers: The End of Public Education?" In LANOUE, GEORGE R. (Ed.), *Education Vouchers: Concepts and Controversies.* New York: Teachers College Press, 1972.

LANOUE, GEORGE R. and SMITH, BRUCE L. R. "The Political Evolution of School Decentralization," *American Behavioral Scientist,* 15(October 1971), 73–93.

LANOUE, GEORGE R., and SMITH, BRUCE L.R. *The Politics of School Decentralization.* Lexington, Mass.: D.C. Heath & Co., 1973.

LASSWELL, HAROLD. "The Structure and Function of Communication in Society," in BRYSON, L. (Ed.), *The Communication of Ideas.* New York: Harper & Row, 1948.

LEVIN, HENRY M. (Ed.), *Community Control of Schools.* Washington, D.C.: The Brookings Institution, 1972.

LIPHAM, JAMES M., GREGG, RUSSELL T., and ROSSMILLER, RICHARD A. "The School Board: Resolver of Conflict?" *Administrator's Notebook,* 17(April 1969).

LUTTBEG, NORMAN (Ed.). *Public Opinion and Public Policy: Models of Political Linkage.* Homewood, Ill.: The Dorsey Press, 1968. 2nd edition, 1974.

LYON, DAVID W. "Capitalism in the Classroom: Educational Vouchers," *Federal Reserve Bank of Philadelphia Business Review,* (December 1971).

MAEROFF, GENE I. "Harried School Leaders See Their Role Waning," *New York Times,* March 5, 1974), 1, 29.

MANN, DALE. *The Politics of Administrative Representation.* Lexington, Mass.: D.C. Heath and Co., 1976.

MARCSON, SIMON. "Decentralization and Community Control in Urban Areas," New Brunswick, N.J.: Rutgers University, January 1971 (ERIC Order Number 049 330).

MARTIN, ROSCOE C. *Government and the Suburban School.* Syracuse: Syracuse University Press, 1962.

McCARTY, DONALD J., and RAMSEY, CHARLES E. *The School Managers.* Westport, Conn.: Greenwood, 1971.

McGIVNEY, JOSEPH H., and HAUGHT, JAMES M. "The Politics of Education: A View from the Perspective of the Central Office Staff," in *Educational Administration Quarterly,* 8:3(Autumn 1972), 18–38.

MECKLENBERGER, JAMES. "Vouchers at Alum Rock," *Phi Delta Kappan* (September 1972), 23–25.

MILLER, WARREN E., and STOKES, DONALD E. "Constituency Influence in Congress," *American Political Science Review,* 57:1(March, 1963), 45–56.

NATIONAL SCHOOL BOARDS ASSOCIATION. *The People Look at Their School Boards.* Research Report 1975-1.

PEAK, G. WAYNE. "Policy Leadership in the Governance of Public School Systems," (Unpublished Ph.D. Thesis, Dept. of Political Science, University of Oregon), Eugene, Oregon, 1971.

PETERSON, PAUL E. *School Politics Chicago Style.* Chicago, Ill.: University of Chicago Press, 1976.

PIERCE, LAWRENCE C. "Teachers' Organizations and Bargaining: Power Imbalance in the Public Sphere," in NATIONAL COMMITTEE FOR CITIZENS IN EDUCATION, *Public Testimony on Public Schools.* Berkeley, Calif.: McCutchan Publishing Co., 1975.

REED, DONALD B., and MITCHELL, DOUGLAS E. "The Structure of Citizen Participation: Public Decisions for Public Schools," in NATIONAL COMMISSION FOR CITIZENS IN EDUCATION (Ed.), *Public Testimony on Public Schools.* Berkeley, Calif.: McCutchan Publishing Co., 1975, 183–217.

SALISBURY, ROBERT H. "Schools and Politics in the Big Cities," *Harvard Educational Review,* 37(Summer 1967), 408–424.

SCHATTSCHNEIDER, E. E. *The Semi-Sovereign People.* New York: Holt, 1960.

SCHUBERT, GLENDON A. *Quantitative Analysis of Judicial Behavior.* Glencoe, Ill.: The Free Press/Bureau of Social and Political Research, Michigan State University, 1959, Chap. 3.

SMOLEY, EUGENE R., JR. *Community Participation in Urban School Government.* Washington, D.C.: U.S. Office of Education, Cooperative Research project S–029, 1965.

SUMMERFIELD, HARRY L. "Cuing and the Open System of Educational Politics," *Education and Urban Society,* 3(August 1971), 425–439.

SUSSMANN, LEILA, with SPECK, GAYLE. "Community Participation in Schools: The Boston Case," *Urban Education*, 7(January 1973), 341–356.

THIBAULT, JOHN W., and KELLY, HAROLD H. *The Social Psychology of Groups*. New York: John Wiley & Co., 1961.

TYACK, DAVID. *The One Best System*. Cambridge: Harvard University Press, 1974.

USDAN, MICHAEL D. "Citizen Participation: Learning from New York City's Mistakes," *The Urban Review*, 4(September 1969), 9–12.

VERBA, SIDNEY and NIE, NORMAN. *Participation in America*. New York: Harper & Row, 1972.

VIDICH, ARTHUR J., and BENSMAN, JOSEPH. *Small Town in Mass Society*. Garden City, N.Y.: Doubleday-Anchor, 1960.

WALTER, BENJAMIN. *Bureaucratic Communications: A Statistic of Analysis of Influence*. University of North Carolina, Institute for Research in Social Science, Sept. 1, 1963.

WIRT, FREDERICK M., and KIRST, MICHAEL W. *The Political Web of American Schools*. Boston: Little, Brown & Co., 1972.

ZEIGLER, L. HARMON. *The Political Life of American Teachers*. Englewood Cliffs, N.J.: Prentice-Hall, 1967.

ZEIGLER, L. HARMON and BAER, MICHAEL. *Lobbying: Interaction and Influence in American State Legislatures*. Belmont, Calif.: Wadsworth, 1969.

ZEIGLER, L. HARMON, JENNINGS, M. KENT, with PEAK, G. WAYNE. *Governing American Schools*. North Scituate, Mass.: Duxbury Press, 1974.

ZEIGLER, L. HARMON, JENNINGS, M. KENT, and PEAK G. WAYNE. "The Decision-Making Culture of American Public Education," in COTTER, CORNELIUS P. (Ed.), *Political Science Annual*, Vol. 5. Indianapolis: Bobbs-Merrill, 1974.

ZEIGLER, L. HARMON, TUCKER, HARVEY J., and WILSON, L.A., II. "Communication and Decision-Making in American Public Education: A Longitudinal and Comparative Study," *National Society for the Study of Education, 1977 Yearbook*. April, 1977a.

ZEIGLER, L. HARMON, TUCKER, HARVEY J., and WILSON, L. A., II. "How School Control Was Wrested from the People," *Phi Delta Kappan*, March 1977b, 534–539.

ZEIGLER, L. HARMON and TUCKER, HARVEY J. *The Quest for Responsive Government*. North Scituate, Mass.: Duxbury Press, 1978.

# INDEX

Affirmative action, 61–62
Agenda(s)
  attitudes and preferences, 43–45
  cabinet meeting, 157–68, 169, 231
  public vs. private, 139–40
  responsiveness, 203–8
  school board meeting, 111–22
  setting, 123–26, 168–69, 231
American Association of University
  Women, 82
American Civil Liberties Union, 32
Andes, John O., 11
Anonymity, 27
Athletics, girls', 48
Attitudes and preferences, agenda, 43–45

Baer, Michael A., 9
Ballard City board meeting, 91–94
Bargaining, 6–7, 13–14, 18–19, 26–27
  as alternative to hierarchy, 16
  ideological, 7, 16
  model, 125
  pluralistic, 7, 45–46
  school official and interest group, 7
  among school officials, 7
  style of school governance, 13–17
Barwig Park board meeting, 80–82
Bensman, Joseph, 9
Bond issues, 94
Boyd, William, 3, 125, 178
Brown, Julius, 109
Budget levy, 94–95, 96
Burns, Tom, 24
Busing, 61–62, 82, 148, 151

Cabinet meeting. See Meetings, cabinet
Callahan, Raymond, 10, 11
Campbell, Alan K., 15
Carlson, Richard, 10, 109
Central office, staff of, 109
Chamber of Commerce, 94–95, 148
Chamberlain, Joseph P., 124
Citizen involvement, 18, 101
Citizen's Advisory Council, 98–99
Clark, Burton, 109
Cobb, Roger, 123
Coldren Corners board meeting, 78–80,
  149–51
Collective bargaining, 91
Committee on Governmental Opera-
  tions, 228

Communications
  data concerning, 24
  expert-lay, 231–32
  intraexpert, 157
  private, 179–202
  professional, 171
Community
  preferences, methodology for deter-
    mining, 23–42
  school, 10
Conflict, 133, 173, 183, 233
  articulation of, 131, 231
  episodes of, 104
  intraboard, 152–53
  resolution, 131
  superintendent and school board, 92
Congruence
  attitude, 46, 68–69
  school, 5–6, 20, 202
Conservatism, 53–56, 63–65
Consolidation ("scientific management"), 10–11
Constituent(s), 185, 187, 203
  articulated preferences of, 19, 41
  communication with, 222–23
  influence, 220, 222
  satisfaction, 211, 213, 214, 219
  unarticulated preferences of, 19, 43
Contacts, private, 180–85, 196–99,
  217–19
Controversy, issues of, 61–65
Corwin, Ronald, 109
Crain, Robert, 9, 109
Curricula, 45, 114, 145

Dahl, Robert, 1, 2, 6, 8, 16, 18
Data collection, 30, 32, 41
  objective, 24–25
  perceptual, 24
  subjective, 24–25
Decision-making
  hierarchical, 6, 8–13, 16, 18–19, 26–27,
    125
  market, 6, 8
  polyarchal, 6, 7–8, 13, 17–19, 26–27,
    125
  routine, 124–25
Demand-Response Log, 24–25, 30, 32–41
Demands, 133, 136–39, 172–73, 174, 176,
  177
  articulation of, 176, 177, 183, 202, 230

Demands (*continued*)
  group, 80, 89
  negative, 83, 134, 137–38
  substance of, 139–40
Discrimination, 45
Discussion, intensity of, 114–15, 117–18, 122
Drummond Falls board meeting, 94–97
Dye, Thomas, 72, 129
Dykes, Archie, 12

Easton, David, 129
Efficacy, questions on, 65–68
Elder, Charles, 123
Elite
  opinion, 205, 208
  preferences, 48, 205
  satisfaction, 37–50
Empirical view, 3
Enrollment, declining, 82
Eulau, Heinz, 4, 5, 208, 211, 226
Expenditures, program, 45–52
Experts, 1–4, 108, 110, 125, 131–132, 152, 155, 185, 194
  preferences of, 43–76, 228, 230–31

Federal
  guidelines, 89–90, 92
  mandates, 48
Field observers
  recruiting, 30
  training, 30–31, 37–41
Friedman, Milton, 8

Gallup Opinion Index, 72
Gittell, Marilyn, 9, 10, 178
Goffman, Irving, 155
Governance, school, 1–22
  experts and laymen in, 1–4
  research on styles of, 8–19
  responsiveness and, 4–8, 19–21
Government officials
  behavior of, 19, 41
  preferences of, 19
Grahamdale board meeting, 99–101
Gregg, Russell T., 12
Greider, Conrad, 11, 143
Gross, Neal, 12, 14
Guidelines, federal, 89–90, 92
Guthrie, James, 122

Hartshorne Hts. board meeting, 97–99
Haught, James, 178
Hess, Robert D., 9

Hierarchical decision-making, 6, 8–13, 16, 18–19, 26–27, 125
Hines, C., 11
Hollander, T. Edward, 9

Iannaccone, Laurence, 15
Ideologies, professional, 228
Industrial revolution, 10
Influence on public officials, indirect, 18
Information exchange, 185, 188
Interest groups, 128–29, 138–39, 182–83

James, H. Thomas, 10, 11
Jencks, Christopher, 8
Jennings, M. Kent, 9, 11, 15, 109

Karps, Paul, 208, 211, 226
Kelly, Harold, 156
Kentington board meeting, 86–89, 151–52
Kerr, Norman D., 11
Key, V. O., 185
Kimbrough, Ralph B., 9
Kirst, Michael, 9
Koerner, Joames D., 16

Labor, division of, 193–94
LaNoue, George R., 18
Lasswell, Harold, 23
Laymen, 1–4, 18, 77
  preferences of, 43–76, 230–31
Leeville board meeting, 83–86, 148–49
Legitimacy, 13–14
Liberalism, 53–56, 63–65
Lindblom, Charles, 2, 6, 8
Linkages, 201
  elite/school official, 69–72
  public/school official, 69–72
Lipham, James M., 12
Luttbeg, Norman, 5, 46

McCarty, Donald J., 3, 12–13
McEachern, Alexander W., 12
McGivney, Joseph, 178
Macktown board meeting, 89–91
Maeroff, Gene I., 3
Mandates, federal, 48
Mann, Dale, 178
Martin, Roscoe C., 9, 13
Mason, Ward H., 12
Meetings, cabinet, 157–78
  agenda of, 157–68
  agenda setting at, 168–69
  communication at, 172–74

demands and, 174–77
participation in, 170–72
Meetings, school board, 77–156
actors and attendance at, 108–11
agenda of, 111–23
agenda setting at, 123–26
communication at, 129–39
issues in, 139–41
participation in, 126–29
selective accounts of, 78–103, 104–52
voting in, 141–44, 152–53
Military education, 150
Miller, Warren, 203
Minority opinion, 216
Mitchell, Douglas E., 18

NAACP, 93
National School Board Association, 201
Nelsonville board meeting, 82–83
News media, 120–21
Nie, Norman, 4, 203
Normative view, 3, 8

PTA, 19, 94
bargaining and, 14
influence of, 16
support of, 15–16
Parents, 181–83, 188, 189, 224
Peak, G. Wayne, 11, 12
Peterson, Paul, 1, 15, 16, 152
Pierce, Lawrence C., 16
Plurality, 7, 46
Policy
implementation, 143
proposals, 140–41, 143, 189
requests, 214, 224
Policy-making
recommendations, 142, 143
as separate from administration, 9
Policy orientation continuum, 190
Polyarchal decision-making, 6, 7–8, 13, 17–19, 26–27, 125
Preferences
articulated, 19, 41
elite, 48, 205
expert-lay, 230–31
of government officials, 19
lay, 43–76
unarticulated, 19, 43
Pre-testing, 31, 32
Prewitt, Kenneth, 4, 5
Professionalism, 232
Professionals, 123, 125, 142, 171, 233

Program
approval, 52–56
expenditures, 45–52
Public
apathy, 230
attendance at meetings, opposition to, 209
concentration of demands, 105
confidence, 15
demands, 80, 81, 83, 86, 89, 90, 93–94, 96, 98, 100, 102, 105, 111, 129, 216
efficacy, elite, 65–67, 211, 230
opinion, 59–61, 199, 204, 208, 216, 232
participation, 110, 124, 126, 155, 171–72, 205, 207, 209, 220, 229, 231, 241
preferences, 46–48, 199–200
satisfaction, 56–57

Quality control, 31

Racial issues, 43, 61–62
affirmative action, 43, 61–62
sexual equity, 84–85
Ramsey, Charles E., 3, 12–13
Recall efforts, 78
Reed, Donald B., 18
Referenda, 80
Regression, linear, 48
Representation, administrative, 68–72, 161, 169–70, 174, 232
Representational school, 5–6, 202
Requests, scope of, 189–95
Research on styles of school governance, 8–19
Responsiveness, 202–28
active, 212, 218
agenda, 203–8
aggregate, 224
congruence, 20, 230
correlates of, 233–41
differential, 223–24
distributional, 216
influence, 219–23
measures of, 206–26
passive, 212, 218
in perspective, 224–28
policy, 214–17
project study, 27, 28
representational, 5, 6, 19, 20
school government, 4–8
service, 211–14
symbolic, 208–11
Rossmiller, Richard A., 12

Salisbury, Robert H., 9, 13
Sample, identifying a, 25–26
Satisfaction, performance, 56–61
Schattschneider, E. E., 123
School
    board. *See* School board
    closure, 82
    districts, choice of, 26–30
    finance, 43, 84, 91, 94, 104, 114, 149,
        230
School board
    agenda, 111, 113, 120, 122
    agenda setting, 123–26
    communications, 108, 181
    decisions, 112
    elections, 17
    erosion of power of, 11
    judgment, 13
    insulation from public demands, 106–7
    meetings. *See* Meetings, school board
    professional role of, 12
    recruitment, 110
    responsiveness of, 202, 203, 207
    superintendent, 142, 144–51
    voting behavior, 142, 144–51
Schubert, Glendon, 153, 156
Service requests, 190, 224
    response to, 217–23, 273
Smith, Bruce L. R., 18
Smoley, Eugene, 14, 155
Stokes, Donald, 203
Strikes
    janitor, 87
    teacher, 64, 91
Student(s)
    achievement, 79, 81
    disciplinary problems, 43, 45, 230
    school board and, 43, 45
Stumont board meeting, 101–3, 145–48
Subcommittee on Intergovernmental Re-
    lations, 72
Summerfield, Harry L., 15
Superintendent, 32, 126, 129, 131–33,
    137, 142–43

agenda setting by, 125
concentration of authority in, 9
domination of school board by, 11, 12
minimizing demands of, 14
private communications to, 181
responsiveness of, 218
Systems theory, 129

Taxpayers' revolt, 83
Teacher(s)
    bargaining by, 14
    influencing, 16
    school board and, 45
    strikes, 64, 91
    unions, 100
Technological model, 2
Thibault, John, 156
Title I, 99
Tucker, Harvey, 72, 142, 143

Unaffiliated individuals
    demands of, 15
    school officials and, 45
Underrepresentation of public opinion,
    59–61
U.S. Department of Health, Education,
    and Welfare, 92, 97
Unity, 133, 144–45, 231

Vandalism, 97–98, 100, 101–2
Verba, Sidney, 4, 203
Vidich, Arthur J., 9
Violence, 91
Vocational education, 51
Votes, unanimous, 144, 216

Ward-based elections, 81
Wilson, L. A., 142

Zeigler, L. Harmon, 9, 11, 13–15, 17, 26,
    72, 109, 110, 122, 124, 142, 143, 152,
    201